written by

Eric A. Johnson & Scott Millard

major photography by

Scott Millard

illustrations by

Don Fox

Editing, Design & Production
Millard Publishing Services,
Tucson, Arizona

Contributing writer
Ruth Rhode Haskell

Proofreading
Mary Campbell

Indexing
Byliner/Pat Hollinshead

Typesetting
The Service Bureau

Printing 10 9 8 7 6 5 4

Printed in Korea

ISBN 0-9628236-1-9

Library of Congress Catalog Card Number 92-73645

Cover photo: *Rudbeckia hirta*

Title page photo:
Centranthus ruber

The information in this book is true and accurate to the best of our knowledge. It is offered without guarantees on the part of the authors, who disclaim liability in connection with the use of this information.

Address inquiries to:

IRONWOOD PRESS
2968 West Ina Road #285
Tucson, Arizona 85741

Additional Photography

Elizabeth Ball
61TR, 61B, 93BL, 93BR, 100B, 109TL

Cathy Barash
96BR

Charles Cresson
113T

Thomas Eltztroth
61TL, 80B, 81BR

Ron Gass
77B

Saxon Holt
13A, 49T, 53BL, 57T, 60T, 85TR, 109TR, 120BL, 121TR

Michael Landis
21, 52B, 69TR, 92TR, 100TR, 109B

Charles Mann
16, 20, 31, 32, 41B, 53BR, 68TR, 73TL, 81T, 92TL, 96BL, 100TL, 101T, 105T, 120BR, 125BL

Sally Wasowski
18, 19

For their patience and understanding, sincere thanks to:

Maxine Johnson,
Palm Desert, CA

and

Michele V. Millard, Tucson, AZ

For their kind assistance, thanks to:

Charles Basham, consultant, Huntington Beach, CA

Melanie Baer, Theodore Payne Foundation, Sun Valley, CA

Dennis Bryson, Theodore Payne Foundation, Sun Valley, CA

Janice Busco, Theodore Payne Foundation, Sun Valley, CA

Don Davis, landscape consultant, Las Vegas, NV

Cliff Douglas, Arid Zone Trees, Queen Creek, AZ

Chris Drayer, Landscape Architect, San Diego, CA

Peter Duncombe, Desert Demonstration Garden, Las Vegas, NV

Ron Gass, Mountain States Nursery, Phoenix, AZ

Ron Gregory, Landscape Architect, Palm Desert, CA

John Harlow Jr., Harlow's Nursery, Tucson, AZ

Fred Lang, Landscape Architect, Laguna Beach, CA

Michael MacCaskey, *National Gardening* magazine, Burlington, VT

Steve Martino, Landscape Architect, Phoenix, AZ

Luann Munns, LA County Arboretum, Arcadia, CA

Bette Nesbitt, horticulturist, Tucson, AZ

Robert Perry, Landscape Architect, LaVerne, CA

W.G. Scotty Scott, landscape consultant, La Quinta, CA

Ken Smith, Landscape Architect, Newberry Park, CA

John Stewart, Albuquerque, NM

Dennis Swartzell, UNLV Arboretum, NV

Lance Walheim, horticultural consultant, Exeter, CA

Sally Wasowski, Landscape Architect, Taos, NM

Margaret West, Landscape Architect, Tucson, AZ

Roger Wyer, landscape consultant, Tucson, AZ

Additional thanks to the botanical gardens and arboretums where many plants and garden scenes in this book were photographed.

Alice Keck Park Memorial Garden, Santa Barbara, CA

Arizona Temple Garden, Mesa, AZ

Descanso Gardens, La Canada, CA

Desert Botanical Garden, Phoenix, AZ

Desert Water Agency, Palm Springs, CA

Filoli, Woodside, CA

Landscapes Southern California Style, Riverside, CA

Los Angeles State & County Arboretum, Arcadia, CA

Quail Botanical Gardens, Encinitas, CA

Rancho Santa Ana Botanic Garden, Claremont, CA

Santa Barbara Botanic Garden, Santa Barbara, CA

South Coast Botanic Garden, Palos Verdes Peninsula, CA

Tohono Chul Park, Tucson, AZ

Tucson Botanical Gardens, Tucson, AZ

University of California Irvine Arboretum, Irvine, CA

Table of Contents

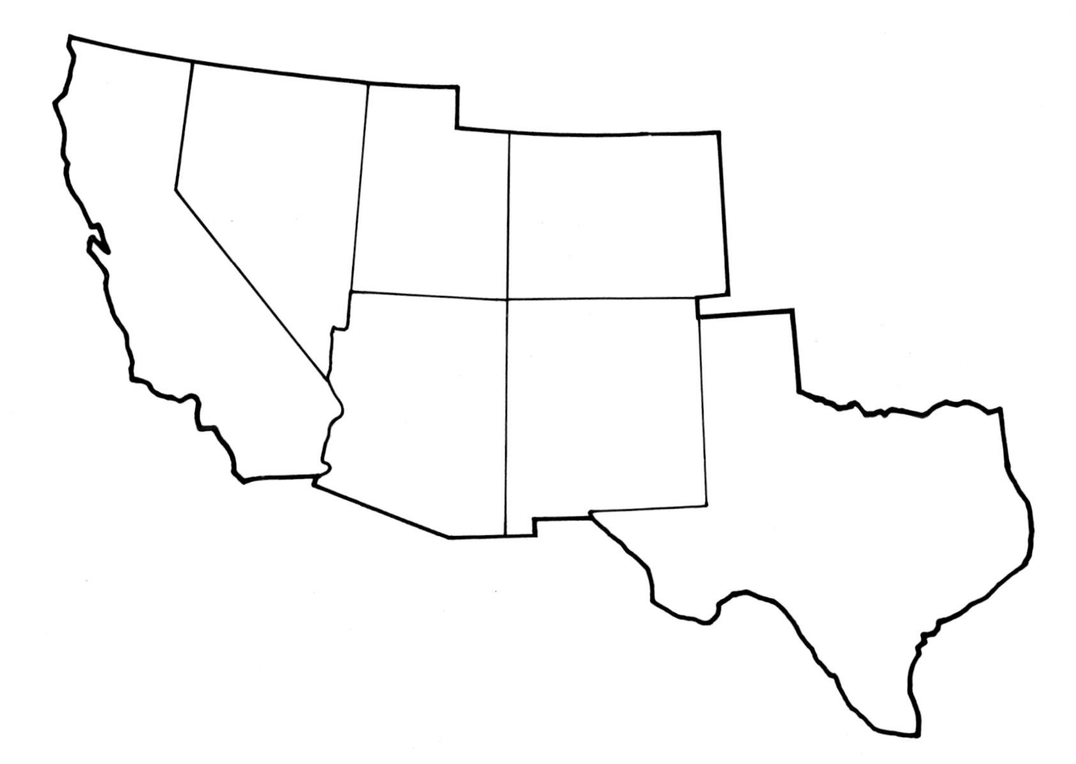

FLOWER GARDENING IN THE ARID WEST

Westerners tend to do things a little differently, and our approach to flower gardening is no exception. This is due in large part to the unique and sometimes adverse growing conditions that face us. Long periods of summer heat, low amounts of rainfall and less-than-ideal soils present special challenges. But adversity tends to breed diversity. Gardeners in the arid West are blessed with an extremely rich palette of plants—in form, flower color and blooming season. And low-water-use plants are available in abundance for every western climate zone.

The following pages will guide you in creating lush, low-water flower gardens composed of *perennials,* flowering *ground covers, ornamental grasses* and *subshrubs*—small shrubs. All bloom year after year—providing color and interest as a permanent part of the landscape.

A Natural Garden Approach

Natural landscapes are designs that take their cues from nature. These informal designs are reflections of casual living, allowing gardeners to include flowering plants in and around their surroundings in ways that go beyond a traditional perennial border. When native plants are used, gardeners renew and develop the unique character of their region and community. As these distinctive landscapes evolve they create a diverse environment that encourages soil, water and wildlife habitat conservation.

A natural garden philosophy blends perfectly with the conservation ethic that is fast becoming part of our everyday lives. And in the arid West, the focus of conservation is, of course, on water. Each chapter in this book is dedicated to providing information on how to enjoy your outdoor space with water-efficient plants and gardening techniques.

Water Conservation: It's Here to Stay

Reducing water use has impact beyond a lower water bill; it conserves a valuable and endangered resource. Conserving water at home can affect how we distribute and store water in the future, reducing the building of canals and dams. Because of dramatic and continuing increases in population, future droughts and increasing demands on western water resources, water conservation will continue to be part of our lives.

A bonus of the natural garden philosophy is the realization that gardeners can have *more with less:* more garden color throughout a variety of locations, more satisfaction knowing you're taking an ecological approach to gardening, using less water and less non-renewable natural resources.

A natural garden scene features yellow *Encelia farinosa,* brittle bush, with pink *Penstemon parryi.*

Above are *Baileya multiradiata* with *Penstemon parryi.*

High Heat in the Arid West: Average Maximum Temperatures in July

Albuquerque	92F
Amarillo	94F
Denver	88F
Fresno	98F
Lancaster	96F
Las Vegas	101F
Los Angeles	83F
Palm Springs	110F
Phoenix	105F
Sacramento	93F
Salt Lake City	91F
San Diego	77F
Santa Barbara	75F
Santa Ana	83F
Santa Fe	85F
Tucson	98F

The Dry-Climate Difference

Sunshine, seasonal temperatures (both high and low), rainfall, wind, soil and other elements create the gardening climate in your own backyard. Understanding these factors, common to every climate, helps you recognize and take advantage of your own garden's unique growing conditions. In other words, when you become a *climate-wise gardener,* you garden with nature instead of against it, planting and caring for adapted plants according to the progression of the seasons. Doing so helps ensure plants will grow and bloom to their full potential, producing a healthy, more attractive, water-efficient garden.

The Sun

The amount of sunshine your garden receives depends on several factors. These include light intensity during the seasons; the direction of exposure (going from highest to lowest: south, west, east, north,) and the amount of shade due to plants and structures. Extreme sunshine and heat can adversely affect the growth of plants, or kill them. High temperatures, intense sunlight and inadequate water stress plants and makes them more susceptible to pests and diseases. This is particularly true of plants introduced to hot arid regions from more temperate climates. They are even more likely to fail if located in southern or western exposures where sunlight and high temperatures are most intense.

In most regions of the arid West, the cool California coast being a notable exception, avoid planting perennials and other landscape plants during late spring and summer. During this time higher temperatures and low humidity greatly increase water need. Fall is the best time to plant, when temperatures are moderate yet the soil is warm to encourage root growth.

Temperatures higher than 90F take a toll on newly planted plants as well as those unadapted to heat. Signs of high temperature damage are browning at edges and tips of mature leaves and wilting of new growth. Plants in fast-draining sandy soils are highly susceptible to heat damage because water drains so quickly. High temperatures also increase the temperature of the upper layer of soil to the extent that roots near the soil surface are killed. Shallow-rooted annuals and perennials are particularly susceptible. Adding an organic mulch—a thick layer of material over the plant roots—cools soil temperatures and insulates roots.

In coastal gardens, *not enough* sunshine and heat can be a problem. Conditions are often too cool, cloudy and foggy for plants that require heat to produce flowers. If you live along the coast, select plants adapted to these conditions, and locate plants in the sunniest locations in your garden—south and west exposures. Reflected heat and light from light-colored walls also increase temperatures.

Cold Temperatures

Every plant has a low-temperature tolerance. When the temperature drops below this point for a certain period of time, plant tissues are damaged. If the cold is severe or prolonged, the plant could be killed. How long cold temperatures last and how quickly they drop affect the extent of the damage. The faster the drop, the worse the injury. Cold that lasts for an hour or less may not hurt plants, but if it stays cold for the whole evening, severe damage is likely. Coldest temperatures often occur just before sunrise.

If the plant is under stress due to lack of moisture, or if it has recently been planted, it is more susceptible to cold injury. The time of year matters as well. When cold temperatures occur late in spring shortly after new, tender growth has emerged, the damage will be much more severe than if the new growth had an opportunity to gradually adjust to cooler temperatures.

Unusual cold waves occur infrequently, dropping temperatures well below normal lows. These "fifty-year freezes," also called *polar waves,* are all-pervading, damaging or destroying plants that would otherwise be cold-hardy. A recent polar wave occured in 1990, when temperatures in Las Vegas dropped to -6F and to 15F in Palm Springs.

Rainfall

With the exceptions of the northern California coast and higher-elevation regions, the West does not receive abundant rainfall, although rainfall can fluctuate greatly from year to year. Yuma, Arizona, has recorded annual rainfall as little as under 1 inch, and as much as 11 inches.

Mountain ranges in the West help determine where rain is distributed. Warm, moist air rises and cools rapidly when it comes in contact with abrupt changes in elevation. The result is condensation and rainfall. After the moisture has been "wrung" from the clouds, there is often little remaining for areas beyond. This is called the *rain shadow effect*. A large-scale example exists in Nevada, where the Sierra Nevada Mountains stand in the way of coastal storms carrying moisture-laden air. The same situation occurs with the San Jacinto Mountains, which block rains from reaching the Coachella Valley.

Throughout much of California, a *Mediterranean* climate prevails, with rainfall coming during winter and spring followed by a warm, dry summer and fall. The lowlands along the coast from Santa Barbara to San Diego are typical. Other regions of the world with this type of climate include South Africa, Chile, western Australia and the Mediterranean. Many native California plants and natives of these similar Mediterranean climates have natural adaptations that allow them to become dormant or semi-dormant during these warm, rainless periods. Because of these adaptations, many native plants may not tolerate regular summer water in a home garden. (An exception is newly planted plants; they should receive regular water until established.)

In southern Arizona, in New Mexico and occasionally in Southern California, summer rains come in the form of intense storms, originating to the south and southeast in the Gulf of Mexico and Gulf of California. These highly localized storms, often no more than three miles across, are capable of dumping large quantities of water in a short time. Much of the rain that falls does more harm than good due to erosion from runoff and the strong surface winds that accompany the storms. High summer temperatures also cause the moisture to evaporate rapidly. Often when it appears that a rainstorm has moistened the soil, the benefit to plants is negligible.

Humidity

How does humidity affect gardening and water needs of plants? In a low-humidity climate, the rate of evaporation of moisture from plants and soil surface can be quite rapid. Low humidity also causes rainfall to evaporate rapidly, to the extent that little actually accumulates in the soil. Low humidity, in combination with hot, dry winds, high temperatures and intense sunlight, causes plants to dry out very quickly. During these conditions, pay close attention to the appearance of your plants. Consider using the hydrozoning principle discussed on page 22; placing plants in groups helps increase humidity around them, thus reducing moisture need.

Wind

Many areas of the West experience high winds—often in spring, occasionally in fall. In much of Southern California, Santa Ana winds sweep through mountain passes into San Bernardino, Riverside, the San Fernando Valley, and Ventura and Orange County. In California's Coachella Valley and in high desert areas, winds up to 40 or more miles per hour are common. Las Vegas experiences winds throughout the year, especially in spring.

Windstorms can turn into sandstorms in many of these areas. Sand blown at a high velocity can seriously damage plants. In some instances the wind-blown sand builds up in watering basins and landscaped areas. Planting living windbreaks and providing protection such as fences or walls, especially for newly planted plants, is necessary in wind-prone regions. Wind, when accompanied by high temperatures, dries out plants rapidly, causing them to require considerably more water. Deep watering, which produces deep roots, helps prevent plants from being toppled over. An extensive root system also draws on a larger reservoir of moisture in the soil.

Microclimates: the Small Climates

Pages 9 to 19 supply a general guide to climates in the arid West. High and low temperatures, wind, sun exposures and rainfall common to general climate zones vary considerably within these climates. Weather variations occur from street to street within a

Cold Temperatures in the Arid West: Average Minimum Temperatures in January

Albuquerque	23F
Amarillo	24F
Denver	14F
Fresno	36F
Lancaster	31F
Las Vegas	33F
Los Angeles	47F
Palm Springs	42F
Phoenix	38F
Sacramento	37F
Salt Lake City	18F
San Diego	46F
Santa Ana	47F
Santa Barbara	42F
Santa Fe	15F
Tucson	38F

In this Tucson garden, heat-tolerant plants were selected to grow in the hot, sunny exposure against a south-facing wall. Featured are lavender-flowering *Verbena*, red *Salvia greggii* and green *Euphorbia rigida*.

city, or from the bottom to the top of a slope, or even among different areas around your house. These small climate variations are called *microclimates*.

In hilly terrain, cold air will flow down hillsides during the evening hours, lowering temperatures in its path. If the flow of air is blocked by a hedge, wall or other barrier, the cold air forms a pool and temperatures drop even lower. For this reason, avoid placing cold-tender plants in low-lying areas.

Areas that stretch laterally across slopes—above valleys but below the crest, especially if they face toward the sunny south—are *thermal belts*. Temperatures in a thermal belt remain much warmer, as much as 10F, than in the valley bottom below. If your home lot is in a thermal belt, you can grow more cold-tender plants than generally recommended for your climate.

Site topography, paved areas, structures and size and placement of existing plants create a broad range of growing conditions, from full shade to reflected sun and heat. Every home lot is different, and changes occur as the plants on site grow and create more shade. Take a walk around your own home to observe microclimates. You'll notice the north side is cooler and the soil is often more moist. It does not receive as much sunshine, especially in winter. Plants that are cold-hardy—able to tolerate cold temperatures of your climate—yet susceptible to sunburn or heat damage—would do best in this location. Now look at your southern and western exposures. Soils here are often hot and dry. If unshaded, plants located here must be tolerant of heat and intense sunlight.

You can modify home microclimates to suit the plants you want to grow, perhaps increasing penetration and reflection of sunlight during cooler winter months and reducing the effects of the hot summer sun. Build overhead structures, install latticework panels or use shade cloth to filter the sun. *Deciduous* trees, which drop their leaves in fall, shade planting beds in summer. In winter, the branches are bare, allowing more sunshine.

Garden Climates in the Arid West

Climates in the West range from the extreme cold of high-elevation, mountainous regions such as those in and around the Rocky Mountains and Sierra Nevada, to moderate coastal climates and to the hot, arid Chihuahuan, Sonoran and Mojave Deserts of the Southwest. The following pages focus on regions where low rainfall, high temperatures, low humidity and other factors prevent moisture from accumulating in the soil.

An excellent way to see firsthand how climate largely determines which plants are able to grow in a given region is by visiting botanical gardens and arboretums. Compare, for example, botanical gardens in Southern California. Tropical plants thrive in coastal gardens such as the San Diego Zoo or Quail Botanical Gardens in Encinitas. Less than 40 miles inland, at Rancho Santa Ana in Claremont, colder temperatures and lack of ocean influence require that more cold-hardy plants be grown. The contrast is even more dramatic when desert regions are considered. The plant palette at the Living Desert in Palm Desert includes many cacti and flowering desert plants that have adapted to survive in extremely hot, arid conditions.

The demonstration gardens on display at botanical gardens and arboretums also offer visitors a wealth of ideas on plant combinations and designs that use little water.

The following pages describe in detail the climates of Arizona, California, southern Colorado, Nevada, New Mexico, southern Utah and Texas. Note that abbreviated codes for each of the climate regions are used in the Gallery of Flowering Plants, pages 36 to 127. (Refer to the bold type information that accompanies each plant listing.) For example, the abbreviation **SSC** stands for Southern California coast. Use these recommendations as a guide to determine which plants are generally adapted to grow in your area.

A display garden at South Coast Botanic Gardens in Palos Verdes Peninsula on the Southern California coast provides visitors with ideas and inspiration for their own gardens. Shown are pink *Cosmos bipinnatus*, orange *Eschscholzia californica*, California poppy, and purple-spiked *Salvia leucantha*, Mexican bush sage.

Average Annual Rainfall in Southern California

Barstow	4.50
Blythe	4.10
Brawley	2.45
Claremont	18.05
Escondido	17.10
Los Angeles	14.75
Needles	4.60
Palm Springs	3.25
Pasadena	20.00
Riverside	11.05
San Bernardino	16.85
San Diego	10.10
Tustin (near)	12.65
Santa Barbara	18.90
Ventura	15.30

Source: *Climate and Man*

Climates of Southern California

In this book, the climates of Southern California are organized into four basic climate zones: *Coastal, Inland Valleys, Low Desert* and *Medium and High Desert*. The following provides an overview; climates here are quite complex. For more specific information on your local climate, contact your state or county cooperative extension service, or consult an experienced nurseryman or Master Gardener in your neighborhood.

Southern California Coast (SCC)— This is the region along the Pacific Coast that includes cities from Santa Barbara in the north to San Diego in the south. The Pacific Ocean rules this climate, and winds and fog are common. An exception occurs when hot Santa Ana winds blow in from nearby deserts, increasing temperatures and drying out plants. Summer sunshine and temperatures are moderate, and humidity is high compared to inland regions, which means plants need less water. Low temperatures are normally quite mild, and tropical and subtropical plants are commonly grown outdoors year-round. Seasonal and day-to-day temperature ranges are small, the opposite of desert regions.

Thermal belts exist near the coast where temperatures are mild but the additional heat allows plants such as avocado to thrive. This is the climate of Camarillo, Beverly Hills, Whittier, Fullerton and Vista.

In the greater Los Angeles area, cold air flows down from hillsides to gather in low valleys below the thermal belts. This reduces the amount of heat available to plants and makes winter lows even lower. Even so, normal winter low temperatures rarely drop below 28F. In summer, morning fog creeps inland as far as Pasadena and Whittier to lower temperatures and increase moisture, usually burning off the same afternoon. This is the climate of Torrance, Inglewood, Lakewood, Gardena and Irvine.

The *growing season*, days between the last and first frosts, is practically year-round, from 330 to 365 days. Generally, as you move inland, the growing season shortens. Rainfall averages range from 10 inches a year in San Diego to 18.90 inches at Santa Barbara.

Problem soils sometimes exist along the coast in the form of heavy clay with a calcareous base. Improving these soils with organic amendments helps increase drainage and workability. See page 130.

In this moderate, forgiving climate, planting can be done year-round. Summer plantings do require closer attention to moisture needs until plants are established.

Southern California Inland (SCI)— This large climate zone is composed of several smaller zones, including the coastal valleys and coastal plains, coastal and interior foothills and the warm thermal belts within. It is a region greatly affected by mountain ranges and local topography. In the northern stretches of Southern California are the *Transverse* ranges, which generally run east and west. In Orange, Riverside and San Diego Counties, the *Peninsular* ranges run north and south. The result is a jigsaw puzzle of diverse climates that are separated, in some instances, by only a few miles.

The nature of climate in inland Southern California largely depends on which imparts the greatest influence—the cool ocean or the hot, inland deserts. In some instances, both may, on a given day, literally depending on which way the wind is blowing.

Winter temperatures are lower inland than on the coast, which means gardeners must be more selective in where they locate tropical and subtropical plants. High temperatures are also higher by comparison—90F to 100F days in summer are common. This, along with the lower humidity, causes plants to demand more moisture. Higher temperatures allow plants that require heat to be grown here where they might fail along the coast. These include flowering plants native to desert regions such as red salvia, *Salvia greggii*, cassia, *Cassia* species, Texas ranger, *Leucophyllum* species and verbena, *Verbena* species.

Rainfall is most prevalent during winter and spring. These are annual averages for selected cities: Riverside, 11.05 inches; Pasadena, 20 inches and Claremont, 18.05 inches.

Escondido, Thousand Oaks, Pasadena, Whittier and Covina are in thermal belts that are regularly involved in a climatic tug of war between the influences of the cool coast and warm inland region. However, winters are generally mild, with normal low temperatures dropping to 36F to 23F, so cold-tender plants can often be grown successfully.

A similar but somewhat cooler climate is found in El Monte, Arcadia and Burbank. In the same situation as described on page 8, cold air tends to gather in low valleys draining down from thermal belts, which further reduces winter lows. In this instance, normal winter low temperatures are 28F to 23F.

Areas of Southern California that are beyond the influence of the coast are affected by the local terrain and inland deserts. Thermal belts in these regions are generally 10F warmer in winter than the low, cool valleys below them. High heat—100F and above—is common. These warmer regions include Chatsworth in the west San Fernando Valley, San Bernardino, Riverside, Moreno Valley, Hemet and Corona. Nearby cities that are not in warm thermal belts and have a slightly cooler climate include Woodland Hills, Pomona and Ontario.

Plant hardy perennials and other hardy landscape plants in fall to early winter. Sow seed of wildflowers in fall to take advantage of winter rains. After last spring frost, set out cold-tender annuals and perennials. Last spring frosts for this area include: Pasadena, February 3; San Bernardino, March 15; Santa Ana, February 7; Riverside, March 6.

Southern California Low Deserts (SCLD)—This is the climate of Palm Springs, Palm Desert, Brawley, Blythe and Indio. Conditions are similar to the low, subtropical desert of Arizona, described on page 14. However, summertime temperatures are typically hotter, and rainfall is even more scarce—a scant 4 to 5 inches a year, often even less.

In the Coachella, Imperial and Borrego Valleys, temperatures reach 110F to 115F in summer (sometimes more) and 26F to 32F in winter. Day-to-night temperature fluctuations can be considerable. In the lower Colorado River basin, temperature swings from the low 60sF to 110F can occur, a difference of almost 50F.

The Colorado River influences a long stretch from Laughlin, Nevada, through Needles, Blythe, Lake Havasu and Parker to Yuma, Arizona. The conditions are hot, dry and humid, with daily and seasonal temperatures similar to those in the Coachella Valley. The rugged terrain accounts for variable wind patterns that are often intense. Rainfall can be erratic, from very little to a lot. Summer rains are sometimes so heavy highways are closed in wash areas.

Soil type plays an important role in watering and garden care. The sandy and alluvial soils that are so prevalent require irrigations be more frequent than in loamy or clay-type soils, particularly for newly planted plants. Drip irrigation is commonly used when the design allows.

Fall planting is the rule. This allows plants to become established before the high heat of summer comes on. The growing season throughout the low deserts is a long 325 to 350 days, with average last spring frosts occurring in mid-January. In most years, less than a half-dozen evenings drop below freezing.

Southern California Medium and High Deserts (SCMHD)—This is the climate of Lancaster, Palmdale, Hesperia, 29 Palms, Yucca Valley and Victorville. The medium desert generally includes areas within an elevation range of 1,000 to 7,000 feet, but is commonly referred to as the "high desert." Climate here is largely affected by the elevation and terrain, and whether your landscape is in the path of cold-air drainage. Climate also depends on which exerts the greatest influence: the cold-winter mountain climates to the north, or the hot, dry subtropical desert regions to the south and west. Valley floors are colder and the growing season is shorter compared to the warm thermal belts on slopes above them.

Summer temperatures are hot, well into the 100sF, but do not reach the plant-wilting highs or occur as frequently as in low-desert regions. Day-to-night and season-to-season temperature variations are almost as extreme as in the lower deserts. At elevations of 1,000 to 2,200 feet, normal winter lows are 20F to 22F; at 2,300 to 3,500 feet, lows range from 15F to 20F,

Climate Adaptation Key

SCC:	**S. Calif. Coastal**
SCI:	**S. Calif. Inland**
SCLD:	**S. Calif. Low Deserts**
SCMHD:	**S. Calif. Medium/ High Deserts**
NCC:	**N. Calif. Coastal**
CACV:	**Calif. Central Valley**
AZLD:	**Arizona Low Desert**
AZMHD:	**Arizona Medium/High Deserts**
NMMHD:	**New Mexico Medium/High Deserts**
SNV:	**Southern Nevada**
TXHP:	**Texas High Plains**
TXEP:	**Texas Edwards Plateau**
TXRRP:	**Texas Red Rolling Plains**
TXTPR:	**Texas Trans-Pecos Region**
CWR:	**Cold-Winter Regions**

Landscape plants in low-elevation desert regions such as Palm Desert, California, must be able to tolerate long periods of high heat and low rainfall. This natural landscape includes yellow-flowering *Encelia farinosa*, brittle bush, and red *Linum grandiflorum* 'Rubrum'.

although extremes are infrequently much lower. This climate has enough days below freezing to provide a definite winter season.

Winds are almost constant, blowing 10 to 20 mph most days. Strong winds 40 to 70 mph occur through the winter and spring months, particularly in areas away from sheltering mountains. Homes and plants greatly benefit from windbreaks and shelterbelts. Arizona cypress, *Cupressus arizonica*, is commonly used. Walls or fences help reduce the impact of wind.

Over half this region receives less than 5 inches of rain each year, with some exceptions. Lancaster receives slightly more. If rains are plentiful in fall and winter as in most regions in the arid West, there's a good chance of seeing spectacular spring shows of wildflowers.

Plant cold-hardy plants in fall so they'll become established during the cool part of the year. Sow wildflower seed in fall as well. Wait until after last spring frost before planting tender perennials and annuals. Last spring frost dates are averages, and late frosts are common. Be prepared to protect newly planted plants in spring. Examples are: Barstow, March 8; and Lancaster, March 31.

This planting of *Heuchera*, coral bells, in a Southern California inland valley garden thrives beneath the shade and protection provided by a wide-spreading *Quercus agrifolia*, coast live oak.

Northern California Climates

Northern California Coast and Coast Ranges (NCC)—The climate of this region, which extends from Santa Maria north, is governed by the ocean. This area is an extremely complex collection of climates, particularly around the San Francisco Bay Area. The following presents an overview. Contact local experts in your region for more complete information.

High temperatures along the coast during summer are quite moderate, normally 60F to 75F, and fog is common many days. This reduces the sun's intensity and also supplies a great amount of moisture. Humidity is also much higher than in inland climates. All these conditions combined reduce the moisture needs of plants. In fact, the additional humidity creates an environment that fosters many plant diseases. The absence of summer sun prevents heat-loving flowering plants, such as crape myrtle, from thriving. Frosts are rare, as is the case on the southern coast.

The Coast Ranges, groupings of ridges and hills, extend from Santa Maria to Eureka. These ridges and the river valleys within them greatly modify the climate of this region. The ranges and valleys nearest the coast tend to be cool and rainy in winter, with high humidity and frequent fog in summer. As you move inland, the daytime temperature increases and fog diminishes. Areas closest to the coast receive afternoon winds during summer. This is the climate of Oakland, Richmond, Hayward and Santa Cruz.

Thermal belts within the coastal ranges moderate winter temperatures in some places, so that cold-tender plants can often be grown. Cities within thermal belts include Saratoga, Piedmont and the Berkeley Hills.

Cold-air basins are located in the many valleys along the coast and between mountain ranges. Cool air drains from the thermal belts above, lowering winter temperatures and causing late spring frosts. These areas include the cities of Hollister, Santa Rosa and

Wildflowers, flowering perennials and ornamental grasses blend with a small lawn to make an attractive garden in Sonoma, California.

Average Annual Rainfall in Northern California and the Central Valley

Bakersfield	6.10
Berkeley	23.10
Bishop	7.50
Fresno	9.40
Livermore	14.00
Marysville	20.70
Merced	11.80
Napa	22.70
Palo Alto	15.20
Red Bluff	23.10
Sacramento	15.90
Salinas	13.40
San Jose	13.95
Santa Rosa	29.10
Visalia	9.60
Stockton	14.10

Source: *Climate and Man*

Napa. Low temperatures generally drop into the the mid-20sF and occasionally to the mid-teens.

Rainfall away from the coast can be erratic enough to help cause drought conditions in certain years. Annual averages for selected cities include: Salinas, 13.40; Santa Maria, 14.10; San Jose, 13.95; Palo Alto, 15.20 inches. In addition, a sampling of last frost dates demonstrates how the coast modifies low temperatures: Oakland, January 11; San Jose, February 10; Salinas, March 17.

Much as on the Southern California coast, planting can be done year-round in most of this region. As you move away from the coast and low temperatures fall, do most planting in the fall. Wait until last spring frost has passed before setting out cold-tender plants.

California's Great Central Valley (CACV)—This climate zone includes the Sacramento Valley in the north and San Joaquin Valley in the south. It covers the heart of northern and central California, from Redding south through the cities of Sacramento, Fresno and Bakersfield. The valley stretches approximately 450 miles and is up to 50 miles wide. It is is completely encircled by mountain ranges.

Climates in the Central Valley are dominated by long, hot summers, with the highest temperatures at both the northern and southern ends of the valley. Daily highs reach well into the 100F range. As a rule, temperatures increase as you travel from north to south in the San Joaquin Valley and from south to north in the Sacramento Valley. As the elevation increases on the gradual slopes of the western side of the Sierra Nevada, winter lows become lower. Temperature ranges are much more severe on the rugged and severe inclines of the eastern slopes.

In low-lying valley areas, cold air drains down from slopes and creates "cold air lakes," lowering winter temperatures. These areas are also subject to dense *tule* fog in winter. This fog can actually serve as an insulating blanket for plants, moderating temperatures to reduce frosts. This is the climate of Bakersfield, Fresno and Merced.

The slopes from which the cold air drains create a climate zone composed of warm thermal belts located along the sides of the valley. This is the climate of Redding, Red Bluff and Porterville. At elevations of 500 to 700 feet, killing frosts are infrequent.

Another climate zone stretches from the San Francisco Bay Area east to Modesto and north to Sacramento, including Stockton, Lodi and Davis. Temperatures in this region are moderated by the marine air, fog and resulting higher humidity that flows inland from the San Francisco Bay. The Sacramento River Delta also has a moderating effect on temperatures causing summers to be somewhat cooler and winters slightly warmer.

Average rainfall and average last spring frosts for selected cities in the valley are as follows: Maricopa, 5.70 inches, February 10; Bakersfield, 6.10 inches, February 21; Fresno, 9.40 inches, February 9; Merced, 11.80 inches, March 9; Stockton, 14.10 inches, February 14; Sacramento, 15.90 inches, February 6; and Davis, 16.45 inches, March 17.

Plant hardy perennials and other hardy landscape plants in fall to early winter. Sow seed of wildflowers in fall to take advantage of winter rains. After last spring frost, set out cold-tender annuals and perennials.

Arizona

Arizona climates range from the cold-winter, high-elevation climates such as around Flagstaff, to the low-elevation Sonoran Desert around Phoenix. Flagstaff, at an elevation of about 7,000 feet, has a growing season (days between last and first frosts) of about 118 days. Average annual rainfall is about 20 inches. Cold temperatures decide which plants can be grown. Prescott, at 5,280 feet, has a definite winter season, but summers are hot. Low temperatures do not drop as low as in Flagstaff, so a greater selection of plants can be grown there.

Arizona Low Desert (AZLD)—This is the climate of Phoenix, Yuma and Casa Grande. It is typified by long, hot summers, mild winters and low rainfall. Phoenix is located in the Sonoran Desert at a 1,200-foot elevation. It is a subtropical desert, similar to Palm Springs in Southern California. Differences include more rainfall (7.60 inches each year compared to 3.25 in Palm Springs) and cooler summers. Daytime temperatures *average* 105F in summer in

Phoenix compared to Palm Springs' 110F to 115F. Winds are generally light, with the exception of high-velocity storms that can be part of the package of the summer rainy season.

Plant hardy perennials and other hardy landscape plants from fall to early winter. Sow seed of wildflowers in fall to take advantage of winter rains. After the last spring frost, set out cold-tender annuals and perennials. Killing frosts are few and the growing season is long. In Phoenix, the average last spring frost is February 5; at Yuma, on the Colorado River, it's January 12.

Arizona Medium and High Deserts (AZMHD)—In the middle-elevation Sonoran Desert (2,200 feet) at Tucson, rainfall averages about 11.15 inches a year. Almost half falls during the summer months. Elevation has a great effect on rainfall. Every 1,000 feet in elevation increases rainfall annually by 4 to 5 inches. During a rainy summer, the foothills come alive as native plants respond to the moisture with fresh new growth and flowers.

Summer temperatures are generally 5F below those of Phoenix due to Tucson's higher elevation. Warmest temperatures occur in late June and early July, just prior to the onset of summer rains. Winter low temperatures restrict the use of many cold-tender, subtropical plants to sheltered microclimates and warm thermal belts on hillsides.

The planting seasons are the same as in the Arizona Low Desert. The growing season in Tucson is 252 days, with a last spring frost of March 15. Wickenburg, at 2,095 feet elevation, has a growing season of 242 days with last spring frost of March 21.

The high elevation deserts of Arizona, 3,300 to 5,000 feet, include the cities of Kingman, Globe, Nogales, Sedona and Douglas. The increase in elevation brings a definite winter season with lower low temperatures and more days below 28F. Summers are hot but are not as extreme as in the low and middle deserts. Rainfall is greater in this region, averaging 15 inches and more per year. Cities in the southeastern part of the state tend to benefit most from the summer rainy season. For example, Nogales receives on the average almost 8 inches of rain during July and August out of total annual rainfall of 16.10 inches; Douglas receives 6.15 inches during the same period out of its average of 12.80 inches a year.

Plant cold-hardy plants in fall so they'll become established during the cool part of the year. Sow wildflower seed in fall. Wait until after last spring frost before planting tender perennials and annuals. Last spring frost dates are averages, and late frosts are common. The last spring frost dates for cities in this zone are: Winslow, May 2; Globe, March 29; Nogales, March 30; and Douglas, April 8.

New Mexico

New Mexico's climates are influenced by a rich mixture of high mesas (plateaus), mountains, canyons, valleys and mostly dry arroyos (washes). Elevations run from 3,000 feet along the southeastern border to about 14,000 feet atop the highest mountain peaks.

New Mexico Medium and High Deserts (NMMHD)—In the southwestern and eastern sections of the state, as well as the Rio Grande Valley, the climate is typically medium to high desert, with elevations ranging from 3,300 to 4,500 feet and more. This is the climate of Albuquerque, Las Cruces, Hobbs and Roswell. Conditions here are similar to those in the high deserts of Arizona and California. Rainfall ranges from an average of 8.40 inches in Albuquerque to 14.40 inches in Hobbs. Summer rains account for almost half.

The higher elevations in New Mexico feature a cold-winter climate similar to that found throughout Colorado, Nevada and Utah. (See following.) Winter temperatures are lower than in Arizona and California; Albuquerque has more than 100 nights of subfreezing weather.

Plant cold-hardy plants in fall so they'll become established during the cool part of the year. Sow wildflower seed in fall. Wait until after last spring frost before planting tender perennials and annuals. Last spring frost dates are averages, and late frosts are common. Be prepared to protect newly planted plants in spring. Last spring frosts for selected cities are: Albuquerque, April 13; Carlsbad, March 29; Santa Fe, April 24; and Roswell, April 7.

Average Annual Rainfall in Arizona

Casa Grande	8.25
Douglas	12.80
Flagstaff	20.90
Gila Bend	5.80
Globe	16.50
Grand Canyon	16.50
Kingman	10.95
Nogales	16.10
Phoenix	7.60
Prescott	20.70
Tucson	11.15
Willcox	12.25
Winslow	8.35
Yuma	3.60

Average Annual Rainfall in New Mexico

Alamogordo	11.25
Albuquerque	8.40
Carlsbad	13.15
Clovis	18.45
Deming	9.20
Farmington	8.45
Roswell	13.05
Silver City	16.85
Santa Fe	14.20
Soccorro	10.35

Source: *Climate and Man*

Nevada, Utah and Colorado

The climate of these three states is largely governed by cold winters, with some exceptions. Snow is common at higher elevations and winter lows drop well below zero. Even in regions above 5,000 feet elevation, summers can get hot—temperatures over 100F are not uncommon.

The Great Basin Desert covers a great portion of Nevada and Utah. Conditions here are almost as cold as in the surrounding high-elevation mountainous regions. Conditions in valleys and deserts are typically dry with bright sunshine and large swings in seasonal and day-to-night temperatures.

Lakes and rivers help modify cold temperatures. For example, the Great Salt Lake warms temperatures around Salt Lake City. The average last spring frost is April 13, and the growing sea-

Average Annual Rainfall in Nevada

Carson City	9.30
Elko	9.45
Las Vegas	4.85
Reno	7.75
Tonopah	4.70
Winnemucca	8.20

Average Annual Rainfall in Utah

Cedar City	13.00
Provo	15.35
Richfield	8.40
St. George	8.75
Salt Lake	15.80

Average Annual Rainfall in Colorado

Boulder	18.20
Colorado Springs	14.20
Denver	14.00
Durango	19.55
Grand Junction	8.75
Pueblo	11.55

Source: *Climate and Man*

A colorful, low-water garden in Santa Fe, New Mexico, includes, from bottom to top: *Verbena* species, *Penstemon strictus,* and yellow *Achillea.* Trees in the background are *Populus* species, aspen.

son is 192 days. Rainfall is 15.80 inches on the average each year. In the Virgin River Valley around St. George, Utah, the lower elevation (2,500 to 3,500 feet) increases the growing season to almost 200 days. The climate is similar to that of the Arizona high desert, although seasonal temperature extremes are greater. River valleys in western Colorado also moderate temperatures, such as around Grand Junction.

Set out plants in spring after danger of frost has passed. The growing season—days between last and first frosts—is usually under 150 days and can even be under 100 days (generally above 6,000 feet elevation). The last spring frost date fluctuates considerably, and gardeners must be aware that damaging late spring frosts are common. Premature fall frosts also damage plants that have not had time to gradually acclimate to the cooler temperatures. Creative use of microclimates can often make the difference between failure and success. Seek out sheltered, sunny south and west exposures when locating more cold-tender plants. See pages 7 and 8 for more on microclimates.

Southern Nevada (SNV)—Las Vegas and nearby Henderson are located in the eastern section of the Mojave Desert in southern Nevada. This area possesses a climate much different from that of the rest of Nevada, with conditions similar to the medium-elevation deserts of California. (See page 11.) At 2,000 feet, the elevation of Las Vegas is about the same as that of Tucson, Arizona, but the growing conditions are more harsh, with normal winter lows to mid-20sF. Soils here are often difficult-to-work caliche and have poor drainage. Summers are hot, with temperatures over 100F normally lasting from late May through August.

Annual rainfall is low, averaging less than 5 inches each year. Hot, drying winds can sap plants of moisture quickly. Windbreaks are helpful for plants as well as people.

Plant hardy perennials and other hardy landscape plants in fall to early winter. Sow seed of wildflowers in fall to take advantage of meager winter rains. After last spring frost, set out cold-tender annuals and perennials. The average growing season for Las Vegas is 239 days, with a last frost date of March 16.

Texas

Texas is the largest state within the continental United States, covering almost 266,000 square miles. It is an area of diverse climates and growing conditions. A broad look at the state divides it into four major geophysical regions: *Coastal Plains, North Central Plains, Great Plains* and the *Trans Pecos Mountain Area.*

This book concentrates on the more arid western half of Texas, approximately bounded by the 98th meridian, the so-called "rainline." This meridian is just east of Witchita Falls and San Antonio. Rainfall increases as you travel east across the state toward Louisiana and can be as plentiful as 50 inches per year in east Texas. Rainfall decreases as you travel west toward New Mexico and the Chihuahuan Desert. A look at rainfall averages of cities traveling east to west tells the story: San Antonio, 26.80 inches; San Angelo, 21.60 inches; Lubbock, 18.80 inches; Midland, 16.75 inches; El Paso, 8.55 inches. These figures are averages; rainfall in Texas can be erratic, with droughts lasting for months in some years.

The Great Plains region of Texas extends from the north and northwest and as far south as Austin. Within the Great Plains are the High Plains of the Panhandle and the Edwards Plateau of southwest Texas.

Texas High Plains—The Panhandle (TXHP)—This is the northernmost portion of the state and the coldest, with elevations ranging from 3,000 to 4,700 feet. Amarillo and Lubbock are located here. Average rainfall is 17 to 20 inches per year, a large portion occurring in early summer. Average winter lows are 20F to 26F, but lows well below zero have been recorded. The higher elevation moderates summer temperatures somewhat, with averages in the mid-90sF. Average last spring frost dates are: Amarillo, April 11; and Lubbock, April 12.

Perennials that do well here include *Penstemon* species, and *Melampodium leucanthum,* blackfoot daisy.

The Edwards Plateau (TXEP)—This is the Hill Country, located in the heart of Texas. The southernmost portion reaches to the *Balcones Escarpment*, a geological fault line that follows a giant semicircle from Del Rio on the

Average Annual Rainfall in Texas

City	Rainfall
Abiline	24.75
Amarillo	20.95
Austin	34.45
Ft. Worth	31.60
El Paso	8.55
Laredo	20.45
Lubbock	18.80
Midland	16.75
San Angelo	21.60
San Antonio	26.80
Witchita Falls	28.55

Source: *Climate and Man*

A planting of *Lupinus texensis*, Texas bluebonnet, and *Yucca* species add color to this Fredericksburg garden in Texas Hill Country.

Rio Grande River to the Red River just west of Gainesville. The plateau extends as far west as the Pecos River. West of the river begins the Trans-Pecos area, described on page 19.

Large cities within this region tend to fall on geological and climatic boundaries (often limestone escarpments), making it precarious to define growing conditions. For example, San Angelo could be included here as well as in the Red Rolling Plains region. (See following.) Eastern portions of Austin and southern portions of San Antonio fall into the Blackland Prairie region.

Rainfall is substantial for cities closest to the 98th meridian, such as San Antonio, which receives an annual average of 26.80 inches. Del Rio, by comparison, located far to the southwest, receives 18.50 inches. Average last frost dates in spring are: San Antonio, February 24; and Del Rio, February 22.

A wide range of perennials are adapted to the Hill Country. In addition to those recommended for the High Plains, *Amsonia* species, blue Texas star, *Aster* species, aster, *Salvia* species, sage, and *Echinacea purpurea*, purple coneflower, are commonly grown.

Red Rolling Plains (TXRRP)— Southeast of the high plains of the Panhandle lie the Red Rolling Plains. Together they mark the southern end of the Great Plains of the central U.S. The region gets its name from the reddish to pinkish color of the soils prevalent here.

As is typical in Texas, rainfall is higher in the eastern portion of the Rolling Red Plains: Wichita Falls, 28.55 inches;

This Midland garden in the Red Rolling Plains features the white annual *Lobularia maritima*, sweet alyssum, and yellow *Coreopsis.*

Abilene, 24.75 inches; San Angelo, 21.60 inches. May and September are normally rainy months. Summers are hot here; average temperatures reach up to 98F for San Angelo and Wichita Falls. This heat is often accompanied by drying winds, greatly increasing evaporation from plants and soil, requiring additional irrigation. Average last spring frosts are: San Angelo, March 25; and Wichita Falls, March 22.

Flowering plants for this region include *Castilleja purpurea*, purple paintbrush, *Verbena bipinnatifida*, prairie verbena, and *Zinnia grandiflora*, yellow zinnia.

The Trans-Pecos Region (TXTPR)— This region is essentially a plateau with elevations ranging from 3,000 to 5,000 feet, but reaching over 8,000 feet in mountain areas. The Chihuahuan Desert is located at lower elevations here. This is the climate of El Paso. Rainfall for the Trans-Pecos region is lowest in the state, averaging 6 to 12 inches a year. El Paso receives 8.55 inches on average. Rainfall is most prevalent in late summer. Summer temperatures are warm; in El Paso they average 95F. In mountain areas at higher elevations, summer temperatures are cooler. Winter temperatures in El Paso tend to be mild by Texas standards, averaging 32F, but have dropped as low as 5F. The average last spring frost is March 21.

Perennials that do well in the higher-elevation regions surrounding El Paso do not necessarily do well in the city due to high temperatures in summer. *Liatrus mucronata*, gayfeather, *Berlandiera lyrata*, chocolate flower, and *Ratibida columnaris*, Mexican hat, accept the heat and growing conditions.

CREATING A LOW-WATER GARDEN

Some call it *low-water* landscape design. Others call it *Xeriscape (zir-i-skap)*. The terms *hydrozoning* and *water-efficient landscaping* are used, as is *natural landscaping*. In one way or another, these terms basically describe the same thing: creative, common-sense gardens composed of native and adapted plants that use water efficiently; landscapes that are attractive as well as practical.

The following pages present a wide range of ideas and design philosophies to fuel your concepts of what a western flower garden could be. You'll discover new ways to combine plants, both native and adapted, in a natural garden design, plus information on creating traditional perennial beds and borders.

As you read this chapter, be aware that your garden requires a unique approach. Every garden is different, so do not attempt to duplicate, plant by plant, successes noticed in catalogs and magazines, or even those of your neighbors. But *do look* for the underlying principles that make a landscape appealing, adjusting the ideas to suit your needs and the qualities of your site. The more you are able to cater to the unique climatic and soil conditions of your landscape, the more likely your garden will thrive.

The innocent promises offered by small, young plants can affect the good judgment in all of us. It's tempting to bring a carload home from the nursery with the idea that you'll surely find suitable spots for them all. But for a long-term flower garden, developing a design and a planting plan ahead of time is well worth the time and effort.

You'll discover that a well-conceived design provides a bonus beyond good looks: It becomes a guide to locating plants according to their inherent cultural needs, as well as proper spacing. Plants in your garden will be easier to water and care for in the years to come.

A planting combination of yellow and gray enhances the entrance to this New Mexico home.

Photo above is *Achillea tomentosa.*

Hydrozoning: Grouping Plants By Water Use

Grouping plants with similar moisture requirements—low, moderate and high—is a simple landscaping principle, but highly useful to gardeners in the arid West. Because plants with like water requirements are situated in one location, it's easier to provide them with the amount of water they need—no more, no less. Zoning plants allows you to budget water use, limiting the most lush, high-water-use plants to small areas close to outdoor living spaces. By grouping plants, maintenance such as pruning and trimming is reduced. Many plants in the low and moderate zones require only occasional selective pruning to control growth.

Irrigation systems are easier to design when plants are zoned by water use. In fact, it is impossible to water mixed plantings of high-water and low-water plants efficiently. Separate control valves or drip irrigation lines for each zone further enhance water conservation and help produce healthier plants.

This zoned landscape in Santa Barbara features blue-flowering *Echium fastuosum* and yellow-flowering *Gazania* species. These low-water plants are placed at the outer reaches of the landscape yet provide masses of color. As a bonus, plant roots bind the soil to help protect the slope against erosion.

Upright-growing *Rosmarinus officinalis*, rosemary, and *Lavandula*, lavender, interweave to serve as backdrop to flowers of *Hemerocallis*, daylily.

Gray-leaved or silver-leaved plants provide opportunities for dramatic contrasts. Shown are *Artemisia pycnocephala*, in the foreground, with *Salvia* species, sandhill sage.

It is not necessary for plants located farthest from your home or patio to be lush in appearance. However, most moderate-water plants—the *transitional* group between lush, high-water plants and low-water plants—are as attractive and colorful as their water-thirsty counterparts. A natural garden design, discussed in the following pages, is an excellent way to put the concept into practice. Natural designs and the plants included in them are usually well adapted to the low and moderate zones of a landscape.

As mentioned, three water-use zones are recommended:

Low-Water Zone—Placed farthest from your home. Select plants that, after becoming established, can live on rainfall (not always possible in extremely low-rainfall, hot-summer climates) or on minimum summer irrigation.

Moderate-Water Zone—Plants that require some irrigation but are not water-greedy. Most are vigorous growers that produce flowers equal to or even surpassing those of high-water plants.

High-Water Zone—Plants requiring the most water but planted in smaller quantities and grouped closely together to get the most out of water applied. This is often called a *mini-oasis*. Like an oasis in the desert, the high-water zone becomes a small, lush spot near your patio or other location where you are able to enjoy your favorite high-water plants and their nuances of fragrance, flowers, color and texture. The high zone is also the place for a water feature, such as a small pool or recirculating fountain. It serves as a focal point in the landscape, and gives your eyes and senses a coolness that contrasts nicely with the surrounding landscape.

Note that each plant in the Gallery of Flowering Plants on pages 36 to 127 is rated according to high, moderate and low water use to assist you with your plant selections. Also refer to page 136 for recommendations on watering according to these zones.

Plant Partnerships

Color, form and *texture* are three basic elements of design to consider when combining and positioning plants. Other design factors are *scale*—how size of plants and garden relate to the whole scene of home and landscape and *balance*—are planting beds in proportion in mass and size with one another?

Color is the most dramatic feature at your disposal and requires some thought (and often restraint!) to be effective. Plant forms, whether they are mounding, vertical, low-growing or weeping, influence landscape design. The relative mature height and spread of plants must also be kept in scale with one another. If positioned incorrectly, taller, more aggressive plants will block your view or even smother smaller ones. Combining plants with contrasting shapes also adds interest. Varying textures of foliage and flowers adds interest to a design, reinforcing a formal or informal theme. See illustrations, page 34.

Color

Many options are available in flower color and bloom periods. It takes thoughtful planning to achieve the effect you want. For example, you may want a sensational display of color during late spring or summer, with a profusion of plants coming into bloom at once. Or you might want your garden to offer something of interest throughout the year, with a few species blooming as others fade. Color can also be achieved with dramatic foliage contrasts, using gray, gray-green or silver-leaved plants in combination with plants having dark-green leaves. The chart on pages 38 to 39 will assist you with your planning, supplying the size, color range and bloom period of plants described in this book.

As you make your choices, keep in mind that color varies according to the surroundings and location. Walls, buildings, garden structures, background plants and even the sky absorb or reflect color, affecting the look of the garden. For example, a white background wall causes light-colored flowers to lose their impact. The quality of light varies according to where you live and so affects the look of your garden. For example, pastel and light-colored flowers look best in the cool, even light of a coastal garden. In the sun-drenched desert, these colors lose their intensity. The bright, warm-colored sunlight creates a scene better suited to rich reds, purples, magentas and yellows.

For a garden that evokes calmness, select and mass plants with complementary foliage colors and textures and similar flower colors. Place plants in natural-shaped drifts rather than a smattering of colors in dribs and drabs. Blue and gray flower colors are good choices for this type of effect. The idea is to blend colors as well as forms and textures together. This works especially well with small gardens, where a simple design visually expands the garden space.

A mass of red *Salvia greggii*, red salvia, combines with *Oenothera berlandieri*, Mexican evening primrose, at home entrance. Lavender *Verbena* and white *Melampodium leucanthum*, blackfoot daisy, are at far right.

A combination planting of fine-texured *Teucrium chamaedrys*, germander, contrasts with the coarse-textured gray leaves of *Artemisia* and yellow-flowering *Coreopsis*.

For the dynamic, create eye-catching combinations with color opposites. A good example is yellow flowers planted with violet. Consider testing color combinations by planting small groups of flowering plants in containers. You can move them about to see how the colors look together, and adjust colors and placement before you commit to a mass planting.

Form

When perennials are a permanent part of the landscape, they can become structural plants, used in place of shrubs for screening, as hedges massed as backgrounds or as permanent borders. This is especially effective in today's small home and condominium lots, where the scaled-down sizes of perennials and subshrubs work to advantage. In mild-climate regions, where plants are commonly on display year-round, select evergreen plants that have attractive foliage. This is one of the advantages of using small shrubs and grasses in a mixed border—they can provide a foundation to the design that herbaceous perennials cannot.

Often it helps to create a focal point in a design by "building" to a dominant element—gradually directing attention to an accent plant or grouping. This focal point can be determined by a plant's position (perhaps at the apex of a curve) or its contrasting color or stature. Another technique involves using various sizes and shapes (being careful not to block plants from view) to "layer" plants in your perennial landscape. As groups of plants gradually merge (but not crowd) into one another, they create a harmonious yet visually interesting scene. As a bonus, weeding and maintenance are often reduced.

Texture

Texture can mean many things in a landscape design. Close up, it defines the surface of leaves and flowers, such as fine-textured, lacy leaves or large, coarse, rough-textured leaves. It can also relate to the whole landscape scene as viewed from a distance, when the form of plants presents a fine or coarse texture. The leaves of evergreen perennials are important to your design, since the foliage is often on display when the flowering season has passed. As you would blend colors, create blends of plants with similar textures. Combine plants with similar fine-textured foliage. For contrast, place them near groups of coarse-foliaged plants. Avoid having too much of one or the other for best interest.

The gray leaves and yellow flowers of *Santolina chamaecyparissus*, lavender cotton, are striking when blended with the bluish purple blooms of *Limonium perezii*, sea lavender. The casual, billowing growth habits of both plants are well adapted to natural garden designs.

Uncommon Garden Spaces

Flower gardens can be located in small, irregular spaces around homes. These can be free-form patterns with simple combinations of two, three or more kinds of plants. Here are a few ideas for small-area garden spaces:

- ☐ Path to the front entry
- ☐ Entry court at front entry
- ☐ Ribbon border along walkway or driveway
- ☐ Filler plants around newly planted shrub areas
- ☐ Narrow areas (side yards) between house and fence or walls
- ☐ Backdrop planting around a pool or spa
- ☐ Along a drainage swale or dry creekbed
- ☐ On a slope as part of rock garden and boulder bed
- ☐ Front yard as natural garden in place of lawn
- ☐ Under low windows
- ☐ Along a long driveway
- ☐ Raised beds for a cutting garden
- ☐ Tree-shaded garden
- ☐ Containers or window boxes on patio or deck

Designing a Natural Garden

Most books on perennial gardening focus on the traditional methods of growing plants in beds and mixed borders. Creating a naturalistic setting requires a different approach, one that can actually be more difficult to carry out effectively. In fact, some gardeners may not enjoy the casual, seemingly haphazard appearance of a natural garden, feeling more comfortable in controlled surroundings. However, natural garden designs, also called *mixed borders,* do work well in selected areas around the home, such as among shrubs and trees located in outlying areas of your landscape.

A natural garden does more than preserve naturally occurring plants that might exist on an undeveloped site. Its goal is to recreate the atmosphere and mood of the surrounding region, including its indigenous colors, textures and forms. It should evoke a natural scene, drawing inspiration from the surrounding countryside. As a bonus, a natural garden provides food and shelter for wildlife.

Many varied natural environments exist in the arid West, from the cool, soft-lighted coast to the sharp lines and bright contrasts of deserts to the rugged, rocky mountain foothills. Natural gardening involves understanding the unique character of plants and terrain that occur in undeveloped areas around your home. By including native plants in your home landscape, the garden becomes a living bridge to your surroundings.

It is not necessary to abandon a traditional landscape for a natural garden design. A natural garden can be blended with existing landscapes, and this is often the best way to begin. In fact, a natural garden fits perfectly into a hydrozoned landscape, described on page 23. Natural design plantings are well suited, both culturally and aesthetically, to low-water or even moderate-water zones. The private, traditional garden is then retained as a small, high-water zone.

Here are some simple ideas to assist you in thinking naturally.

Observe Wild Landscapes in Your Region—Visit areas near your home where undeveloped landscapes still exist. Arboretums and botanical gardens offer many opportunities to learn about natural garden design and native plants. Plants are in mature stages of growth and are accurately identified. Many botanical gardens also have undeveloped areas as well as interpretive displays and demonstration gardens that show examples of attractive, low-water landscapes. Take photos of plants and scenes that interest you to serve as inspiration at home.

Take Advantage of the Surrounding Landscape—Today's home lots are often small and crowded. You might be able to "borrow" from the surrounding natural landscape to visually expand your garden. For example, frame a view of a natural scene with shrubs and small trees. A good design also intrigues the visitor to explore, to want to know what lies around the curve in the path. As you install your landscape, include walkways, paths and benches. Make it interesting to continue; make it comfortable to stay.

Develop Your Region's Sense of Place— As mentioned, this requires an understanding of the unique, native vegetation, terrain and architectural history of your area. Every place has these distinct characteristics—whether you live in the desert, in the mountains or on the coast. A sense of place provides a focus to develop a landscape style that fits with local traditions and history. Even within general climate zones, there are many differences. The subtropical desert of Palm Springs is much different than the medium-elevation desert of Lancaster.

Select Plants with Casual Growth Habits—Ornamental grasses, for example, are excellent because of their informal shapes, textures and colors. When assisted by the wind, they add sound and movement. In fact, the majority of native and adapted plants look best when left to their own devices and allowed to mature unpruned into their natural forms.

Space Plants and Materials Randomly—Place plants in groups or clusters as they would appear in nature. Allow plenty of depth and space for the planting area. One of the best ways to carry out this theme is by creating natural, undulating earth berms and rolling terrain. This eliminates the common, flat lot. Use of

A Low-Water Landscape Design

The landscape plan shown here presents many of the options available to homeowners in the arid West. The low-water-use plants included perform multiple landscape functions. Evergreen, deciduous and native trees provide shade and color, as well as food and shelter for wildlife. The location of plants and gardens are carefully considered. The lawn is placed at the rear of the home where it can be best used as a play surface. A water dish for wildlife is positioned so it can be viewed from indoors. Several special gardens, including a rose garden, vegetable garden and perennial border, are tucked into small-space areas. Walkways link the landscape and make all areas accessible.

Many landscape designers—professionals as well as amateurs—begin the design process with graph paper, using the squares to equal a unit of measurement so the landscape can be drawn to scale. Existing features such as property lines, residence, patios, drives and walkways are drawn on the graph paper. Then, using tracing paper, you can sketch in the locations, sizes, shapes and designs of your planting beds. Experiment as much as you want. Soon, your ideas will take shape. They can be finalized to create a detailed design to guide you with your plant selection and placement. Also see the illustrations on page 34.

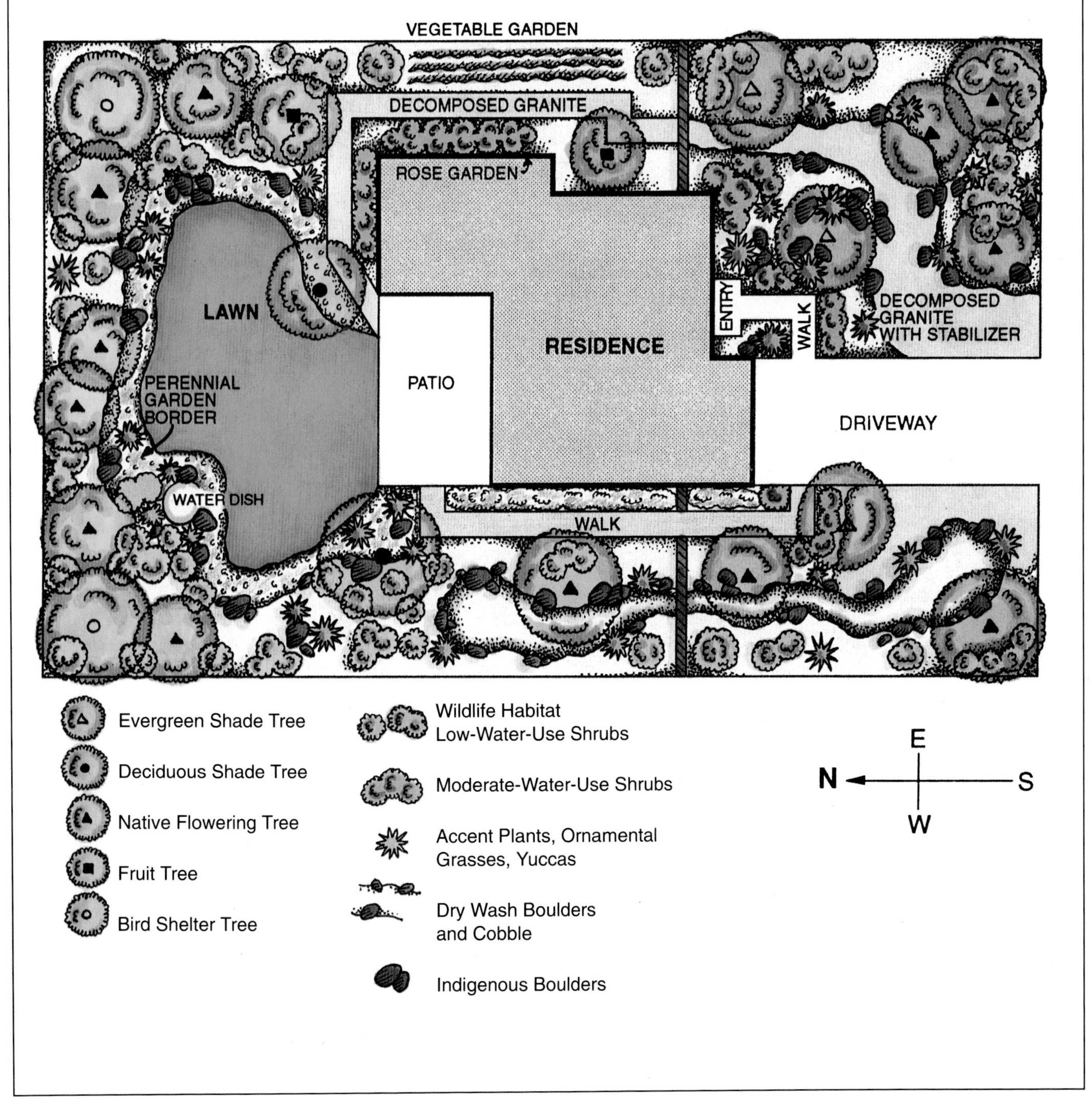

Developing a meadow is just one way to include wildflowers in the landscape. On a smaller scale, consider combining wildflowers with perennials for spectacular color displays. See photo, page 9.

stones and boulders common to your region, partially buried in the ground, supports the effect. Bury some rocks more deeply than others to suggest the natural rock formations indigenous to your area. If slopes and drainage areas exist on your lot, imagine the action runoff of rainfall would have on the soil, rocks, gravel and plants, and arrange them accordingly.

Wildflowers in the Natural Garden

In a natural garden, wildflowers fill a gap in the flowering season, blooming earlier in the season than most perennials. In warm-climate regions, wildflowers are generally at their prime from February to mid-April. After the last of the wildflowers fade, perennials begin to take center stage. You can use the early flowering season to your advantage by interplanting wildflowers among your perennials. Be prepared to be diligent the first year in controlling weeds and getting desirable plants established. Avoid disturbing the soil as much as possible. When the soil is heavily cultivated, weeds sprout from buried seeds brought to the surface, where they are able to germinate, claiming your site before your wildflowers can become estabished. Purchase seeds or transplants of native plants grown locally—they will be best adapted to your climate region.

Recreating a meadow as part of your landscape is one kind of natural garden, but requires considerable space. Most meadow gardens are composed of annual and perennial wildflowers as well as various kinds of ornamental grasses, although the appearance and plants included vary considerably from region to region. A meadow of mixed wildflowers is especially appealing if the background

is simple, such as green foothills or a grove of trees.

For complete information on using wildflowers in the landscape, both perennial and annual species, refer to the IRONWOOD PRESS book, *How to Grow the Wildflowers.*

Wildlife in the Natural Garden

One of the pleasurable aspects of living in the arid West is observing wildlife in their natural habitats. However, as urban and suburban areas develop, wild natural habitats are rapidly being lost. You can create a substitute for lost habitats by including areas for wildlife cover and food in your natural garden. Generally speaking, the more native plants you can include in your landscape, the more birds you'll attract.

The garden area shown in the photograph shown above, located in Tucson, Arizona, contains the basic elements that attract a multitude of birds and butterflies. The small, shallow water dish is the center of attraction. It is sloped to allow animals to move in and out of water easily. The dappled shade of a palo verde tree provides cover and the tree itself is an upper-story retreat. Cacti, dense, low native shrubs and grasses provide ground-level interest and close-by protection. Flowering shrubs and perennials with red and yellow colors are especially attractive to hummingbirds and butterflies.

Many birds that cohabit around a water supply require the protective cover of low-growing flowering shrubs. *Encelia farinosa,* brittlebush, *Ambrosia deltoides,* bursage, *Salvia greggii,* red salvia, and *Justicia spicigera,* desert honeysuckle, are a few favorites that supply cover as well as nectar. Boulders and grassy accent plants supplement the habitat.

A shallow concrete pool serves as a focal point and water source in this wildlife habitat garden. Featured plants include *Verbena* and *Agave* species. The yellow-flowering tree, *Cercidium* species, palo verde, provides shelter and protection.

Lantana species is one of the many flowering plants known to attract butterflies. Creating a wildlife habitat garden in your own backyard helps provide cover and food for a wide range of animals, birds and insects.

Locate a habitat garden where it can be viewed from a patio or indoors. You'll be surprised how quickly the local bird population will discover your garden, even if your home is miles away from a natural area. A habitat garden can easily be tucked into part of a natural, low-water-use garden.

A wildlife garden is appropriate in all areas of the arid West. It attracts not only birds, but reptiles, butterflies and animals as well. The birds and other creatures also help keep insect pests in control without use of chemical sprays. Maintenance requirements are not much different than in the balance of your garden, except that the water basin should be checked every other day or so. Installing a simple water delivery system and float will help maintain the water level. Evaporation and use by birds and animals can deplete the water supply quickly, and in hot climates the water can develop a layer of algae. Clean by washing or brushing out the basin as needed.

Scattering seed will feed local birds, but populations may expand beyond what you may desire, attracting hordes of unwanted gregarious species. The birds may also become dependent on this extra food if overdone. When it's well-planned, you can create a balanced and self-regulating wildlife garden by including a wide selection of plants that supply nectar, seeds and fruit.

Rocks and Boulders in the Natural Landscape

Including boulders and rocks in your home landscape provides a dramatic linkage with the natural dry washes and rock-studded hillsides common to the arid West. The form, color and texture of boulders provide an ideal setting for native and adapted low-water-use plants. In addition to their aesthetic value, boulders create moisture-retentive areas for plant roots. And, as garden seasons progress and plants move through flowering cycles and into dormancy, the boulders provide stability to the scene.

Choices for rocks and boulders should be small (1-1/2 to 2 feet), medium (3 feet) and large (4 feet). Arrange them in odd numbers in random clusters, burying at least one-fourth of each rock, so they appear as they would in the natural environment. Avoid huge boulders for small-area gardens, much as you would avoid using towering trees or wide-spreading shrubs. Step back and view the scene you are creating, and don't include too much.

Tucking plants among rocks and boulders, such as this red-flowering *Penstemon pinifolius*, is a simple and effective way to create a colorful, natural scene. Use rocks native to the region and bury them about one-quarter beneath the soil so they will appear more natural.

Due to their size and weight, large boulders must be set in place with a crane or heavy equipment. Hire a landscaping firm to do this after all rough grading is completed. Stake the location of groupings in advance, digging out holes. After positioning, backfill around the bases of boulders to create a natural look.

Vertical accent plants with sword-shaped leaves are dramatic when combined with boulders. Low-growing, flowering ground covers flow over the ground and around the boulders. Consider grass-like plants with native shrubs, ground covers or perennials planted on the sides of slopes and among the boulders. Carpets of prostrate rosemary, gazania, lavender cotton, Mexican primrose, germander, verbena, and trailing indigo bush stabilize the soil and provide color and texture.

Dry Stream Beds

A simulated dry stream bed helps give your natural landscape a focal point. Stream beds can be 12 to 18 inches deep and 3 to 6 feet wide, depending on space available. In addition to being a design element, they can perform a valuable function by channeling excess rainwater runoff through the landscape or into retention basins. To create the most natural appearance, use boulders of various sizes in clusters on the edges of banks. Add small, 1- to 3-inch pebbles or cobblestones to stabilize soil between boulders in the bottom and sides of the stream bed swale. Make the stream bed appear as natural as possible. Take photographs or make sketches of dry stream beds in nature and use these as a guide to randomly place rocks and boulders.

Rock Gardens

Rock gardens differ from boulder gardens in that they are usually developed on mounds, terraces and hillsides to stabilize the soil. They are low profile, emulating rock outcroppings in nature, interplanted with low-growing perennials, herbs and ground covers.

Rocks should be combined carefully to create cool, moist, sheltered areas for plant roots. Improve the soil among rocks by adding organic amendments. A drip irrigation system works well in a rock garden design by providing water to each plant. This avoids overhead sprinkling and reduces weed growth and water stains. The drip tubing can be concealed beneath the soil or covered with a mulch such as decomposed granite.

Traditional Borders and Beds

Borders and planting beds are traditional ways of growing perennials, and this may be your preference. A border, as its name suggests, is a planting (usually an edge or strip) that serves as a border to a lawn area or against a wall or hedge. It often makes the transition from lawn or ground cover to shrubs and trees, allowing the different elements of the landscape "floor" to flow into the garden "walls" and "ceiling." A similar planting bed design, sometimes called an *island bed,* is a garden within. In this sense it is an island of flowering plants surrounded by lawn, mulch, brick, concrete or similar paving.

The extent and shape of the border or planting bed is highly dependent on the individual site. Try to keep shapes simple, creating a shape that will fit into the overall design. Use of raised beds and terraces allows for interesting grade changes and separation of planting beds. For a more informal appearance, allow plants to merge together.

This mixed border of perennials and annuals provides a casual, relaxed and colorful display. Taller species are placed in the background and low-growing species are located in the foreground so all plants can be seen and have room to grow.

If you are a beginning gardener or are gardening in a new location, start small and expand as you gain experience. If you make mistakes in plant selection or positioning, a small garden is more easily corrected. It's also easier to expand a garden than redo it completely. Plant only the number of plants you'll have time to take care of. Also, be sure plant sizes are in scale with each other. See Plant Partnerships, page 23.

Most borders are typically 4 to 6 feet in depth, ranging up to 12 feet or more long. This size makes it easier to plant, weed, water, fertilize, stake and divide. Narrow beds are easy to overplant and plants have a tendency to grow out of bounds and crowd one another. Installing a small walkway behind the border allows you to reach all parts of the garden without stepping on the soil, which causes unwanted compaction around roots.

When designing the border, adding flowing curves will give it interest. Test your designs by laying a rope or garden hose along the ground on the intended site. Unless your goal is a formal garden, avoid straight, geometric patterns and experiment with smooth, undulating lines.

Combining Annuals with Perennials

A newly planted perennial bed often takes a season or two before plants fill in. Including fast-growing annuals or annual wildflowers in the planting scheme the first year provides color and interest while perennial plants are maturing. Consider annuals as temporary color filler plants, and select those with flower colors that will complement the flower colors of your perennials. Be aware, too, that annuals generally require more water than the perennials listed in this book.

Select low-growing, compact varieties, and keep them at least 12 inches away from perennial plants. Most annuals, such as alyssum, petunias, phlox and snapdragons are rapid, aggressive growers and are quite capable of crowding the basal growth of slower-growing perennials. This is particularly true when perennials are dormant during winter. If annuals are allowed to grow unchecked, they will retard the regrowth of perennials the following spring.

As an option to annuals, apply a layer of mulch over the bare planting area until perennials are established.

A traditional English garden features *Papaver nudicaule*, Iceland poppy.

Low-growing annuals such as these pansies fill in nicely in the foreground with red-flowering *Salvia greggii*, red salvia, and ornamental grass *Pennisetum setaceum* 'Cupreum'.

Flowering Plants in Containers

Most flowering plants can be grown in containers. It's a matter of keeping the plant's height and spread in scale with the size of the container, and planting in well-draining soil.

One of the greatest benefits of container gardening is mobility. You can move plants to suit the time and place. Plants in flower can be displayed in a highly visible location, such as near the patio or entry. After bloom is spent, plants can be moved off center stage until they bloom again.

Compared to in-ground plantings, the soil dries out much more quickly in containers. Moisture loss can be extremely rapid in hot windy locations. In hot-summer regions, plants in containers might need watering every day. In these instances, drip irrigation is a wise way to water.

Provide container plants with afternoon shade during the summer months to help reduce water need. This is practically a necessity in hot-summer regions. Locate plants where they receive exposure to the less-intense morning sun, receiving shade during the hot afternoon hours. Turning the container one-quarter turn each week helps keep plant growth even.

Soil for Containers—Soil mixes for perennials should be loose and well draining. Several kinds are available. Some gardeners use a sterile potting soil straight out the bag. Others mix the potting soil with equal parts of sand and ground bark or peat moss. The added weight of the sand is helpful in windy regions, preventing plants from being blown over. A house plant potting soil is lightweight and recommended for hanging plants.

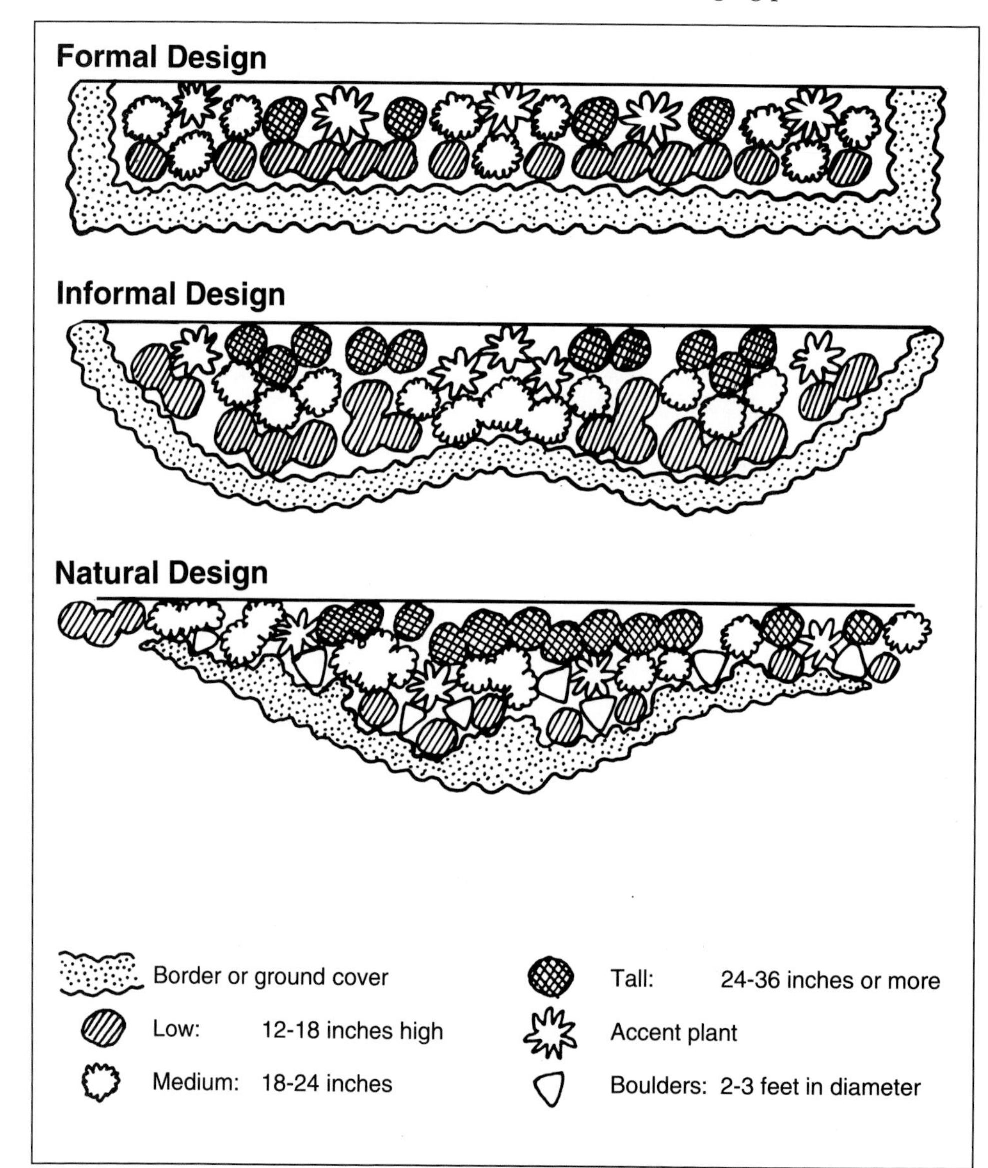

Formal design has a geometric shape and plants are arranged somewhat symmetrically. Growth is kept controlled.

Informal design is curved and plants are arranged randomly. Plants with informal growth habits are included.

In a natural design, plants are grouped randomly in odd numbers. Contours, mounds and boulders are often included.

Operation Facelift

It had been almost two decades of trimming hedges, hauling clippings, mowing and fertilizing extensive lawn areas and viewing woody, overgrown shrubs that no longer produced flowers or berries. The owners of the Springs, a home development in Rancho Mirage, California, felt it was time to renew and invigorate the common-area landscaped grounds that surrounded the 817-home complex. The goal was two-fold: improve the appearance of the grounds with perennial flowering plants and accent plants while drastically reducing maintenance costs.

With professional guidance, a plan and budget for retrofitting was developed. This included the removal of all common-area hedged plants, refurbishing the soil and cultivating it deeply with organic amendments, and bringing in new plants. Plants were selected to provide long seasons of color throughout the year, without relying solely on water-thirsty annual bedding plants.

This program led to upgrading the irrigation system to zoned water use, reducing overspray onto surrounding sidewalks, streets and driveways, and controlling overwatering of existing plants. Native and adapted perennials, flowering subshrubs, ornamental grasses and accent plants were selected and combined to create highly colorful yet more natural garden settings. Turf areas were reduced and planting areas were expanded into flowing, undulating beds. Groups of granite boulders two to three feet in diameter were added in clusters to provide naturalistic settings for accent plants and to reduce the visual impact of utility equipment.

Plants were carefully selected to provide staggered bloom periods so flowers would be abundant most of the year. Perennials and flowering subshrubs provided the majority of color; more than 60 species were used. Star performers included *Salvia greggii*, red salvia, *Salvia farinacea*, blue salvia, yellow and orange *Hemerocallis*, daylily, *Coreopsis*, *Euryops pectinatus*, *Rudbeckia*, *Lantana montevidensis*, lantana, *Pennisetum setaceum* 'Cupreum', purple fountaingrass (noninvasive), and *Kniphofia*, redhot poker plant. Annuals were used in the foreground and as fillers while the perennials were becoming established.

Planting was done primarily in the fall, winter and early spring months so the planting beds would be well on their way to being established before the long, hot summer ahead. After only one year, the result was a spectacular sequence of color, as one perennial species came into bloom after another.

Maintenance chores now include removing spent flowers and dead foliage, as well as weeds and debris from the planting beds. It was discovered that weeds were less of a problem because they were shaded out by the lush, healthy perennials and annuals. Some of the more vigorous plants are pruned to natural forms on occasion to prevent overcrowding.

Reducing turf and other plants led to a reduction in water use by 30 to 40 percent, due in large part to the improved soil, removing competing shrub and tree roots and installation of appropriate sprinkler heads. Costs of trimming and hauling debris to landfills were reduced considerably, as were use and maintenance of power equipment.

Operation Facelift resulted in a spectacular sequence of color, as one perennial species comes into bloom after the other. Best of all, the great majority of the 1,600 residents love the fresh, colorful new look. Many even incorporate the design themes and use the same flowering plants in their own courtyards and patios.

See photo, page 33 (right).

GALLERY OF FLOWERING PLANTS

This chapter describes over 270 species of flowering perennial plants adapted to grow in the arid West. You'll discover these pages offer much more than garden variety perennials; they include a wide selection of small flowering shrubs, as well as ornamental grasses and flowering ground cover plants. The flowering plants shown and described here are interesting in their contrasts and literally range from A to Z. Old favorites, such as *Achillea,* are included with relative newcomers such as *Zauschneria.* Each has its place in the western landscape. Note that plants are listed in alphabetical order according to botanical name. If you know a plant by its common name only, refer to the index at the end of the book.

For Fast Information—For easy reference, each plant has a column set in bold type that lists "fast facts." Learn the plant's origin, seasons of bloom, regions where the plant is adapted to grow, its average mature height and spread, plus preferences for soil, water and sun exposure. The narrative description provides detailed information on the plant's features and describes superior species or cultivars, suggestions on where and how to use, and plants that work well in combination. Finally, we offer recommended planting times and methods, as well as instructions on how to water, maintain and propagate plants.

About the Water Requirements—Each plant's water need is indicated for established plants, as *low, moderate* or *high.* These amounts are relative and vary according to season, exposure, soil type and climate region. The recommendations are based on research conducted by the University of California Cooperative Extension Service via its *Water Use Classification of Landscape Species (WUCOLS)* project. These classifications were developed from field observations by more than 50 landscape architects, horticulturists, nurserymen and irrigation consultants.

About the Adaptaptions—Climate adaptations accompany each listing, providing a guide as to where the plant can be grown in the arid West. Western climate zones, as described on pages 9 to 19, are designated by letter codes due to space limitations. An adaptation key, shown on page 49, defines the letter codes and the corresponding climates. This key is also supplied throughout this chapter for ease of reference. Note that climates will vary greatly even with a zone, and microclimates can have a great effect on the success of your plantings.

In discussing plants for an area as large and climatically diverse as the arid West, plant appearance, mature growth and cultural requirements will vary according to climate and location in the garden. For example, full sun may mean just that in many regions, but in hot desert areas and warmer inland valleys, many plants do better with some afternoon shade. When possible, specific information has been provided. Ultimately, however, you as gardener and caretaker of your plants become the final judge in supplying them with what they need to grow.

The flowers in this natural garden create a mosaic of color, combining with *Fouquieria splendens,* ocotillo, and *Opuntia ficus-indica,* spineless cactus.

Above are *Encelia farinosa,* brittle bush, with *Bougainvillea.*

Plant Selection Guide

BOTANICAL NAME	HEIGHT (IN FEET)	FLOWER COLORS	SEASONS OF BLOOM Winter Spring Summer Fall
Achillea	2-3	Y, O-R, R-P, W	
Agapanthus	1½-5	B, W	
Alcea rosea	6-8	Y, Y-O, P	
Alstroemeria	2-5	Y-O, R, P, W	
Anisacanthus	3-5	Y-O, R	
Aquilegia	1-3	Y, R, P, B, W	
Armeria maritima	<1	P, W	
Artemisia	1-6	Y, W, GF	
Asclepias	2-3	O, W	
Aster	2-4	R-P, B	
Aurinia saxatilis	1-1½	Y	
Baileya multiradiata	1-1½	Y	
Bergenia cordifolia	1-2	R-P, P, Pur, W	
Bougainvillea	3-5	O, R, P, Pur, W	
Calylophus hartweggi	1-1½	Y	
Campanula	1-3+	B-Pur, W	
Centaurea	1-4	Y, P, B, Pur, GF	
Centranthus ruber	2-3	P, W	
Cerastium tomentosum	<1	B	
Chrysanthemum	1-4	Y, R, P, Pur, W	
Cleome isomeris	3-4	Y	
Convolvulus	2-4	P, B	
Coreopsis	1½-2	Y	
Dianthus	1-2	Y, R-P, P, W	
Dictamnus	2-3	R-P, W	
Dietes	2-4	Y, P, W	
Echinacea purpurea	2-4	Y, O, P, W	
Echinops	2½-4	B	
Echium fastuosum	4-6	Pur	
Encelia	3-4	Y	
Ericameria laricifolius	1-3	Y	
Eupatorium	1-6	P, W	
Euphorbia	1-4	Y, R-P, R, B, G	
Euryops	4-6	Y	
Felicia amelloides	1½	B	
Gaillardia aristata	1-4	Y, R	
Galvezia speciosa	3-5	R	
Gaura lindheimeri	3-4	P, W	
Gazania	<1	Y-O, R-P, Pur, W	
Gerbera jamesonii	1½	Y-O, R-P	
Gypsophila	3-3½	P, W	
Helianthus	7	Y	
Heliopsis scabra	2-5	Y	
Hemerocallis	1-6	Y-O, R-P, L, W	
Hesperaloe parviflora	6+	R-P	
Heuchera	1-2	O, R, P, W, G	
Iberis sempervirens	<1	W	
Ice plants	1-1½	Y-O, R-P, R, Pur, W	

Use this chart to help plan your garden, selecting plants according to size, flower color and bloom seasons. Note that mature sizes, bloom periods and even colors of plants will vary according to your climate and the particular season. In general, plants tend to flower *later* into summer in coastal regions, and begin *earlier* in late winter and spring in mild, hot-climate areas.

BOTANICAL NAME	HEIGHT (IN FEET)	FLOWER COLORS	SEASONS OF BLOOM Winter Spring Summer Fall
Iris	1-3	Y, P, B-L, W	
Justicia	2-6	O, R-P	
Kniphofia uvaria	2-4	Y-O, R, W	
Lantana montevidensis	2-3	Y, L	
Lavandula	1½-4	B, L	
Leonotis leonurus	3-6	O	
Liatris	1½-5	P, L, W	
Ligularia	1½-6	Y-O, R-O, Y	
Lilium	3-6	Y-O, R-P, W, G	
Limonium perezii	2-3	Pur	
Linum	1-2	Y, R, B	
Lobelia	2-4	O, R, B	
Lupinus	1-4	Y, R, B, Pur	
Lychnis	1½-3	O, R-O, R-P, Pur-W	
Lythrum	2-4	R-P, Pur	
Melampodium	<1	W	
Mimulus	1-3	Y-O, O, R	
Mirabilis	2-4	Y, P, L, W	
Monarda didyma	2-4	R-P, R, W	
Nepeta	1-2	B-L	
Nierembergia violacea	<1	B, Pur	
Oenothera	1-2	Y, P, W	
Papaver	2-4	O, R-P, W	
Penstemon	1-6	Y, R, B-Pur, W	
Perovskia atriplicifolia	3-4	B-L	
Phlox	1-3	O, P, B-L, W	
Physostegia	2-6	Pur-R, Pur-P, L, W	
Platycodon grandiflorus	1-3	P, B, W	
Primula	<1	O, R-P, B-Pur, W	
Psilostrophe	1-2	Y	
Romneya coulteri	6-8	W	
Rosmarinus officinalis	2-5	B	
Rudbeckia	2½-7	Y, O	
Ruellia	2-4	B, Pur	
Salvia	2-4	R, B-Pur	
Santolina	1½-2	Y	
Scabiosa	1½-2	B-L, W	
Sedum	1-1½	Y, R-P	
Stachys byzantina	1-1½	Pur-L, GF	
Tagetes	3-4	Y	
Teucrium chamaedrys	1-2	R, Pur, W	
Thalictrum	2½-6	Y, P, Pur-L, W	
Trichostema lanatum	3-5	B	
Verbena	<1	O, R, P, Pur, L	
Veronica	1-2	R, B, P, Pur, W	
Watsonia	3-4	O, R-P	
Yucca	2-7	W, G-W	
Zauschneria californica	1-3	R	

Color codes:
B=Blue G=green GF=gray foliage L=lavender O=orange
P=pink Pur=purple R=red W=white Y=yellow

Achillea — Yarrow

Native to many regions; see individual species descriptions

Perennial; blooms in summer and again in fall

Adapted to all regions of the arid West

Grows 2 to 3 feet high, spreading 1-1/2 to 2 feet wide

Provide with average, well-draining soil

Moderate water use; tolerates dry conditions

Plant in full sun; provide afternoon shade in low-desert regions

Yarrows are tough, persistent, dependable plants for the sunny border or rock garden. Most bloom May to August, some later, especially if cut back. Plants form spreading clumps of gray-green, pungent leaves that are finely cut and sometimes ferny. Flowers on most species are flat or slightly rounded umbels carried on stiff stalks. Typical flower color is yellow, but white, red and pinkish red are also available. Recently introduced varieties of *A. millefolium* have red, orange-red and salmon flowers.

All yarrows make excellent cut flowers. They dry easily, keeping their color well. Use yarrow in the border. Low-growing kinds make wonderful edging or rock garden plants and are fire-retardant.

Recommended Species—
A. x 'Coronation Gold' bears bright yellow flowers on 3-foot plants.
A. millefolium comes in a variety of shades. 'Moonbeam' has pale yellow, flat flowerheads on 2-foot plants. 'Red Beauty' is pinkish red. Plants are strongly aromatic. Native to North America, Australia and New Zealand.
A. ptarmica 'The Pearl' bears double, button-sized, white blossoms. A good substitute for baby's-breath. Leaves are smooth, dark green spears. If deadheaded, flowers bloom until frost. The 2-foot plants have a floppy growth habit and need support. Native to Europe and Asia.
A. tomentosa, woolly yarrow, forms a wide-spreading mat of ferny, dark green leaves. Bears yellow or white flowers. Native to Europe and western Asia.

Planting & Care—Plant from containers in fall or spring. Space plants 12 inches apart, 18 inches for tallest varieties. Cut plants back after main bloom (midsummer for most varieties), and plants will often rebloom later on. Yarrow can be divided and transplanted successfully during much of its growing season, but best time is fall.

Agapanthus — Lily-of-the-Nile

Native to South Africa

Tuberous-rooted perennial, blooms in summer

Adapted to SCC, SCI, SCLD, NCC, CACV, AZLD, SNV

Grows 1-1/2 to 5 feet high, spreading 3 to 4 feet wide

Provide with fertile, well-draining soil; accepts clay soils

Moderate water use during growth periods; low while dormant

Accepts full sun on coast; needs afternoon shade in hottest regions

This is a showy, eye catching perennial for garden plantings in mild-winter areas. A member of the lily family, lily-of-the-Nile has arching, strap-like leaves and large, round, prolific, globe-shaped flowers in shades of blue and white supported by strong vertical stems. It is a heavy feeder and needs rich, deeply prepared soil. *Agapanthus* increases rapidly and is a strong grower. When planted in containers its roots can break clay pots if they become crowded. Accepts full sun, but best with afternoon shade in hot-summer areas. Will accept northern exposures and competes well with tree roots.

Recommended Species—
A. africanus (A. umbellatus) grows to 1-1/2 feet, bears blue flowers in midsummer to early fall. Evergreen. 'Headbourne Hybrids' are hardy to about -20F. Sky-blue flowers come on stalks 2-1/2 to 3 feet tall. Deciduous.
A. orientalis is most commonly grown, has flowers in blue or white on stalks 4 to 5 feet tall. Evergreen.
A. 'Peter Pan' is a dwarf selection with blue flowers that grows 1 to 1-1/2 feet high. 'Peter Pan Albus' has white flowers. Useful in the shaded border.

Planting & Care—Along the coast and in inland valleys, set out plants from containers in early spring. In colder regions, plant in pots, 3 plants per 12-inch pot. Cover crowns with 2 inches of soil. Plants flower best when clumps are crowded. Water enough to keep plants from wilting. Soft rot can occur with too much water in winter. In spring, increase water and feed freely. Divide to replant only when clumps become crowded. The less plants are disturbed, the more profuse the flowers. Slugs and snails are occasional pests.

Achillea millefolium, yarrow, is a tough, dependable plant for the sunny border or rock garden. Plants generally bloom late spring and into summer.

Agapanthus, lily-of-the-Nile, is a showy perennial in mild-winter areas. Flowers are available in shades of blue and white and bloom during summer.

Alcea rosea, hollyhock, is a reliable, old-fashioned biennial or short-lived perennial. Flowers are most prolific during the summer season.

Alcea rosea — Hollyhock

Native to Asia Minor

Biennial or short-lived perennial; blooms mid-summer to fall

Adapted to all regions of the arid West

Grows 6 to 8 feet high, spreading 2 to 3 feet wide

Accepts most soils, deep soils necessary for deep rooting

Moderate water use, provide with deep irrigation, reducing frequency as plants mature

Locate in full sun to reduce risk of rust infection

(Also known as *Althaea rosea*)

Hollyhock has been a favorite for many generations of home gardeners. The mission fathers brought seed to the missions of California, and eastern settlers traveling to the West brought seeds and planted them around their new homes.

Hollyhock is a reliable, old-fashioned biennial or short-lived perennial. Single, 3- to 6-inch flowers are available in pink, apricot, copper and yellow, and are most prolific during the summer season. Leaves are large and lobed, covering stalks that reach up to 6 to 8 feet high. It may be necessary to stake plants in windy areas. Ideal locations for hollyhocks are against south, west or east walls or fences where height can work as a strong vertical element.

Dwarf strains include 'Majorette' at 2-1/2 feet high with 3- to 4- inch flowers, and 'Pinafore', mixed colors, which branches freely from the base.

Planting & Care—Sow seed in fall where you want plants to grow. Sometimes you'll have flowers the first year. Plants are also occasionally available in containers at nurseries. Plants enjoy full sun and dry conditions. Supply young plants with moderate moisture. Mature plantings prefer deep, infrequent waterings. Avoid splashing leaves with water to reduce the chance of rust disease infection. If leaves become infected, remove them to slow spread. Cut existing plants back to near ground level in late fall after flowering for renewed growth the following spring. Propagate plants by removing new shoots that develop around the root crown, and replant them as new plants.

Alstroemeria — Peruvian Lily

Native to South America

Perennial; azalea-like blooms in late spring through summer

Adapted to SCC, SCI, SCLD, NCC, CACV, CALD, AZLD, AZMHD, SNV

Grows 2 to 5 feet high, spreading 2 to 3 feet wide

Best with well-drained loam or sandy soil

Moderate water use; provide with regular irrigation spring and summer during bloom

Accepts full sun along coast; needs afternoon shade inland and in low-elevation deserts

The delicate, exciting, azalea-like flowers of *Alstroemeria* bring a riot of color to the perennial border. The tall plants, 2 to 5 feet high, are excellent in the background, blooming late spring into summer. The lily-like foliage has an airy effect that supports flowers in colors of white, cream, yellow, orange, shades of pink, rose and red. Some selections have streaks of darker colors.

A cluster of three to five plants provides abundant color after annuals and spring-blooming perennials have completed their burst of bloom. Use other perennials such as four o'clock, false dragonhead and meadow rue in companion plantings. *Alstroemeria* is also a popular flower for cutting, and many gardeners grow it so they can bring the beauty of the garden indoors.

Planting & Care—Plants are sometimes available in containers, or sow seed in place. In low-elevation desert regions, sow seed in the fall. In other areas, set out plants in the early spring. Plants reseed readily after flowering and beds may need to be thinned by spring. Prefers loam or sandy soils, although adding organic amendments helps improve most any soil to retain moisture. Plants are heavy feeders and respond to slow-release fertilizer applied in early spring.

Peruvian lily spreads 2 to 3 feet wide with aggressive roots, so provide adequate growing space. In hot-summer areas, locate in partial shade; full sun is acceptable along the coast. Keep soil moist in the spring and apply a mulch to cool soil in summer when plants are growing and during their flowering period. Plants go dormant after flowering in the fall. Reduce watering and cut back withered leaves. Plants do not need to be divided for many seasons, but large crowded clumps can be divided in fall to extend plantings.

Anisacanthus — Desert Honeysuckle

Three *Anisacanthus* species share the common name of desert honeysuckle. However, each species offers a different growth and flowering habit, adding lush foliage and colorful flowers to the landscape during spring and into fall. Hummingbirds and butterflies flock to plants, attracted by the tubular, orange to red flowers that are loaded with nectar. Plants are in bloom up to four months during spring and summer. All are deciduous, losing their leaves in winter.

Plant in groups where plants can naturalize. Excellent for wildlife habitats. Use as companions with other low-water-use plants such as Texas ranger, red salvia and brittle bush. Allow plenty of space so plants grow to their normal height and spread.

A. thurberi, desert honeysuckle, is indigenous to Arizona, New Mexico and Texas. It grows 3 to 5 feet high with an equal spread. Sturdy branches with orange or yellow tubular flowers bloom in spring and summer months.

A. quadrifidus var. *brevilobus* 'Mountain Flame' is native to the Chihuahuan Desert of Texas and Mexico. It is similar to *A. thurberi,* with gray-green leaves. It produces prolific numbers of orange-red, tubular flowers from spring to fall. In higher-elevation deserts, most flowers occur in summer and into fall. Plants normally grow 4 to 5 feet high and as wide. Hardy to 10F. *A.q.*var. *wrightii,* Mexican flame, is native to Texas and Mexico. It is also hardy to cold in the 10F range. Plants grow to 3 to 4 feet high. The tubular, brilliant orange flower clusters are at their best during the high heat of late summer, blooming until frost.

Planting & Care—Plant from containers in fall or early spring in well-draining soil that has been pre-moistened. Water thoroughly after planting. Reduce irrigation to a weekly deep application. Cut plants to ground in winter for renewed growth the following spring. Can be propagated by cuttings or layering.

Native to southwest U.S. and northern Mexico

Deciduous subshrub; blooms spring into summer

Adapted to SCLD, SCMHD, CACV, AZLD, AZMHD, NMMHD, TXHP, TXEP, TXRRP, TXTPR

Grows 3 to 5 feet high and 6 to 8 feet wide

Provide with well-draining soil; coarse alluvial soils preferred

Low water use

Plant in full sun to part shade

Aquilegia — Columbine

Columbines are delightful garden plants, admired for their refreshing appearance and ease of growth in tough conditions. The flowers attract hummingbirds and are available in a wide range of colors and sizes. Big, brightly colored flowers stand out in the perennial border; airy species complement the woodland garden, and low-growing specimens are well suited for the rock garden. Most species are upright or mound-forming, with gray-green or blue-green, lobed leaves and graceful, usually spurred flowers on erect branching stems. Bloom periods range from spring through early summer in shades of blue, yellow, pink, red and white, often in combination.

Recommended Species—*Aquilegia caerulea,* Colorado or Rocky Mountain columbine, has white-centered flowers in shades of blue to purple. Grows 1-1/2 to 2 feet high.
A. chrysantha, one of the best for the border, blooms longer and is longer-lived than most columbines. Yellow flowers top plants 2 to 3 feet tall. Native to Texas.
A. flabellata 'Nana', dwarf blue columbine, grows to 1 foot high and bears fat little flowers of lilac-blue with white centers. 'Nana Alba', the white form, is a superb plant. Both are good in rock gardens. Native to Japan.
A. longissima 'Maxistar' grows 2 to 2-1/2 feet high and has large yellow flowers with long spurs. Native to Texas.

Planting & Care—Plants are easy to start from seed and are occasionally available in containers at nurseries. Set out transplants in fall or spring. Plant in full sun; best with partial shade in hot-summer areas. Space plants 12 to 15 inches apart. Mulch root zone to keep upper soil area cool. After first flush of flowers, cut back old stems to encourage additional blooms. If plants are bothered by leaf miners, cut foliage to about 4 inches high after bloom is over.

Native to north temperate regions and western states

Perennial; blooms in spring; flowers on tall stems develop over 1 to 2 months

Adapted to all regions of the arid West

Grows 1 to 3 feet high, spreading 2 to 3 feet wide

Provide with well-draining sandy or loam soil enriched with organic matter

Low water use on north coast and Central Valley; moderate other regions

Plant in full sun along coast to filtered shade in inland and desert regions

Aquilegia species, columbine, are easy to grow, tolerating tough soil and climate conditions. Add their big, bright flowers to the perennial border for a splash of color.

Below left: Locate *Armeria* maritima, sea pink, where they can be viewed up close, such as near the patio or in containers. Plants also work well as an edging or in the rock garden.

Below right: *Artemisia* species are grown for their gray-green or silvery leaves that contrast so well with green-foliage plants. Here, the upright leaves weave with *Baccharis* 'Centennial' to control erosion on a sandy slope.

Armeria maritima — Thrift, Sea Pink

(Sometimes listed as *Armeria laucheana;* all plants sold in the trade are *Armeria maritima.*)

These plants are easy to grow. Sprightly little tufts of stiff, upright, grassy leaves bear white or pink pompon flowers on slender 6-inch stems. Plants are usually evergreen, with flowers borne year-round in warmer regions, in spring and early summer in colder areas.

Sea thrift is a small-stature plant. Locate where it can be viewed up close, such as near the patio or in containers. It also works well as an edging or in the rock garden, clustered around the bases of large boulders.

A. maritima has pink flowers and grows 4 to 8 inches high. 'Alba' is slightly smaller, with white flowers. 'Dusseldorf Pride' has deep, pinkish red flowers. It grows 6 to 8 inches high. After flowering, trim back spent blooms for neat appearance. 'Bloodstone' forms neat mounds to 10 inches high. Stiff stems support rosy red flowers in abundance during the spring.

Planting & Care—Plant from flats or containers or sow seed in place during fall months in sandy loam in full sun. However, seed-grown plants are variable. Mulch in winter in cold areas. Propagate by division in early spring. Pull old plants apart, discarding the woody center, and replant vigorous outer portions. Plants quit flowering when they get woody in the center.

Native to Europe, Asia Minor, Spain and North Africa

Perennial; blooms year-round in warm coastal climates, during spring and early summer in cold regions

Adapted to SCC, SCI, NCC, CACV, CWR

Grows to 8 inches high, spreading 12 inches wide

Best with sandy, well-draining soil

Low to moderate water use

Plant in full sun; provide afternoon shade in hottest regions

Artemisia — Wormwood, Southernwood, Dusty Miller

Artemisia species comprise a delightful group of woody perennials, grown for their gray-green or silvery leaves that blend so well with many arid-land plants. When leaves are brushed, they produce a bitter-aromatic, medicinal scent. In fact, *Artemisia* was used medicinally in the past. Plants grow from under 1 foot to 6 feet or more. The insignificant flowers are yellow or white.

Artemisia works well in the herb garden, natural garden and the perennial border. Use them to tame brightly colored flowering plants, and integrate unharmonious ones. Smaller types, especially *A. schmidtiana* and its dwarf form, 'Nana', are well adapted to the rock garden. Varieties that attain larger stature can be used as small shrubs.

Fascinating leaf patterns and the silvery gray or white aromatic foliage are highly effective in a natural garden setting. Plants combine exceedingly well with other low-maintenance and low-water-use plants. Established plants can be kept on the dry side and will accept full sun.

Recommended Species—*A. abrotanum,* southernwood, grows to 4 feet high. Flowers are yellowish white.

A. californica 'Canyon Gray', California sagebrush, is a dense, ground-hugging plant. Its stems produce a two-toned, 6-inch, layered carpet of shiny, silvery gray, young leaves over darker, metallic gray, finely cut, aromatic mature leaves. Flowers are inconspicuous.

A. caucasica, silver spreader, has silky, silver-green leaves. It is low-growing, from 3 to 6 inches high, spreading 2 to 3 feet wide—ideal for rock gardens or slope plantings. Space at 2-foot centers. Good drainage is desirable, and it's best to minimize summer moisture after establishing. Plants tolerate heat and cold and are known to be fire-retardant.

A. dracunculus, French tarragon, is a true perennial herb used for seasoning.

Native to western North America and Europe

Perennials grown for their fascinating leaf patterns and white or silvery foliage color

Adapted to all regions of the arid West

Grows to 1 to 6 feet high, spread varies with species

Accepts most any well-draining soil, even poor soils

Low water use

Plant in full sun

Artemisia, continued

Artemisia schmidtiana

It has a low creeping habit to 2 feet high with glossy, green, narrow, aromatic leaves and clusters of greenish white flowers. Plants spread with creeping rhizomes and can become invasive. Use as a container plant or plant in a contained bed to control growth. It becomes dormant in winter.

A. lactiflora, white mugwort, grows 4 to 6 feet high, has dark green, lobed leaves and white flowers in late summer. Plant in well-prepared soil. A superior foliage plant.
A. ludoviciana (A. albula), silver king artemisia, has silvery white, slender, spreading branches. Lobed 2-inch leaves are attractive in combination with gray-green ground covers. Graceful stems are excellent for cut foliage arrangements. Its aggressive growth and deep roots work well on banks and slopes to control soil erosion, but it can also be invasive.
A. pycnocephala, sandhill sage, is best adapted to coastal regions. It grows to 2 feet high and almost as wide. Luxurious soft, silver-gray leaves provide a vertical accent.
A. schmidtiana 'Silver Mound' is probably the best known, growing 6 to 8 inches high, spreading to 12 inches wide. Leaves are silver-green and finely cut.
A. stellerana, perennial dusty miller, is a good plant for seaside gardens as well as hot-climate regions. It grows to 3 feet high.

Planting & Care—Select well-established container plants and set out in fall or early spring. Locate in full sun. They aren't picky about soil as long as it's well draining, thriving even in poor, dry locations. Plants actually develop better in unimproved soils. Cut back in late winter and again in midsummer if heat affects the plant's looks. Also can be easily propagated by division in spring or fall, or by cuttings or layering in late summer.

Asclepias — Butterfly Weed

Native to prairies of North America

Perennial; blooms during summer

Adapted to SCC, SCI, CACV, AZLD, AZMHD, SNV, NMMHD, TXHP, TXEP, TXRRP, TXTPR

Grows 2 to 3 feet high, spreading 2 to 3 feet wide

Accepts most well-draining soils

Moderate to low water use

Plant in full sun

Introducing members of this group of plants will add a new dimension to your landscape, particularly a natural garden design, one you'll quickly notice when butterflies and hummingbirds begin to flock to plants.

Asclepias linaria, pine-leaf milkweed, is native to Arizona. It has a typical milkweed habit of growth, with a woody base and herbaceous, thin, needle-like leaves. The clusters of white flowers in late spring and summer develop into inflated fruit pods in the fall. Plants become rounded, 3-foot subshrubs. Cold-hardy throughout the West.
A. subulata, desert milkweed, is a novel Arizona native with narrow, almost leafless stems. The 3-foot plants are enhanced with cream-colored summer flowers at the tips of the vertical stems. The flowers are followed by inflated pods that hold the seeds; plants reseed readily. Plants are low water users and accept exposure to full sun. Use as vertical accents in a natural garden, placed in groups at the base of boulders.
A. tuberosa, butterfly weed, has bright orange flowers that appear from July through September on plants 2 feet tall. Occasionally flowers are red or yellow. As its common name suggests, it attracts butterflies as well as hummingbirds. Reduce water during summer.

Obvious choices for wildlife gardens, *Asclepias* also work well in the perennial border, the meadow garden and informal herb gardens. When used in the border, situate in the middle and surround with plants that will mask the coarse qualities of the leaves.

Planting & Care—Plants are difficult to transplant because of long taproots. Grow from seed and set plantlets out in permanent locations when they are small. Pre-chill seed in the refrigerator, then sow indoors in spring or outdoors in late summer. Take cuttings in early spring and root them in moist sand. Allow established plants to self-sow.

Aster — Hardy Aster, Michaelmas Daisy

These charming flowers were once a standby in old-fashioned gardens. Asters today remain one of the mainstays of the late-blooming perennial border, providing tumbling masses of color in August and September. Woody-based plants grow 2 to 4 feet high. Stalks must either be pinched back or staked. Secondary blooms can be encouraged by cutting off spent flowers. Asters are good for cutting for use in indoor bouquets. Smaller varieties can be used in rock gardens and in containers. Plant clusters in a single color or in drifts in a border garden.

Recommended Species—Nurseries that are perennial specialists are good sources for new selections. Some superior species include:
Aster x frikartii 'Wonder of Stafa' grows 2-1/2 feet high, has lavender-blue flowers. Native to the Himalayas. Adapted to coast and inland valleys.
A. novae-angliae 'Alma Potschke' grows to 3 feet high. Flowers are bright, pleasing pink. 'Harrington's Pink' grows to 4 feet high; flowers are clear pink. Adapted to all regions. Excellent in cold climates and tolerates wet conditions.
A. novi-belgii 'Crimson Brocade', 3 feet high, has semi-double crimson flowers. Adapted to all regions. Not always readily available.

Planting & Care—Culture is similar to chrysanthemums. Plant from containers in fall or spring in well-draining soil in full sun. The common native asters can be grown from seed, but cultivated varieties, cultivars, can be variable, so propagate them by division. Pinch stems twice to induce bushiness, pinching off half the stalk each time. To lengthen the flowering time and promote a less regimented appearance, don't pinch all the stems at once. Allow plenty of room between plants for spreading growth.

A virus, aster yellows, is transmitted by leafhoppers and aphids. Plant resistant varieties.

Native to five continents

Perennial; blooms summer into fall

Adapted to all regions of the arid West

Grows 2 to 4 feet high, spreading 3 to 4 feet wide

Accepts most any well-draining soil

Moderate water use

Plant in full sun

Aurinia saxatilis — Hardy Alyssum, Basket-Of-Gold

(Also known as Alyssum saxatile.)

A low-growing, mat-forming plant with cascades of tiny, bright yellow flowers, hardy alyssum blooms with the spring bulbs, and, when planted with them, makes a striking display. It is an excellent plant for edging, tumbling over railroad ties or nestled among boulders in the rock garden. Flowers look much like those of the annual alyssum—pale to bright yellow, producing a billowing bloom in early spring that usually lasts for over a month. Tongue-shaped leaves are gray-green and persistent on prostrate, thickened, woody stems.

Hardy alyssum grows well in most climates. A short-lived perennial, it normally is replaced every few years. Starts easily from seed and readily self-sows. Use in the rock garden, at the front of the border, as an edging and among spring bulbs. Looks spectacular in drifts.

Recommended Varieties—'Citrina' grows 12 to 15 inches high, with pale yellow flowers. 'Compacta' has flowers of deeper yellow on plants 6 inches tall. 'Sulphureum' grows to 1-1/2 feet, with light yellow flowers.

Planting & Care—In cold-winter regions, sow seed in place in early spring. If you want a jump on the season, sow indoors in late winter 1/4 inch deep in trays; transplant seedlings in spring. In mild-winter areas sow seed in place outdoors during fall. Plants will bloom the following spring. Plant 2 feet apart in light, moderately rich soil. Plants self-sow readily. Fertilize lightly in early spring. Cut back spent flowerheads as they occur for neat appearance. In late winter, pull away tattered leaves.

Native to south and central Europe, Turkey

Perennial; blooms in spring and into summer in cooler regions

Adapted to SCC, SCI, NCC

Grows 6 to 18 inches high, spreading 18 inches wide

Provide with average, well-draining, garden soil

Moderate water use; tolerates short dry periods

Plant in full sun; afternoon shade preferred in hottest regions

Asclepias linaria, pine-leaf milkweed, produces clusters of white flowers in late spring and summer that develop into inflated fruit pods in the fall. The seedpods (shown above) burst to disperse the fluffy seedheads.

Baileya multiradiata, desert marigold, is a perennial wildflower known to bloom for a long period even in tough conditions. Here it makes a colorful combination with *Verbena* species.

Aster x frikartii grows 2-1/2 feet high and produces lavender-blue flowers. It is well adapted to coastal and inland valleys.

Climate Adaptation Key

SCC:	**S. Calif. Coastal**
SCI:	**S. Calif. Inland**
SCLD:	**S. Calif. Low Deserts**
SCMHD:	**S. Calif. Medium/ High Deserts**
NCC:	**N. Calif. Coastal**
CACV:	**Calif. Central Valley**
AZLD:	**Arizona Low Desert**
AZMHD:	**Arizona Medium/High Deserts**
NMMHD:	**New Mexico Medium/High Deserts**
SNV:	**Southern Nevada**
TXHP:	**Texas High Plains**
TXEP:	**Texas Edwards Plateau**
TXRRP:	**Texas Red Rolling Plains**
TXTPR:	**Texas Trans-Pecos Region**
CWR:	**Cold-Winter Regions**

In regions where freezing temperatures occur infrequently, bougainvillea can often be grown in warm microclimates, such as beneath overhangs on warm south exposures.

Baileya multiradiata — Desert Marigold

Native to deserts of Southwest U.S.

Perennial; blooms spring through fall

Grows 6 to 18 inches high, spreading 18 to 24 inches wide

Adapted to SCLD, SCMHD, AZLD, AZMHD, NMMHD, SNV, TXHP, TXTPR

Accepts most any well-draining soil; prefers loose, deep, sandy soil

Low water use once plants are established

Plant in full sun

Desert marigold is an admirable perennial wildflower, blooming for a long season in tough conditions and locations. It can naturalize along rocky slopes and sandy washes. Its showy yellow flowers are most noticeable alongside highways where rainfall can run off and accumulate. You'll see desert marigold in the Mojave Desert, low elevations of Arizona's Sonoran Desert, and as far east as Texas and north to Utah for a long period—from spring into the fall months. The basal leaf growth bears stems 6 to 18 inches long that produce an abundance of bright yellow, daisy-like flowers an inch or more in diameter. Reseeding occurs rapidly, and volunteers increase the color show each season. Remove weeds carefully so as not to disturb seedlings.

Natural companion plants include brittlebush, *Encelia farinosa*, blue ruellia, *Ruellia peninsularis*, ocotillo, *Fouquieria splendens*, *Opuntia* species and creosote bush, *Larrea tridentata*. All have similar soil and moisture requirements. Use on level land or slopes, among native or adapted plants for a long term effect. Excellent for desert revegetation. Often included in wildflower seed mixes. Desert marigold blooms on through the hot summer when the annual wildflowers have long since faded.

Planting & Care—Sow seed in place in fall or early spring. Pre-moisten soil prior to applying seed. Rake lightly after seeding. Seed can be sown as late as June or July if you water seeded area regularly. Plants are also often available in containers at native plant nurseries.

Trim back spent flower stems during the winter months to basal growth to stimulate new growth. Simulate summer rainfall by applying 1 inch of water monthly to encourage continued growth and flowers. Maintain moderate moisture; excessive moisture causes weak succulent growth.

Bergenia cordifolia — Bergenia

Native to China

Perennial; blooms in spring

Adapted to SCC, SCI, NCC, CACV

Grows 1 to 2 feet high, spreading in clumps to 3 feet wide

Provide with organic-rich, moisture-retentive soil

Low to moderate water use, depending on exposure to sun and humidity

Plant in full shade to partial shade; accepts some sun along coast

Bergenia has thick, succulent, glossy, dark green, leathery leaves. In harsh winter climates, they often look tattered by the time spring comes on. Plants are low growing with leaves emerging from a basal rosette, and will colonize to form thick ground cover. Clusters of reddish pink flowers open in March or early April reaching up to 1 foot high. Plant form is casual and creates a strong pattern. Use near the front of the border, as an edging, in the rock garden or under canopy trees and shrubs.

Recommended Varieties—'Bressingham White' grows 1-1/2 to 2 feet tall. It is considered the best white selection. 'Bressingham Salmon' blooms a month later on shorter plants, to 1 foot tall. Leaves are blushed pink and purple in winter. 'Perfecta' grows to 1-1/2 feet. It bears deep, rose-pink flowers. 'Silberlicht' bears tightly culstered white flowers on plants 1 foot tall. Hybrid 'Evening Glow' blooms are deep rose-red on 1-foot stalks. *B. crassifolia* has 8-inch-wide, dark green leaves with attractive wavy edges. Clusters of purple, lilac or rose flowers rise above the leaves during January and February—when color is appreciated.

Planting & Care—Bergenia can be planted from containers almost any time, but best planted in fall. Plants succeed in a range of soils, from acid to alkaline. Plant in groups spacing plants 12 to 18 inches apart. Plants will spread to form thick colonies. Remove dead or damaged leaves during the summer to maintain appearance. Divide after flowering or in the fall, when plants begin to die out in the center. One of the names for Bergenia is *neigborhood plant,* because root cuttings are often passed from neighbor to neighbor.

Bougainvillea — Bougainvillea

The colorful shrub forms of bougainvillea have long been grown in frost-free coastal and subtropical inland valleys and low desert regions in Southern California. After they're established, bougainvillea can be kept on the dry side, which slows growth and helps produce more prolific blooms with darker richer colors. Note that the color of bougainvillea is not flowers but specialized leaves called *bracts* that surround tiny flowers.

In regions where freezing temperatures occur infrequently, utilize warm microclimates, such as beneath overhangs on warm south exposures. In cold regions, try planting dwarf forms in containers, which allows you to move them to shelter when frost threatens.

Recommended Varieties— 'Crimson Jewel' is a vigorous, sprawling, profusely flowering form with red bracts. Effective in containers. 'Hawaii', with red flowers, is more shrubby and mounding. New leaves are tinged in red; mature leaves have golden yellow margins. During a freeze in 1990 in the Coachella Valley in Southern California, plants showed less frost damage than other varieties. 'La Jolla' has more compact and shrubby growth with bright red bracts. 'Temple Fire' is shrub-like with bronzy red flowers to about 4 feet high. Growth is vigorous and spreading. Plants are partially deciduous, so use in combination with evergreen perennials or shrubs.

Planting & Care—Plant from containers, being careful when handling the rootball. Roots are not fibrous and the rootball is fragile. Select well-established plants. Remove rootball gently from container and place in holes twice the width and equal to depth of rootball. Add soil gently around rootball and water in thoroughly to remove air pockets. Do not place excessive pressure on rootball. Avoid overwatering at any time. Shrubby dwarf selections tend to send out long leaders. Remove them so plants maintain their dwarfish look.

Native to subtropical regions of South Africa

Subshrub or ground cover; blooms primarily during summer; also in winter and spring in relatively frost-free regions

Adapted to SCC, SCI, NCC, SCLD, AZLD

Grows 3 to 5 feet high with varying widths

Provide with well-draining soil

Low to moderate water use

Plant in full sun

Calylophus hartweggi — Calylophus 'Sierra Sun Drop'

In some ways, *Calylophus hartweggi* looks a lot like yellow flowering *Oenothera*, described on page 104, but there is a difference in how the soft yellow, 1-inch flowers open up around sunset. The moth-pollinated flowers remain open until sunset, just before the new crop of flowers open. Bloom is profuse in spring beginning in March, with strong intermittent flowers until November.

Plants grow 1 to 1-1/2 feet high, spreading by underground rhizomes and creeping branches that send out roots. The narrow, 1-1/2-inch leaves create dense growth below the short-stemmed flowers. The plants are effective when used among boulder-strewn rock garden plantings and as an underplanting among taller shrubs.

The range is extensive and includes high elevations—2,000 to 7,000 feet—throughout west Texas and Colorado. Plants are hardy to about 0F. Gardeners in the hottest desert regions throughout the Southwest have had good results with plants in full sun locations, but those located in afternoon shade often have improved health and appearance.

Planting & Care—Set out plants from gallon-size containers in fall in mild-winter regions; wait until spring in cold climates. Space new plantings 2 to 3 feet apart on center. A light, organic mulch over the soil surface around plants seems to help increase spread of underground rhizomes. Do not overwater new plants or fungus problems may occur.

In cold-winter climates, trim back foliage as plants go dormant in late winter. This renews plants for the upcoming season.

Native to west Texas, New Mexico, Arizona

Perennial; blooms primarily in spring, with sporadic blooms until late fall

Adapted to SCI, SCLD, SCMHD, CACV, AZLD, AZMHD, TXTPR

Grows 1 to 1-1/2 feet high, spreading 3 to 4 feet wide

Accepts most any well-draining soil; prefers unamended soil

Low to moderate water use

Accepts full sun, but plants in light afternoon shade perform better during periods of high summer heat

Calylophus hartweggi is similar in appearance to a yellow-flowering *Oenothera.* Bloom is most profuse in spring, with occasional flowers until late fall.

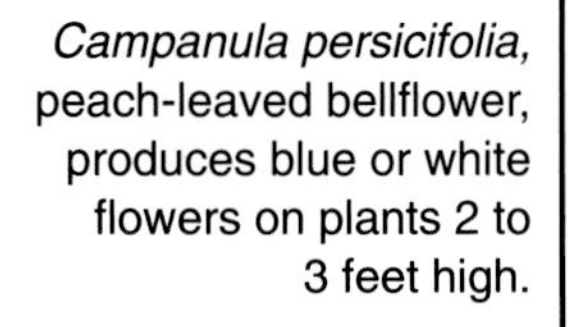

Campanula persicifolia, peach-leaved bellflower, produces blue or white flowers on plants 2 to 3 feet high.

Centranthus ruber, red valerian, is an old-fashioned perennial at home in traditional gardens, entries or patio plantings where its fragrance can be enjoyed. Plants are widely adapted and perform well in most areas of the arid West.

Below left: *Centaurea macrocephala* has large, yellow, thistlelike flowers on 4-foot plants. Use as a distinctive specimen plant in the natural border.

Below: *Chrysanthemum leucanthemum* (newly reclassified as *Leucanthemum maximum)* produces classic, oxeye daisy flowers, with white petals and yellow centers.

Campanula — Bellflower

Native to the Mediterranean

Perennial; blooms in summer

Adapted to SCC, SCI, CACV, SCLD, NCC

Plant sizes range from 6 inches to 3 feet or more. See individual species descriptions

Provide with most any well-draining soil

Moderate to high water use

Plant in full sun along coast, afternoon shade elsewhere

This large genus is an important and reliable group of plants, with a wide selection of fine annuals and perennials adapted to a variety of garden settings. Flowers shaped like cups or bells, some facing up, others down- or out-facing, open June to October, depending on variety. Flower colors are shades of blue, purple and white. In most cases, plants form a mat or basal rosette of leaves. The flowering stem that rises from this has smaller leaves. These old-fashioned favorites make good cut flowers.

Recommended Species—*Campanula carpatica* is low growing to 8 inches, producing blue or white flowers all summer. This species prefers moist soil. Use as edging or in the rock garden.
C. glomerata has the most unusual form in this genus, bearing dense clusters of purple or white double flowers in June and July on stalks 1-1/2 feet tall. It tolerates poor dry soil better than other species.
C. lactiflora grows to 3 feet or more, has flowers blue to lilac that bloom June to September. Well-adapted to hot, dry, shaded locations.
C. persicifolia, peach-leaved bellflower, blooms June to July with white or blue flowers on plants 2 to 3 feet tall. Remove shriveled flowers to extend bloom period.
C. portenschlagiana blooms from May through August in coastal or inland valley areas. Its erect, bell-shaped, 1-inch, violet-blue flowers are colorful companions with other perennials that thrive in shade or partial shade. Grows just 6 inches high with deep green, toothed leaves. Moisture needs are moderate to high.

Planting & Care—In mild-winter regions, plant from containers in fall or early spring. In cold-winter areas, plant in spring. Prefers slightly acid soil. In hot-summer areas, situate plants so they are exposed to morning sun but receive afternoon shade. Feed monthly with acid plant food. Cut off spent flower stems to extend bloom and keep plants neat. Divide plants about every three years to keep plantings vigorous.

Centaurea — Perennial Cornflower

Native to the Mediterranean and Near East

Perennial; blooms in summer

Adapted to all regions of the arid West

Grows 1 to 4 feet high, spreading 2 to 3 feet wide

Accepts most any well-draining soil

Moderate water use; do not allow soil to dry out completely

Plant in full sun

The perennial *Centaurea* species brighten landscapes with their cheerful blossoms all summer long. These durable plants tolerate various soil and moisture conditions, making them good candidates for low-water, low-maintenance plantings. *Centaurea* are naturals in the border of cottage and old-fashioned gardens and in rock gardens. They also make fine cut flowers.

Recommended Species—
C. cineraria, dusty miller, is an old-fashioned favorite with velvety, white-lobed leaves. Plants grow in clumps to 1-1/2 to 2 feet high, producing yellow blooms during summer. The foliage provides great color and texture contrasts. Well adapted to Western gardens.
C. hypoleuca flowers are deep rose, blooming June to September on 1-1/2-foot plants. 'John Couts' has brilliant, rosy flowers from June to August.
C. macrocephala has large, yellow, thistle-like flowers on 4-foot plants in June and July. A distinctive plant to use as a single specimen. Adapted to all regions.
C. montana flowers are one of the darkest blues in the garden. Plants grow 1-1/2 to 2 feet tall. Undersides of leaves are often covered with fine white hairs. Flowers 2 to 4 inches across come in white, yellow and shades of blue, purple and rose. Thrives in heat, but accepts some shade.

Planting & Care—Plant from containers or sow seed in fall in mild-winter regions. Sow seed or plant from containers in spring in cold-winter regions. Select only fresh plants at the nursery; old woody plants are slow to establish. Space 1-1/2 feet apart in full sun. Plants self-sow easily. Soil should be well draining. Plants do best if soil is not allowed to dry out completely. Remove spent flowers to groom plants and for repeat blooms. Divide plants in early spring or fall every three to four years to keep them vigorous.

Centranthus ruber — Red Valerian, Jupiter's Beard

Centranthus produces highly perfumed flowers from early summer until frost. Plants are short-lived but easy to grow from seed. Primary flowering occurs in early summer; thereafter plants bloom intermittently until frost. Flowers are prolific in shades of rosy pink or white, clustered at ends of stems. Leaves are pale blue-green on lush, mounding plants.

This is an old-fashioned favorite and a fine choice for traditional gardens, entries or patio plantings where its sweet scent can be most enjoyed. *Centranthus* has a wide range of adaptation, performing well in the cool, foggy mornings and the clay soils along the California coast, to hot desert areas. Plants can become rank and invasive, so be aware.

Locate plants in clusters 18 inches apart at the bases of large boulders or as an underplanting among yuccas or other accent plants, where their lushness and bright flower colors can stand out. *Centranthus* combines well with other plants that have dark green, glossy foliage.

Recommended Varieties—
C. ruber grows to 2 feet high; flowers are glowing pink. The cultivar 'Albus' is a white form. Plants grow 2 to 3 feet high and spread 2-1/2 feet wide. 'Coccineus' blooms a deep reddish pink.

Planting & Care—These are short-lived plants. Plant new seed in spring every four or five years. *C. ruber* self-sows and can naturalize. Performs best in sun, but tolerates partial shade (avoid excessive moisture in shaded areas). Pruning plants back after first flush of bloom promotes flowering later in the season. Thinning stems and deadheading spent flowers occasionally helps produce more flowering wood. Divide established clumps in spring.

Native to all continents except Antarctica and Australia

Perennial; blooms June through September

Adapted to all regions of the arid West

Grows 2 to 3 feet high, spreading 2 to 3 feet wide

Provide with average garden soil

Low water use; moderate in low deserts

Plant in full sun to light shade

Cerastium tomentosum — Snow-in-Summer

The low, neat, woolly foliage of snow-in-summer creates a silvery carpet for its small, 1/2- to 3/4-inch, white flowers that bloom in profusion during the spring and summer months. This superior ground cover has many landscape uses, including borders along walks, small space plantings, flower bed borders, cascading from a terrace, in rock gardens and as a foreground to shrub beds. Plants grow only 6 to 8 inches high but spread as much as 2 to 3 feet wide.

Snow-in-summer is most striking when combined as a foreground to dark-foliaged plants such as lavender, gaillardia, swan river daisy and tufts of blue fescue. Plants can become invasive. They are dormant during cold weather and often look sparse at this time, but they recover quickly with warmer temperatures. Interplant with evergreen perennials to lessen the sparse appearance.

Planting & Care—Snow-in-summer is often available in flats but can be difficult to transplant due to interwoven root growth. Best to use transplants grown in pots or containers. Or sow seeds in well-cultivated planting beds in spring, just as temperatures begin to warm. Seeds germinate in about two weeks. Overwatering can cause problems with rot, so well-draining soil is required. Adapted to all climate zones when given sun and good soil drainage. Provide afternoon shade in hot-summer regions. Shear off spent flowers to keep planting looking neat. Reseed or replant beds as needed to renew sparse aging plants.

Native to the Mediterranean

Perennial ground cover; blooms in late spring and summer

Adapted to all areas of the arid West

Grows 6 to 8 inches high, spreads 2 to 3 feet wide

Provide with most any well-draining soil

Low water use

Plant in full sun; provide afternoon shade in hottest areas.

Chrysanthemum

Chrysanthemum

Native to China

Perennial; blooms summer and fall

Adapted to all regions of the arid West

Grows 1 to 4 feet high, spreading 2 to 4 feet wide

Prefers fertile, well-draining soil

Moderate to high water use

Plant in full sun

The chrysanthemum originated in China, and for many centuries has been a favored plant in that country, as well as in Japan and Korea. The genus is huge, providing flower gardeners with many important garden plants.

C. maximum (C. x superbum) is the popular Shasta daisy. It is available in a variety of forms, from simple single flowers to frilled, crested and double flowers that range from small to gigantic on plants to match. Others include painted daisies, the oxeye daisy (or marguerite), varieties of hardy *C. rubellum* and countless hybrids of the fall-flowering *C. x morifolium.* All are available in a wide range of flower forms and colors.

For a brilliant fall display, a bed devoted to chrysanthemums cannot be excelled. Growing plants *en masse* makes a bigger impact than individual plants and also makes pinching easier. (See following.) Once established, mums are fairly drought-tolerant. With fall-blooming mums, the most-important thing to remember is to grow varieties adapted to your climate, so plants have the opportunity to attain full bloom before frost comes on.

Recommended Species—
C. coccineum (Pyrethrum) 'Robinson's Hybrids' grow 2 feet tall, with flowers in red and white. Also available in a double form.
C. frutescens, marguerite, may persist as a perennial in coastal temperate climates. Plants do not do well in hot or cold temperatures; grow as an annual in these areas, where they will provide a rich source of lush growth in spring and early summer. Small plants set out in early spring can develop into 4-foot, well-rounded plants by early summer.
C. leucanthemum (newly reclassified as *Leucanthemum maximum)* 'May Queen' grows 2 to 2-1/2 feet tall with classic, oxeye daisy flowers—white petals and yellow centers.
C. maximum 'Alaska' bears single flowers on vigorous plants 2 to 2-1/2 feet tall. 'Miss Muffet' is a dwarf, 12 to 15 inches tall, with semi-double flowers. 'Polaris' grows 3 to 4 feet high, bearing large single flowers.
C. x morifolium is the fall-blooming chrysanthemum, not necessarily hardy in all gardens. The hybrids developed by the University of Minnesota with names such as 'Minnautumn', 'Minnpink', and 'Minnyellow' are cushion types that are particularly hardy.
C. pacificum is not planted for its tiny, yellow, button flowers, but for striking, blue-green leaves finely edged in white. Compact plants grow 1 foot tall, spreading to 3 feet. Place this one in the front of the border, where you can admire it.
C. x rubellum 'Clara Curtis' covers itself from late summer until frost with clear pink, daisy flowers. Plants grow to 2 feet high.

Planting & Care—Select plants at the nursery that are succulent and have fresh growth. Locate in full sun. Regular moisture is important to keep plants growing vigorously. Eastern exposure is best in warm-summer areas. Plant in well-draining soil. Blend organic matter into soil before planting to increase its moisture- and nutrient-holding capacity. Stake tall-growing varieties; the heavy flowerheads can cause plants to bend over. Prune plants lightly; heavy pruning creates hard wood that regrows slowly. Plants bloom up to first frost in cold climates. Remove plants after frost. Shasta daisies: Plants normally last about three years. For best bloom, divide and reset in spring each year, or in late fall in warmer climates. Grow in full sun in loamy, well-draining soil. Supply with regular water. Painted daisies and *C. x rubellum*: Divide and replant every three to four years in early spring.

New plants need protection if set out early. Fall-blooming mums: Divide established clumps each spring when shoots are 4 to 6 inches tall, discarding weak or woody growth. Replant individual leafy shoots and roots in fertile, well-draining soil in full sun. When plants reach 10 inches, pinch tips. Pinch two more times but stop by mid-July. Water regularly, and side-dress with well-rotted manure. After plants are established, feed weekly with water-soluble fertilizer. The fall-flowering chrysanthemums are heavy feeders.

Climate Adaptation Key

SCC:	S. Calif. Coastal
SCI:	S. Calif. Inland
SCLD:	S. Calif. Low Deserts
SCMHD:	S. Calif. Medium/ High Deserts
NCC:	N. Calif. Coastal
CACV:	Calif. Central Valley
AZLD:	Arizona Low Desert
AZMHD:	Arizona Medium/High Deserts
NMMHD:	New Mexico Medium/High Deserts
SNV:	Southern Nevada
TXHP:	Texas High Plains
TXEP:	Texas Edwards Plateau
TXRRP:	Texas Red Rolling Plains
TXTPR:	Texas Trans-Pecos Region
CWR:	Cold-Winter Regions

Chrysanthemum coccineum grows to 2 feet high, with red and white flowers.

Coreopsis species are workhorse plants, highly decorative and heavily blooming. They look attractive when tucked in clumps among boulders, or as a border. Flowers are favored for cutting, and they create lavish bouquets.

Cleome isomeris — Bladder Pod

Native to central California to Baja California

Perennial subshrub; blooms early spring to early summer

Adapted to SCC, SCI, SCLD, SCMHD

Grows 3 to 4 feet high, spreads 3 to 4 feet wide

Provide with most any well-draining soil

Low water use; moderate water produces more luxuriant plants

Plant in full sun

(Formerly known as *Isomeris arborea*)

Bladder pod, also known as burro fat, is a little-known plant that, despite its rather unflattering names, deserves a more prominent place in the arid landscape. Divided, oblong to elliptic, gray-green leaflets and bright yellow, snapdragon-like flowers are borne in clusters at the tips of branches. They cover the 3- to 4-foot evergreen shrublet from January through May. Large, inflated capsules, the bladder pods, create interesting clusters that enclose and shelter the seeds.

Flowers are a source of nectar for bees and hummingbirds. Foliage has a slight odor that is unpleasant to some. Locate plants on slopes or away from frequent garden traffic to avoid.

Plants native to bluffs and hillsides in coastal regions from central California to San Diego often have elongated pods. Plants are also native to the western edge of the Mojave Desert and the low-elevation Coachella Valley. Some can also be found in the Caliente Creek area of Kern County. Best examples are along Old Woman's Spring Road that begins in Yucca Valley, through Johnson Valley to Lucerne Valley.

The light green foliage and rounded form combine well with brittle bush, *Encelia farinosa,* desert marigold, *Baileya multiradiata* and red salvia, *Salvia greggii.* All have similar moisture needs. This is also a valued plant for revegetation.

Planting & Care—Sow seed in place in the fall. Seedlings emerge in a week to ten days; thin plants to 3 to 4 feet apart. Plants thrive in most any well-draining soil and tolerate minimum moisture after they're established. Little pruning is required in dry situations. Plants given moderate moisture may need periodic thinning or topping. Do not water heavily during the summer months since this is their dormant period.

Convolvulus — Bush Morning Glory

C. cneorum native to southern Europe; *C. mauritanicus* native to Africa

Perennial and subshrub; bloom from late spring into early fall

Adapted to SCC, SCI, NCC, CACV, SCLD, SCMHD, AZLD, AZMHD

Grows 2 to 4 feet high, spreads 3 to 4 feet wide

Provide with well-draining soil

Low to moderate water use

Plant in full sun

These two *Convolvulus* species produce morning-glory-like flowers and are blessed with soft, silvery gray leaves. *C. cneorum,* bush morning glory, is compact and shrub-like, growing 2 to 4 feet high. Leaves are silvery gray and as smooth as silk. Funnel-shaped flowers tinged white to pink appear from late spring through summer. The gray foliage and form blend well in perennial and shrub plantings as foreground for taller *Cassia* species, *Leucophyllum,* Texas rangers, or at the base of *Yucca pendula* for a prostrate, shrub-like pattern. They are excellent in a natural garden, particularly if boulders are a primary part of the scene.

C. mauritanicus, ground morning glory, is better as a low foreground plant, growing just 1 to 2 feet high, spreading 2 to 3 feet wide. The rounded leaves are soft gray-green and are more evergreen than *C. cneorum.* Lavender-blue flowers, 1 to 2 inches in diameter, bloom over a long season from summer into late fall. Both plants combine well with *Cerastium tomentosum,* snow-in-summer, and as foreground companions to red and blue *Salvia* species, sage.

Planting & Care—Plant from containers in fall in mild-winter regions; wait until spring in cold-winter areas. Locate in full sun in well-draining soil. Prune and thin plants in late fall months to renew growth and to prevent woody growth. Avoid overhead irrigation with spray heads; irrigate with drip irrigation emitters when possible.

Coreopsis — Tickseed

These easy-to-grow plants produce a profusion of cheery, yellow, daisy flowers. They are native to open meadows of the U.S., primarily east of the Mississippi and in the South. The seeds are beloved by goldfinches. These are workhorse plants, decorative and heavily blooming. Given a sunny spot, *Coreopsis* will thrive in almost any soil. Remove spent flowers for continuous bloom. If you have a lot of plants, use hedge shears to trim the dead blooms away. Flowers are favored for cutting, creating lavish bouquets.

Recommended Species—
C. auriculata is native to the south-eastern U.S. Plants grow 1-1/2-feet high with single, yellow, 1-1/2- to 2-inch flowers.
C. grandiflora 'Early Sunrise' blooms the first year from seed, unlike other coreopsis, and was the first flower to win gold medal awards in both America and Europe. It has divided leaves and yellow, semi-double flowers on plants 2 feet high. Tolerant of a wide range of soil types.
C. lanceolata is the common *Coreopsis.* It self-sows profusely and can take over the garden if not controlled.
C. verticillata 'Moonbeam' has thread-like leaves and pale yellow flowers. It grows to 2 feet tall. A choice plant with a long bloom season, it requires low water after establishment.

Planting & Care—Easy to grow from seed. Plant 'Early Sunrise' in place in fall and there's a good chance you'll have flowers the first year. Plants are also often available in containers at nurseries; set out in fall or spring. Space plants 2 to 3 feet apart. Grows best in full sun and in ordinary soil. Divide every few years in early spring to expand plantings. Dig up clumps and cut into three or four sections. Cut back leaves and replant plants, watering thoroughly.

Native to North America

Perennial; blooms late spring through summer

Adapted to all regions of the arid West

Grows 1-1/2 to 2 feet high, spreading 1-1/2 feet wide

Accepts almost any well-draining soil

Moderate to low water use

Plant in full sun

Dianthus — Pinks

Dianthus flowers between the first spring flush of bloom and the major display of summer flowers. This relative lull in between gives the gardener a chance to appreciate the charm of these delightful plants. They form tufts of spiky, gray-green leaves, or mats of small, dark, evergreen leaves. Flowers vary from single fringed ("pinked") petals to dense heads similar to miniature carnations. The florist's carnation, *D. caryophyllus,* is in this genus. Flowers are spicily fragrant and come in red, white, yellow and shades of pink. Long stems need staking to support the large flower-heads. Prune back after first flowering for repeat bloom. Remove faded flowers as they decline. Pinks are at home in the cutting garden, perennial border, rock garden and historical garden. They are among the most satisfying perennials to grow.

Recommended Species—*D. x allwoodii* has mostly double, highly fragrant flowers in white and pink.
D. deltoides, maiden pink, forms 6-inch mats of short, dark green leaves with rosy pink or white flowers on 12-inch stems in summer.
D. gratianopolitanus (D. caesius) is the Cheddar pink, with mats of blue-gray foliage and fringed pink flowers on 12-inch stems during May and June. Flowers are highly fragrant.
D. plumarius is the cottage pink, old-fashioned, hardy, with spicily fragrant flowers. Blooms June to October.

Planting & Care—Plants are available in containers at the nursery in fall and spring, ready to flower. Species *Dianthus* are easy to grow from seed. Space plants 6 to 9 inches apart in full sun. Mulch plants with composted manure to supply additional nutrients. Cut flowers for bouquets frequently. This creates new flowering wood and more flowers as the season progresses. Prune straggly branches after the flowering season for new growth the next year. Divide existing plantings in spring or fall to keep plants vigorous, or, take cuttings of nonflowering shoots in midsummer.

Native to Eurasia to South Africa

Perennial; blooms in early spring and into summer

Adapted to all regions of the arid West

Grows to 6 to 18 inches high, spreading 12 inches wide

Prefers fertile, well-draining soil

Moderate to high water use, but avoid overwatering

Plant in full sun; but best with afternoon shade in desert regions

Dianthus species bloom between the first spring flush of bloom and the major display of summer flowers. Flowers vary from single fringed ("pinked") petals to dense heads similar to miniature carnations.

Right: *Cleome isomeris,* bladder pod, is a 3- to 4-foot evergreen subshrub producing interesting inflated capsules, the bladder pods, which enclose and shelter the seeds. Yellow flowers bloom from early spring to early summer.

Far right: *Convolvulus mauritanicus,* ground morning glory, is excellent as a low foreground plant, growing just 1 to 2 feet high, spreading 2 to 3 feet wide. Leaves are more evergreen than *C. cneorum.* In the background is *Alyogyne huegelii,* blue hibiscus.

Far left: *Dictamnus* ('Albus' is shown here) is an old-fashioned plant well adapted to adverse conditions.

Left: *Echinops ritro* 'Taplow Blue' produces interesting metallic blue flowers. It is better behaved than the species, growing 2-1/2 to 3-1/2 feet high.

Below: *Echinacea* are handsome although somewhat rangy to 4 feet high, with dark stems and deep green leaves. The flowers are marvelous for cutting.

Dictamnus — Gas Plant

Native from southern Europe to northern China

Perennial; blooms in early summer

Adapted to SCI, SCMHD, CACV, AZMHD, NMMHD, SNV, CWR

Grows 2 to 3 feet high, spreading 2 to 2-1/2 feet wide

Provide with loose, improved garden soil

Moderate water use

Plant in full sun to partial shade

An old-fashioned plant with a cast-iron constitution, *Dictamnus* earns its common name by the fact that, under the right conditions (a warm, windless day), the lemony, aromatic, resinous leaves will ignite if a lighted match is held close by. Foliage on this upright, shrubby, long-lived perennial is glossy olive-green. Flower spikes are white or reddish pink. The green stamens of the flowers are quite prominent and create an unusual, interesting effect in contrast to the white flower petals. Seeds and plant parts are poisonous.

Recommended Varieties—*D. albus* has white flowers, grows to 2 to 3 feet high. *D. a. 'Purpureus'* is a pink form.

Best use is in the background of the perennial border, or interplant in the natural garden among shrubs or small trees. Dried seed pods add interest to indoor arrangements, but be aware that pods and leaves are poisonous.

Planting & Care—*Dictamnus* grows easily from seed sown in place in fall or spring. Be aware that plants establish slowly. After plants are up and growing, provide with moderate water. They are self-supporting and do not require staking. Established plants resent being moved and will take a few seasons to recover from transplanting. It's best to set out young plants, 2 feet apart, where you want them to grow.

Dietes — Fortnight Lily

Native to South Africa

Perennial; blooms spring through fall

Adapted to SCC, SCI, SCLD, AZLD, NCC, CACV

Grows 2 to 4 feet high, spreads 2 to 3 feet wide

Tolerates all soils

Moderate water use

Plant in full sun along the coast, in partial shade inland and desert regions

Accent plants are valuable features in low-water landscapes and natural gardens. *Dietes vegeta* has a special quality, producing strong, vertical, narrow, 2-inch, dark green leaves and white, 3-inch, iris-like flowers. Plants grow as clumps to 3 to 4 feet high and are topped with flower stalks that grow well above the foliage. Flowering occurs for many months from spring through fall, coming in waves at two-week to four-week intervals.

D. bicolor has similar, vigorous, vertical, narrow green leaves to 2 to 3 feet high. Flowers are iris-like and are a distinct yellow with maroon spots. Most effective when used in rock gardens adjacent to large boulders, in clusters for accents and at the bases of trees as plants develop into vigorous clumps. Clean out dead interior leaves as they occur to provide a crisp, fresh look. Treat flowering stems the same as *D. vegeta*. Do not cut back vertical green leaves at any time, because brown tips and regrowth will be unsightly.

Planting & Care—Plants grow from rhizomes and are generally available in containers. Plant almost any time along coast or inland; plant in fall or early spring in desert areas. Well adapted to most soils. Plants tolerate heat, wind, full sun or partial shade. However, avoid reflected sun in a western exposure in desert and inland areas. Provide deep watering at regular intervals once plants are established. As plants age and show decline, cut out leaves at the bases of plants to maintain a clean appearance. Flower stalks live for years and should be removed at the base only when they die out. Remove seed pods on flower stalks as they develop to encourage more flower production. After several years, divide oversize plants to extend plantings, or pass some along to friends.

Echinacea purpurea — Purple Coneflower

The Greek name *Echinacea* means "hedgehog," and the spiny cone of this composite does indeed look like a hedgehog. As flowers open, the center is a flat disk of pliable orange spikes, the rays tiny. As it develops, the center grows to make a large cone, with tiny, yellow, disk flowers between the spikes. Ray flowers usually curve downward. Cones persist long after the pink or white petals have dropped.

This native of the American prairie makes a handsome though somewhat rangy plant 2 to 4 feet high, with dark stems and deep green leaves. Bumblebees love the flowers, which are marvelous for cutting.

Recommended Varieties—'Bright Star' grows 2 to 2-1/2 feet high, with rosy pink ray flowers held outward. 'Alba' is the white form. 'White Lustre' has ivory petals that curve downward and a bright orange cone on plants 2-1/2 feet tall. Flowers appear August to September. 'Magnus' has vivid, true pink blooms all summer and into fall on plants 2-1/2 feet tall. Plants are the ideal size for the rear of the perennial bed or along a fence or wall. Plant in clusters for the best show.

Planting & Care—*Echinacea* is easy to grow from seed. In warm desert and inland regions, sow seed in place in fall. In other mild-winter regions, sow seed in spring. In cold-winter regions, sow in spring in trays indoors, and set out seedlings in early summer. Space plants 2 to 3 feet apart in a sunny location. Because it is native to the prairie, grow in ordinary soil; accepts slightly alkaline soil. Do not overwater after plants are established. Plants self-sow readily and can also be divided.

Native to prairies of U.S. Midwest

Perennial; blooms late spring and early summer

Adapted to SCI, SCLD, SCMHD, NCC, CACV, AZLD, AZMHD, TXEP, TXTPR

Grows 2 to 4 feet high, spreading 2-1/2 feet wide

Provide with most any well-draining soil; accepts slightly alkaline soil

Low water use; do not overwater after plants are established

Plant in full sun

Echinops — Globe Thistle

Like *Echinacea,* this, too, is a hedgehog plant. *Echinops* species gives a bold and unusual effect in the back of the perennial border. From the middle of summer into fall, it produces round flowerheads of deep, steel blue that rise on prickly stems from a basal rosette of leaves. The thistle-like plants grow 3-1/2 to 4 feet high or more and are somewhat coarse in appearance, making globe thistle excellent for the natural garden or in low-water areas of the landscape. Highly effective when combined with yellow-flowering perennials. Leaves have prickles along the edges and are covered with white hairs on the underneath side. Plants are long-lived, needing little maintenance. Be aware, too, they can become overly aggressive in the border.

The space-age flowers are wonderful additions to arrangements—they last long and dry well, retaining their blue color. Wear gloves when handling flowers and stems to protect your hands from the prickly thistles.

Echinops ritro 'Taplow Blue' is similar to the species with deep, metallic blue flowers. Plants are better behaved, growing 2-1/2 to 3-1/2 feet high.

Planting & Care—In mild regions sow seed in place during fall. In cold regions, sow seed in trays indoors in late winter to early spring, and transplant seedlings when weather begins to warm. Space plants 3 feet apart. Grows best in full sun and when given low water. Avoid planting in low-lying areas where the soil may remain soggy. It is difficult to divide plants because of deep roots, but you can propagate by root cuttings in spring.

Native to eastern Europe to western Asia

Perennial; blooms midsummer to fall

Adapted to all regions of the arid West

Grows 2-1/2 to 4 feet high, spreading 3 to 4 feet wide

Provide with light, well-draining soil

Low water use

Plant in full sun to light shade

Above: *Encelia farinosa,* brittle bush, is one of the most widely distributed native flowering plants in the Southwest deserts. Yellow flowers on tall, 12-inch stalks can literally cover the gray, mounding plant with bouquets of blooms.

Above right: *Encelia californica,* California encelia, is similar to brittle bush, but growth is more open. It is well adapted to the cooler coast and foothills of the coastal ranges.

Echium fastuosum, pride of Madeira, is a large, shrublike perennial that does best in the mild Mediterranean climate along the coast.

Echium fastuosum — Pride of Madeira

This is a dramatic large-scale perennial with tall, spike-like flower clusters composed of 1/2-inch purple flowers. Plants are vigorous and shrub-like, blooming in abundance during May and June. In the mild Mediterranean climate along the coast, plants grow in full sun or light shade. The large, coarse branches 3 to 4 feet long are covered with hairy, narrow, gray-green leaves. Plants are wide-spreading and need ample space. In inland valleys beyond the coastal hills, locate where plants will be protected from hot sun and avoid placing in low-lying areas that might be more susceptible to frost.

Pride of Madeira is a favorite for slope plantings and helps reduce soil erosion. Use ice plant as a ground cover around plants to increase soil binding action and to extend the season of color. Also excellent as a tall background in wide perennial beds.

Planting & Care—Nurseries near the coast generally have plants available in containers. Plants reseed and with time can create a natural landscape effect on their own. Remove flowering stems after bloom period and prune branches selectively to maintain a natural appearance. In winter, cut plants back to 1-1/2 to 2 feet high to create structure for new spring growth. Along the coast, plants are low water users once they're established. Inland, be ready to supply additional water (moderate, not high) during warm summer months. Plants in sandy soils require more frequent watering.

Native to the Mediterranean

Perennial; blooms late spring to early summer

Adapted to SCC, SCI, NCC, CACV

Grows 4 to 6 feet high, spreading 6 to 8 feet wide

Accepts a range of soils, from gravelly to clay

Low to moderate water use

Full sun along the coast, partial shade in inland valleys

Encelia — Brittle Bush, Encienso

Encelia farinosa, brittle bush, is one of the Southwest desert's most widely distributed native flowering plants. It can be seen throughout low-elevation desert areas of California and Arizona and mid-elevation regions of southeastern Nevada—wherever temperatures do not fall below 30F for too long a period. It is almost herbaceous in character, with a growth pattern that ebbs and flows according to how much rainfall or irrigation plants receive. Flowering is most profuse mid-March to April, but can begin as early as November in frost-free areas. Yellow flowers on tall, 12-inch stalks can literally cover the 3- to 4-foot, gray, mounding plant with bouquets of blooms.

E. californica, California encelia, has similar characteristics, but growth is more open. It is well adapted to the cooler coast and foothills of the coastal ranges. Several other species of *Encelia* are distributed in the Southwest deserts, but these two are most readily available and best adapted.

Brittle bush blends with plants in the natural garden that have similar moisture needs. Companion plants include: *Fouquieria splendens*, ocotillo, *Larrea tridentata*, creosote bush, and *Melampodium leucanthum*, blackfoot daisy. Use California encelia in combination with *Salvia clevelandii*, *Artemisia* and *Lavandula* species.

Planting & Care—Easy to start from seed when planted in place during fall or early spring. Brittle bush is also included in wildflower mixes. Container plants are commonly available and can be planted at any season, but fall is ideal. With time, landscape plants often develop heavy woody branches. Thin and cut back soft branches at least one-third, maintaining natural form, for renewed growth after flowering. After shearing, selectively thin inside branches to allow sunlight into the plant's interior. Plants have low to moderate water requirements, and when water is abundant plants can become weak.

Native to U.S. Southwest

Perennial; blooms in spring

Adapted to SCC, SCI, SCLD, AZLD, SNV

Grows 3 to 4 feet high with an equal spread

Accepts most any well-draining soil

Low water use; goes dormant in extreme drought

Plant in full sun

Ericameria laricifolia — Turpentine Bush

Native to Arizona, New Mexico and west Texas

Perennial; golden flowers and foliage in fall months

Adapted to SCI, SCLD, AZLD, AZMHD, NMMHD

Grows 1 to 3 feet high or more, spreads 2 to 3 feet wide

Provide with average, well-draining soil

Low to moderate water use

Plant in full sun

Ericameria larcifolia, turpentine bush, produces profuse, small, golden flowers in fall, in combination with resinous, refined, turpentine-scented leaves that turn to gold as winter approaches. When given low water, mature height is about 1 to 3 feet. With moderate water, plants can develop to twice that size.

Many other species not often found in home landscapes dwell in natural habitats throughout the Southwest, even into the San Joaquin and sage-brush chaparral of the California coast. These plants reclaim disturbed soil areas and establish themselves on alluvial plains and rocky slopes. In many areas the numerous species of turpentine bush constitute the primary vegetative cover.

The special flowering traits, colorful fall foliage, size and adaptability to landscape use with low-water requirements make turpentine bush a valuable low-water-use plant for the natural garden and revegetation projects. To create a more colorful mass foreground effect, group plants in clusters at 2- to 3-foot triangulated spacing. Companion plants include tall-growing Texas rangers, *Leucophyllum,* as well as *Artemisia* and *Justicia* species.

Planting & Care—Plant from containers any time but best in fall or spring. Provide moderate water until plants are established, then low water. Almost any well-draining soil is acceptable. Avoid overhead spray irrigation and use drip irrigation if possible. If growth sprawls or becomes tall and rangy, or after flowers have completed their cycle, cut back selectively in winter or in the late spring to control form.

Eupatorium — Mistflower

Native to west Texas

Deciduous perennial; white flower clusters bloom during fall months

Adapted to CWR, SCLD, SCMHD, AZLD, AZMHD, NMMHD, TXEP, TXTPR

Grows 1 to 6 feet high and spreads as wide

Accepts loam, sandy or clay soils

Low to moderate water use depending on location in sun or partial shade

Plant in full sun in higher elevations; in partial shade of trees in high-temperature areas

Mistflowers, with their white to pale pink fragrant flower clusters, add a special, refined, delicate look in perennial beds after the summer season. We've found butterflies and hummingbirds enjoying the prolific 2-inch flower heads even into the fall season. Both species described here are native to Texas hills and ravines in the Edwards Plateau and are adapted to other dry climate areas.

E. havenense, mistflower, has light pink to white clusters of flowers set among triangular serrated leaves. When dry, the flowers are an attractive feature. Growth is more vigorous and expansive to 4 to 6 feet high.
E. wrightii, white mistflower, grows 1 to 2 feet high when given low water, but plants may grow to 3 feet with moderate moisture. Small, 2-inch, dark green, serrated leaves provide a dense background for the white fragrant flowers in fall.

Plant in perennial beds in clusters of three to five plants among tall perennials. This helps support the overall structure of the garden during the fall months at a time when many other perennials have completed their cycle.

Planting & Care—Plants are easiest to establish when planted in fall. Space 3 to 4 feet apart in average, well-draining soil. Both species adapt to low water use. However, in hottest regions additional summer irrigation is recommended. After flowering and during the deciduous season, prune plants back about one-third (but retain the natural form) to encourage new growth the following spring.

Euphorbia — Spurge

This large, diverse group includes trees, shrubs, and tender succulent plants. The so-called flowers are actually *bracts*— brightly colored leaves just below the true flowers, which are usually small and insignificant. The leaves are often more attractive than the flowers. Euphorbias have a milky sap that can irritate the skin like poison ivy. This is not usually a problem, because plants don't need pinching or cutting and are best left undisturbed.

Recommended Species—
E. epithymoides (E. polychroma) has chartreuse bracts on plants 1-1/2 feet tall.
E. milii (E. splendens), crown of thorns, is a favorite in containers or in a mini-oasis garden. It grows 1-1/2 to 3 feet high and as wide. Red bracts are colorful all year round in sunny locations. Plants are cold-tender; in inland or low-elevation desert areas, grow in containers and move to shelter when frosts threaten.
E. myrsinites grows 6 inches tall and spreads wide. Leaves are scaly, blue-gray, bracts are yellow in spring then turn coral-pink in summer.
E. rigida (E. biglandulosa), gopher plant, has the reputation of keeping gophers out of the garden. Growth is low, to 2 feet high and spreading. Leaves are fleshy gray-green, 1-1/2 inches long. Chartreuse flower clusters appear winter to spring. Strangely, after seeds ripen in spring, stems die back and need to be removed. New stems grow back quickly.
E. wulfenii (also known as *E. characias)* has more upright stems. Plants develop into a dome shape almost shrub-like to 3 to 4 feet. Large, dense, chartreuse and blue clusters bloom during the late winter and spring.

Planting & Care—Plant from containers in fall or spring. Space plants 1-1/2 to 2 feet apart to allow for natural spread. Locate in full sun in light, gritty soil that is not too fertile. Divide or take root cuttings in fall or early spring, or take cuttings of basal shoots in midsummer.

Native to subtropical regions of South Africa, Asia Minor, Mexico

Perennial; blooms in spring

Adapted to SCC, SCI, SCLD, NCC, CACV

Grows 6 inches to 4 feet high

Provide with gritty, well-draining soils, even poor soils

Low water use

Plant in full sun

Euryops — Golden Euryops

Euryops pectinatus and *E. p. viridis* are two African perennials that have become garden favorites due to their long blooming season in regions as diverse as the foggy coast to desert and inland valley areas. Plants are valued for the bright, 1-1/2 to 2-inch, yellow, daisy-like flowers that grow above the finely divided foliage.
E. pectinatus, with gray-green foliage, grows 4 to 6 feet high with an equal spread and is more cold-hardy.
E. p. viridis (often called 'Green Gold') also has the vigor and size of the parent plant, but foliage is brighter green and flowers are more attractive. Plants colorful in the background in perennial beds, or in foreground to taller shrubs and in containers.

Both species blend with other perennials and annuals. Perennials with similar moisture requirements include *Kniphofia, Artemisia, Felicia* and *Verbena* species.

Planting & Care—Plant from containers any time along the coast, but wait until fall or early spring in inland regions. Purchase fresh, vigorous plants at the nursery, avoiding overgrown, root-bound plants. Space 3 to 5 feet apart. Due to their vigor, plants require thinning and cutting back to trim off spent flowers and to control size after flowering. In cool coastal areas, prune in early summer. Prune in fall in hot summer regions so plants will regrow to flower during late winter and spring. If growth is rapid, cut long vigorous branches to side growth to create more flowering wood. Strip away interior dead leaves on lower stems in the fall for a clean, neat look (dense growth causes interior foliage to die out).

Both species prefer good drainage. After establishing, plants respond to moderate water. A location in full sun is ideal along the coast; supply afternoon shade in inland valleys and in low-elevation desert areas.

Native to South Africa

Perennial; blooms fall, winter, to early spring

Adapted to SCC, SCI, SCLD, NCC, CACV, AZLD, AZMHD

Grows 4 to 6 feet high with an equal spread

Provide with fertile, well-draining soil

Moderate water use; best with deep irrigation

Plant in full sun along the coast; provide afternoon shade in hot inland valleys and desert regions

Above: *Euphorbia rigida (E. biglandulosa),* gopher plant, has a low, spreading growth habit, which makes it an interesting specimen for containers. Chartreuse flower clusters appear winter to spring.

Above right: *Euphorbia epithymoides (E. polychroma)* produces chartreuse bracts on plants that mound to 1-1/2 feet high.

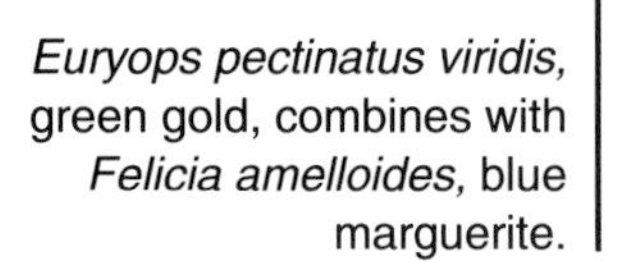

Euryops pectinatus viridis, green gold, combines with *Felicia amelloides,* blue marguerite.

Far left: *Gaillardia aristata* blooms for a long period—from spring to frost. The flowers are good for cutting, especially those of taller varieties.

Left: *Galvezia speciosa* is native to the Channel Islands, located just off the Southern California coast. Although shrub size, the 3- to 5-foot, wide-spreading plants blend into garden borders, on slopes and with other low-water-use landscape plants.

Below: *Felicia amelloides,* blue marguerite, with geraniums. The sky blue, yellow-centered flowers of blue marguerite are special attractions in the perennial border, cherished for their long blooming period.

Felicia amelloides — Blue Marguerite

Native to South Africa

Perennial; blooms in summer

Adapted to SCC, SCI, SCLD, NCC, CACV, AZLD

Grows to 1-1/2 feet high, spreading 3 to 4 feet wide

Provide with well-draining soil

High to moderate water use

Plant in full sun; some afternoon shade in desert areas

The sky blue, yellow-centered flowers of blue marguerite are special attractions in the perennial border, cherished for their long blooming period. Plants are shrubby in form, growing 1-1/2 feet high and spreading 3 to 4 feet wide. They are highly compatible with other plants in mini-oasis gardens where their luxuriant growth blends with other favorite high-water-use plants. Many new selections have been recently introduced that have larger flowers and darker blue color.

Plants excel in containers and look exceptional combined with *Euryops, Hemerocallis* and other yellow-flowering perennials of similar size and culture. A well-draining soil is necessary. Select a 16- to 20-inch-diameter container for best results.

Planting & Care—Where adapted, plant from containers in the fall to establish plants before hot weather comes on. Locate in full sun along the coast; in hot climates, locate plants where they'll receive filtered afternoon shade. Plant in soil with good drainage. After summer heat and in early fall, thin and prune to stimulate new growth for late winter and spring flowering season. Plants will develop scraggly appearance if not pruned and thinned. Deadhead spent flowers frequently during bloom season to encourage more flowers.

Gaillardia aristata — Blanket Flower

Native to central and western U.S.

Perennial; blooms begin in spring and continue until frost

Adapted to all regions of the arid West

Grows 6 inches to 4 feet high, spreading 18 to 24 inches wide

Prefers well-draining sandy or loam soil

Low water use

Plant in full sun

Gaillardia is one of the few perennials that bloom continuously from spring to frost. Even warm-climate plants in a southern exposure persist. The composite flowers have a large rounded, bristly center. Rays are brightly marked in shades of red and yellow. The flowers are good for cutting, especially those of taller varieties.

The colors of *Gaillardia* don't blend well with some flowers, notably pink ones, but they can be used successfuly alone or surrounded by gray-leaved or blue- or yellow-flowering plants. Plants range in height from 6 inches to 4 feet. Common uses include foreground borders in perennial beds, meadows, wildflower gardens and rock gardens.

Recommended Varieties—The following are recommended selections of *G. aristata:* 'Burgundy' has deep, wine-red flowers on 2-foot plants. 'Dazzler' grows 2 to 2-1/2 feet high. Flowers have a maroon center with yellow edge. 'Goblin' is a dwarf at 12 inches, with red flowers that have a yellow edge. 'Monarch' strain is a color mixture including solids and bicolors, growing 2 to 3 feet high.

Planting & Care—Plant from containers or sow seed almost any time; summer plantings require more water. Fall is the ideal time to plant in mild-winter regions. Space 12 inches apart in full sun. Well-draining soil is essential for plants to survive through winter. *Gaillardia* has a floppy growth habit, and tall varieties need staking. Deadhead spent flowers regularly to encourage more blooms. Propagate from division or stem cuttings made in late summer or by root cuttings made in early spring.

Galvezia speciosa — Bush Snapdragon

This is one of eight rare species native to the Channel Islands (located just off the Southern California coast) that have adapted to mainland gardens. Although shrub size, the 3- to 5-foot, wide-spreading plants blend into garden borders, on slopes and with other low-water-use landscape plants. The bright scarlet, 1-inch, tubular flowers cluster at the tips of gray-green branches. They create a vivid scene during the spring months and sporadically through the summer and fall. Hummingbirds are attracted to the flowers.

The plant form, size and foliage color of bush snapdragon blend well with *Echium fastuosum*, pride of Madeira, *Romneya coulteri*, matilija poppy, and *Encelia californica*, brittle bush, all of which have similar moisture and soil requirements.

Planting & Care—Plant from containers in fall or early spring in well-draining soil. Plants bloom more frequently along the coast. They will perform well when given partial shade or morning sun in inland or hot desert regions. Cut back summer watering to moderate or low after plants are well established. This simulates the rainless summers of its native region. Deadhead flowers after flowering season. Prune lightly (do not shear) to maintain natural form and produce new flowering wood.

Native to the Channel Islands—offshore Southern California

Perennial subshrub; blooms spring and summer

Adapted to SCC, SCI, NCC, CACV

Grows 3 to 5 feet high, spreading as wide

Provide with well-draining soil

Low to moderate water use

Locate in full sun in coastal areas; partial shade in inland valleys

Gaura lindheimeri — Gaura

This native of the Southwest U.S. is gaining recognition as a superb garden plant. The 1- to 3-1/2-inch, lance-shaped leaves form a bushy plant 3 to 4 feet high. From early summer until fall, branching spikes bear white starry flowers that gradually turn to pink. Gaura is a long-lived plant and is easily grown, doing well in hot conditions and dry soils.

Flowers are sparse and do not appear in profusion at any one time, yet they bloom for a long period through the season. Each flower drops off after blooming leaving a clean look on the stem. As the season progresses, it's best to cut off the seed-bearing spikes to reduce abundant quantities of the self-sowing seeds. The ideal location is full sun, but accepts partial shade.

In perennial beds, take advantage of the 3- to 4-foot mature height and place a cluster of plants at the back of a border. Gaura adds an informal touch to the perennial border, or include it in the natural or wildflower garden.

Planting & Care—In mild-winter regions seed can be sown in place in fall. In colder areas sow seed in trays indoors in early spring, and set out seedlings later in the season. Space plants 2 feet apart in well-draining sandy soil. In cold regions, apply a layer of mulch over the root area during winter to help extend plant life. If flowering ceases in midsummer due to lack of water, cut back to about 1 foot high to create bushy regrowth and more flowers will appear later in the year. Divide existing plants in spring or fall.

Native to the U.S. Southwest

Perennial; blooms from early summer until fall

Adapted to all regions of the arid West

Grows 3 to 4 feet high with an equal spread

Provide with light, well-draining, sandy soil

Low water use

Plant in full sun

Gazania — Gazania

Native to South Africa

Evergreen perennial ground cover; blooms spring and fall; occasionally throughout the rest of the year

Adapted to SCC, SCI, SCLD, SCMHD, NCC, CACV, AZLD, AZMHD, SNV

Grows 6 to 12 inches high, spreading 24 to 36 inches wide; clumping types to 15 inches

Provide with well-draining soil

Low water use

Full sun in all locations

Gazanias are popular perennial ground covers in the arid West that are grown as annuals in cold-winter regions. They provide a long season of color, require relatively little water and blend well with most dry-climate landscape plants. Clumping and trailing forms are available, both thrive in full sun and tolerate a wide range of soils. Clumping types can be seeded; trailing types are generally planted from rooted cuttings. Both work well in borders, as foreground accents and ground covers for large areas.

Recommended Species—*G. rigens leucolaena*, trailing gazanias, spread with long trailing stems and are ideally used for covering slopes as well as level areas. Prime flowering periods in desert areas are winter and spring. Along the coast and in inland valleys, plants flower intermittently all year. Recently introduced hybrids have soft, pleasing green foliage. Flower colors include yellow, white, orange or bronze. Favorites include 'Sunburst', orange with a black eye, and 'Sunrise Yellow', with large, black-eyed flowers. *Gazania splendens* are clump-forming. Superior cultivars include multi-colored 'Aztec Queen', 'Mitsui Yellow', 'Burgundy', 'Copper King', 'Daybreak Orange', 'Daybreak Yellow' and 'Fiesta Red'. Recent introductions include 'Pixie Dwarf White' and 'Pixie Dwarf Yellow'. These are most effective in small-scale plantings as fillers in color borders and rock gardens. Mixtures of clumping hybrids in seed mixes or plants are available in several colors and foliage forms. Plants have great vigor, establish easily from transplants and reseed readily.

Planting & Care—Sow seed of hybrid clumping forms in place in fall, late winter and spring months. Plant trailing forms from containers in fall in mild-winter regions; wait until spring in colder areas. Both forms perform well in most any soil that has good drainage. Plant in full sun; flowers close on cloudy days and at night. Overwatering can sometimes cause problems with die-back.

Gerbera jamesonii — Transvaal Daisy

Native to South Africa

Perennial; blooms over a long season; most profuse early summer to fall

Adapted to SCC, SCI, SCLD, CACV, AZLD

Grows to 1-1/2 feet high, spreading 18 inches wide

Provide with well-draining soil

Moderate water use

Plant in full sun along coast; provide afternoon shade in inland and desert regions

The glowing flower colors of this South African introduction are valued by gardeners throughout the arid West. In cool coastal areas, grow in full sun. In hot inland valleys and deserts, plant in a location that receives filtered afternoon shade.

Slender, 1-1/2-foot stems support the large, single daisy flowers that grow to 4 inches in diameter. Colors range from red, orange and yellow to coral. Double flowers are also available. They bloom early summer and fall and are especially prized as cut flowers.

Planting & Care—Select plants when in bloom at the nursery to get the flower color you desire. Plant from containers in fall or spring in mild-winter areas; wait until spring in cold regions. Handle with care when transplanting. Plants can be grown from seed, but it is a slow process, taking up to 18 months.
Well-drained soil is important, as is deep irrigation. If your soil is a slow-draining clay, plant in raised planters, on mounds or in containers. Most important, plant the rootball high to supply the necessary drainage at the plant's crown. Also keep rootball crown free of moist organic mulches. After a deep watering, plants do best with a brief dry period. When planning planting locations, arrange plants in moderate water zone separate from other perennials that require high water.

Far left: *Gaura lindheimeri,* gaura, is native to the Southwest U.S. From early summer until fall, branching spikes bear white, star-shaped flowers that gradually turn pink. Here it is shown in combination with silver-blue *Festuca ovina glauca.*

Gazania species are colorful flowering plants with a long bloom season that can be enjoyed up close, shown at left with gray-leaved *Artemisia.* They also work well as ground covers for large areas (see below).

Ornamental Grasses

Refer to individual descriptions for information on each plant adaptation, mature size, soil, sun and water preferences

As a group, ornamental grasses are gaining wide acceptance as prime choices for perennial gardens—to mix with flowering plants and shrubs and as accents and in mass plantings. Combining grasses with low-maintenance, long-flowering shrubs and perennials is highly effective in today's natural design gardens.

Grasses such as those described here offer subtle beauty throughout the year—their fine-textured leaves and softly colored flower spikes lend a special quality to the garden. They are particularly striking when located where they will be backlit by morning or afternoon sun. They also provide shelter for birds and for other wildlife. In addition, shorter types of grasses can be used as ground covers; other kinds have utilitarian use in revegetation projects and for erosion control.

Billbergia mitans, queen's tears, is an exotic, evergreen perennial grass from Brazil. It evokes a tropical look in the mini-oasis garden. Give it a location sheltered from direct sun and plant in containers or under the shade of canopy trees. Other landscape uses include a solid planting under the shade of trees as a ground cover effect. Plants can also be grown indoors. The spiny-toothed leaves grow as basal clusters. Flowers grow out of these clusters and droop gracefully with spikes of rose-red bracts tinged with deep, blue-green edging along the petals. The basal growth holds a funnelled reservoir of water, which makes overhead irrigation necessary to get water into the reservoir. Adapted to coastal climates and in sheltered locations inland.

Briza media

Briza media, quaking grass, is an annual grass, producing fascinating green tufts from May through June with 12- to 18-inch, white, rattlesnake-like seedheads above the light green foliage. Allow plants to grow naturally to avoid a crowded effect so the unique seedheads can move unencumbered with the breezes. Also useful in dried arrangements. *B. maxima,* big quaking grass, is also an annual. It grows to 2 feet high, producing light yellow panicles from May through August. Both *Briza* species prefer full sun with moderate water, and both are adapted to all regions.

Calamagrostis x acutiflora 'Stricta', feather reed grass, forms an attractive clump of thin green leaves in early summer. Upright tan to yellow flower spikes reach 5 feet or more. Due to their height, use as a background or as a strong vertical accent. This is a sterile form, so it will not reseed, but it can be divided in spring. Adapted to all regions of the arid West, but requires acidic soil.

Carex buchananii, fox red curly sedge, also fox red cherry sedge, is native to New Zealand. It grows erect to 1-1/2 to 2 feet high, with unusual, narrow, reddish bronze leaves. Growth is dense and tufted, with curly tips. This is a grass with controlled growth, requiring minimum moisture and maintenance. Avoid shearing; plants look best when growth remains natural. Propagate by division or seeding. Moderate water use. *C. morrowii* 'Aurea Variegata', Japanese sedge grass, has striking borders of green on each side of the pendulous leaves, which have bright yellow centers. Plants are also often grown and sold as 'Old Gold'. Evergreen, it grows 12 to 18 inches high and spreads gracefully. A valued plant in sheltered mini-oasis garden settings and around small waterfalls and pond areas, or in shaded rock gardens possessing a rich organic, acidic soil. Maintain soil moisture at moderate to high. Widely adapted. Plant in sun to shade along the coast, in partial to full shade in inland areas.

Elymus condensatus 'Canyon Prince', giant blue wildrye, has graceful, blue-gray leaves, excellent in providing a blue accent massed as a striking ground cover. Low water use, hardiness and adaptability to heavy soils in most any climate are valued attributes, as is its ability to control erosion. plants can become invasive. Control spread with root barriers when used in perennial beds. A location in full sun is ideal. *E. glauca,* blue lyme grass, grows 1-1/2 to 2 feet high with attractive blue leaves. Low water use. Adapted to all regions, thriving in high heat.

Festuca cinera 'Elijah Blue' produces intense blue, needle-fine foliage, providing dimensions of color and texture to the striking flower garden. Cut back plants to just above ground

Ornamental Grasses, continued

level after flowering to renew growth. Best planted in full sun. Low water use after established. Adapted to all areas. *F. ovina glauca,* blue fescue, forms graceful tufts of fine, blue-gray leaves 6 to 10 inches high. It is most useful in the foreground in flower borders, in pattern plantings and in clusters among boulders. Divide every few years to renew growth. Adapted to all regions of the arid West, but prefers cool coastal conditions. Low water use.

Hakonechloa macra 'Aureola', golden Japanese forest grass, is a recent introduction from Japan. Graceful, variegated, slender, arching leaves are soft and satiny, growing to 2 feet high. Most effective in filtered sun or light shade. Use in drifts, as shrub filler, accent in perennial border or planted in containers. Plants thrive in well-draining soil when given moderate moisture. Best in coastal regions; protected locations in mild-winter inland areas.

Imperata cylindrica 'Red Baron', Japanese blood grass, has striking, blood red leaves that reach 1-1/2 to 2 feet long. Slow-growing, not highly invasive. Best adapted to coastal regions.

Miscanthus sinensis 'Gracillimus', eulalia or maiden grass, is native to eastern Asia. It forms a dominant clump of slender, silver-striped green leaves 4 to 5 feet high. 'Purpurescens' grows 3 to 4 feet high, has reddish purple leaves and red flower spikes. 'Zebrinus' is an unusual variegated form, with broad gold stripes that run *across* the leaves. Moderate water use; ample water can cause rampant growth. Cut back in late winter to renew plants for next season. All are adapted to grow throughout the arid West.

Muhlenbergia dumosa, bamboo muhley, has fine-textured leaves that become more interesting with maturity when the interior reveals bamboo-like stems. Form is soft and mounding, reaching a height and spread of 4 to 5 feet. During the April bloom period, plants take on an attractive tan look while the green leaves are hidden. Plants are low-water users and thrive in most any soil. Plantings mature over several seasons, gradually increasing their density. Plants remain much more attractive if they are not cut back. Evergreen in many mild-climate regions.

M. emersleyi 'El Toro', bull grass, features graceful evergreen leaves that grow in clumps to 3 feet high. Straw to reddish flower plumes can reach 4 to 5 feet high. They bloom in the fall with open flower stalks, and are even showier than *M. rigens.*

M. lindheimeri 'Autumn Glow' reaches 1-1/2 to 2 feet high and 3 to 4 feet wide with open flower stalks. Many light tan stalks are produced on each plant in the fall months, giving it a dense, fluffy appearance. Native to Texas; adapted throughout the arid West.

M. rigens, deergrass, is a native of Arizona and California. It is evergreen and well adapted to the rigors of western climates. It is at home in both perennial and natural gardens. This is a valuable erosion control plant for slopes and to revegetate disturbed areas. Graceful, 2- to 3-foot, mounding tufts can spread up to 5 feet wide, making it an attractive alternative to the much larger pampas grass. Cut back to 6 to 9 inches every year—in early spring you'll be rewarded with fresh new foliage. Grows in clay, loam or sand. Water requirement is low. Locate in sun to part shade.

Nolina lindheimerana, devil's shoestring, produces slender leaves and slender spikes of flowers that are held high above 3-foot plants. Plants evoke a soft grace among perennials or in the natural garden, especially in combination with large boulders. Well-draining soil important. Low water use. Locate in full sun or partial shade. Adapted to the varied climates of Texas through New Mexico, Arizona and the California deserts.

Ophiopogon jaburan, often sold as *Liriope gigantea,* is an important ornamental grass, lending a lush, evergreen effect in flower borders. Dark green, 1/2-inch leaves arch up and out 1-1/2 to 3 feet high. Small, white flower clusters are hidden in the lower part of the plant by the profuse leaves. Use in Oriental gardens, among bamboo in containers, in perennial and boulder beds. Ideal location in desert areas is shade or partial shade. Along

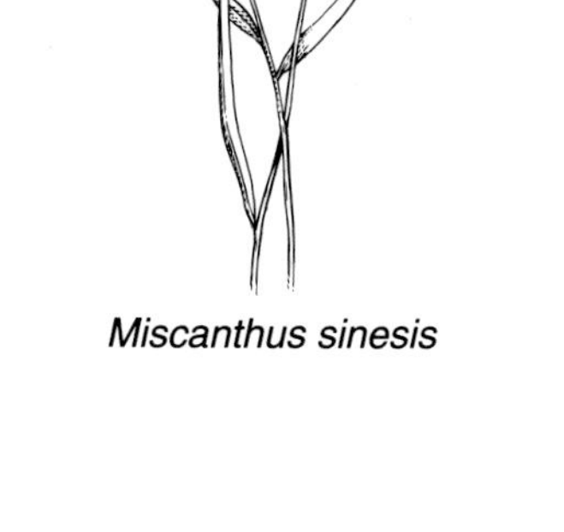

Miscanthus sinesis

Sisyrinchium bellum, California blue-eyed grass, is a native perennial grass with striking, bright blue flowers. It is excellent in a natural garden design.

Right: *Carex morrowii* 'Aurea Variegata', Japanese sedge grass, has striking borders of green on each side of the pendulous leaves, which have bright yellow centers. Plants are also often sold as 'Old Gold'.

Far right: *Elymus condensatus* 'Canyon Prince', giant blue wildrye, has graceful, blue-gray leaves, excellent in providing a blue accent or massed as a ground cover.

Stipa gigantea, giant feather grass, is shown in background. Attractive seedheads are striking, blooming on 4- to 5-foot spikes. These make a graceful, billowy, cut flower during the summer months. In the foreground is *Festuca* species.

Muhlenbergia lindheimeri 'Autumn Glow' (left) with 'Regal Mist'. Both grow 1-1/2 to 2 feet high and 3 to 4 feet wide with open flower stalks that give plants a dense, fluffy appearance.

Climate Adaptation Key

SCC:	S. Calif. Coastal
SCI:	S. Calif. Inland
SCLD:	S. Calif. Low Deserts
SCMHD:	S. Calif. Medium/ High Deserts
NCC:	N. Calif. Coastal
CACV:	Calif. Central Valley
AZLD:	Arizona Low Desert
AZMHD:	Arizona Medium/High Deserts
NMMHD:	New Mexico Medium/High Deserts
SNV:	Southern Nevada
TXHP:	Texas High Plains
TXEP:	Texas Edwards Plateau
TXRRP:	Texas Red Rolling Plains
TXTPR:	Texas Trans-Pecos Region
CWR:	Cold-Winter Regions

the coast, locate plants in full sun. Prefers well-draining soil and regular water. Divide mature plants to extend plantings. Cut out dead leaves only at base of plant as they occur. Do not shear plants; tips of cut leaves turn brown and do not regrow. New growth develops from base of plant.

Pennisetum alopecuroides, Australian fountain grass, forms clumps of slender leaves 2-1/2 to 4 feet high. Rose-pink flower spikes that look like foxtails are produced late August through October and often into winter. Of the many fountain grasses available, this has the best proportioned growth habit for garden use. Does not reseed.

P. setaceum 'Cupreum' ('Rubrum'), grows 3-1/2 feet high, with nodding, purple-pink flower spikes to 1 foot high. New plantings are less cold-hardy than established plants. Cut back to 6 inches high after frosts to develop new growth. Does not reseed. Both *Pennisetum* species can be divided in early spring.

Phalaris arundinacea picta, ribbon grass, gardener's garters or reed canary grass, has flat leaves striped green and cream. Plants grow to 2 to 3 feet high. Flourishes in a variety of soils and climates. Prefers shade but accepts morning sun. Spreads to make a good ground cover. Moderate water use, tolerates very moist to dry conditions. Cut back in late summer when plants become shaggy for fresh new growth.

Phormium tenax, New Zealand flax, creates a bold point of interest with many wide, sword-like, green leaves that can reach as high as 6 to 9 feet. Allow ample space for this large-scale plant to develop—locate 6 to 8 feet on center. Variations in leaf color range from green to bronze, dark purplish red to variegated. Flowers are dull red on stalks that grow well above the leaves. Many dwarf hybrids are available for smaller gardens, some grow to only 18 inches high. Moderate water use. Full sun exposure along coast; partial shade in hot climates. Remove dead leaves at base of plant only. No leaf pruning is necessary.

Sisyrinchium bellum, California blue-eyed grass, is a native perennial grass with distinctive, iris-like leaves. Dainty, silky, 6-petaled, bright blue flowers bloom at the ends of 16-inch stems in spring and summer. Locate plants in full sun; they accept dry conditions once they're established. Plants become dormant during summer with dry weather, but recover with cooler winter and spring temperatures.

Stipa gigantea, giant feather grass, develops into gray-green, rounded mounds of leaves 1 to 2 feet high. Attractive seedheads are striking, blooming on 4- to 5-foot spikes. This selection is worth including as a garden specimen or cluster planting of choice in perennial beds, and also makes a graceful, billowy cut flower for the summer months. Locate in full sun in cool climates, in partial shade in hot climates. Low to moderate water use. Plants may go dormant in late summer. Cut back at this time to near ground level; plants revive and regrow quickly.

Planting & Care—Ornamental grasses are easy-care plants, requiring less maintenance than perennials or garden shrubs. Many are becoming available in containers for planting in fall or spring. Plants can also be started from seed. One method is to sow seed in pots and bury pot and all to control growth and identification. Most grasses prefer a rich, light soil; adding gritty sand and amending with ground organic bark products helps improve the soil's water-holding capacity. Most tolerate poor soil and dry conditions, but plants will not reach full mature height. In general, supply plants with moderate water during warm weather; low water during the cool late fall and winter months.

Grasses are vigorous-growing plants, rapidly increasing by offset shoots. These are easy to separate and propagate to extend plantings. Divide established clumps in spring. Extremely vigorous types may require frequent division. Unless otherwise noted in the descriptions, grasses usually benefit by cutting old tops back to ground level in late winter to early spring before new growth emerges for fresh new leaves and renewed vigor and appearance.

Gypsophila — Baby's-Breath

For clouds of pale pink or white flowers, there's no better choice than *Gypsophila*, the perennial baby's-breath. Plants form dense clumps 3 to 3-1/2 feet high, with thick, slightly fuzzy leaves that are completely hidden by the billowing blooms.

Use among or between taller-growing shrubs and perennials. When plants are in bloom the lack of leaves creates a need for a background. Its value as a cut flower is well known.

Recommended Species—*G. paniculata* 'Bristol Fairy' is a double white form. All of these cultivars grow 3 to 3-1/2 feet high. 'Pink Fairy' has double pink flowers. 'Perfecta' has the largest double flowers in pure white. *G. paniculata* has a taproot and can't be moved once established.
G. repens is a trailing plant, growing 6 to 10 inches tall, spreading 2 to 3 feet, perfect for rock gardens. 'Alba' has white flowers; 'Rosea' has pink flowers.

Planting & Care—Sow seed in place in spring. Plants have a long taproot and are fussy about transplanting. Space plants 3 feet apart in organic, moderately fertile soil that has a pH of 7.0 to 7.5.

Plants often need support to prevent them from being blown over in wind or rain. Stake tall varieties of baby's-breath by placing several bamboo stakes or other support around each plant so stakes extend about 2 feet above the ground. Do this in spring when plants are 1 to 1-1/2 feet high. Tie firmly with twine to form a webbing.

Native to Caucasus Mountains of Russia to central Asia

Perennial; blooms in summer

Adapted to SCC, SCI, SCMHD, NCC, CACV, AZMHD, NMMHD, CWR

Grows 3 to 3-1/2 feet high, spreading 3 feet wide

Provide with well-draining, organic-rich soil

Moderate water use

Plant in full sun

Helianthus — Perennial Sunflower

This is the perennial form of the common, roadside annual sunflower. *Helianthus annuus* native to North America, it is excellent for naturalizing or as a rough accent at the back of the border. Plants grow to 5 feet or more and usually need staking. Late summer through early fall, plants are covered with single or double, showy yellow sunflowers. This bloom period provides color in the garden at a time when most others have completed their flowering cycles.

Sunflowers combine well with purple coneflower, *Echinacea purpurea*, which has a similar coarse growth habit and cultural requirements. They also make fine cut flowers.

Recommended Species—*Helianthus maximiliani*, Maximilian sunflower, grows 4 to 6 feet high, but can reach even higher. Flowers bloom in fall.
H. x multiflorus 'Flore Pleno' grows to 6 feet high, has bright yellow, double flowers. Blooms July to September.
H. salicifolius grows 5 to 7 feet high but does not need staking. Plants are topped with yellow flowers from late summer through fall.

Planting & Care—Seeds sown in spring generally take a year before they develop flowers. Space plants 4 to 5 feet apart. Remove spent flowers to maintain appearance and to encourage additional blooms. Cut back plants in winter while plants are dormant for renewed growth in spring. Tolerant of tough conditions. Divide established plants each year in early spring.

Native to North America

Perennial; blooms in summer

Adapted to all regions of the arid West

Grows to 7 feet high or more; spreading 3 to 4 feet wide

Accepts most any well-draining soil

Moderate water use; tolerates dry conditions

Plant in full sun or partial shade

Pennisetum setaceum 'Cupreum' ('Rubrum'), purple fountain grass, grows to 3-1/2 feet high, with profuse, arching, purple-pink flower spikes. Yellow ground cover in foreground is *Lantana camara.*

Gypsophila paniculata 'Bristol Fairy' produces double white flowers. Plants form dense clumps to 3-1/2 feet high, with thick, slightly fuzzy leaves that are completely hidden by the billowing blooms.

Helianthus maximiliani, Maximilian sunflower, grows 4 to 6 feet high but can reach up to 10 feet high. Flowers bloom profusely during fall. Place in the back of the border, or include with tall-growing grasses.

Below left: *Hesperaloe parviflora,* red yucca, is a favorite flowering accent plant in desert gardens. Large clusters of pink to rose-red flowers rise on slim stems 4 to 5 feet above the plant.

Below: *Heliopsis helianthoides scabra* 'Summer Sun' has double flowers of rich yellow that cover plants from the middle of summer until frost. It performs well in dry soils but has more luxuriant growth with moderate moisture.

Heliopsis helianthoides scabra — Golden Sunflower

Native to North America

Perennial; blooms from summer until frost

Adapted to all regions of the arid West

Grows 2 to 5 feet high, spreading 3 to 4 feet wide

Provide with average garden soil

Low water use; better with moderate water during bloom period

Plant in full sun

Heliopsis, like *Helianthus,* belongs to the sunflower family, and all are native to North America. Each is well adapted to the dry climates of the West. They excel in wildflower gardens, in the background of perennial borders or in natural landscape designs. Their low to moderate water use, easy maintenance and long flowering season make them easy to grow and like.

Heliopsis is a stalwart plant, covered with sunflower-like blossoms from the middle of summer until frost. It performs well in dry soils but has more luxuriant growth with moderate moisture. The double or semi-double flowers are 3 to 4 inches wide, and good for cutting. Plants are generally maintenance-free and grow 2 to 5 feet high, with serrated leaves that are beautiful deep green. The shrubby growth is self-supporting.

Recommended Species—
H. helianthoides scabra 'Summer Sun' has double flowers of rich yellow from mid to late summer on 4-foot plants. 'Gold Greenheart' grows to 3-1/2 feet and bears double yellow flowers with green centers.

Planting & Care—Sow seeds in place in spring after last frost. Space 1-1/2 feet apart in average soil and full sun. *Heliopsis* is drought-tolerant, but moderate moisture when the weather is dry produces better plants and flowers. Too much water, however, particularly overhead irrigation, can blemish foliage and flowers. Water by flooding basins or use drip irrigation. After flowering has ceased in winter, cut plant stalks to just above ground level for renewed growth the following spring. Divide plants about every three years.

Hemerocallis — Daylily

Native to Central Europe, China, Japan

Perennial; blooms mid-spring to early fall, depending on variety

Adapted to all regions of the arid West

Grows 1 to 6 feet high, spreads 2 to 3 feet wide

Accepts most any well-draining soil

Low water use when not in bloom; regular when flowering

Plant in full sun to partial shade; afternoon shade in hot climates

Daylilies are one of the toughest and prolific garden perennials. They are also one of the easiest to grow, flowering year after year. Members of the lily family, plants form stemless clumps of narrow, strap-like leaves. Flowers appear in clusters at the ends of branches. A wide variety of colors are available, with yellow, pink and near-white shades predominating. Flowers last one day only; pick a single blossom and it will stay fresh, out of water, throughout the day. Some varieties are evergreen in mild-winter areas.

Recommended Varieties—
Hundreds of hybrids in many colors and color combinations are available. Here is a selection of the most popular: 'Stella D'Oro' has an unprecedentedly long flowering season, beginning in late spring and continuing, almost without hiatus, into early fall. Plants are 2 feet tall, the 2-1/2 inch flowers deep yellow. 'Hyperion' has fragrant yellow flowers produced from midseason to late on 3-1/2-foot plants. The 'Chicago' series offers a wide variety of colors in flowers with ruffled petal edges. 'Starburst Orange' with bright orange flowers, and 'Starburst Salmon' with ruffled petals and salmon blooms add their bright colors. 'Zaraheima' has shell pink and lavender flowers.

Planting & Care—Plant rhizomes about 1 inch below soil in fall or early spring. Plants are also available in containers in spring. Space 2 to 3 feet apart. Daylilies are tolerant of soil type, but do best in fertile, well-prepared soil. Water regularly during blooms when weather is dry.

Apply a light application of low-nitrogen fertilizer in late winter or early spring. Note that the thick roots are near the soil surface and can be damaged with cultivation. If the leaves turn brown it may indicate an infestation of spider mites. Daylilies are also attacked by aphids. Knock off light infestations with a stream of water and control large populations with a soap and water spray. See page 139.

Hesperaloe parviflora — Red Yucca

Red yucca is a favorite flowering accent plant in desert gardens, gaining in popularity in warm inland regions. Its flamboyant clusters of pink to rose-red flowers rise on slim stems 4 to 5 feet above the plant for a dramatic and colorful effect. The narrow, gray-green leaves look like those of a yucca and grow 3 to 4 feet long. This Texas native has an inherent hardiness, and works well in combination with other dry-climate plants. The flowering period is long, beginning in late March and extending into late summer. Plants in large containers create strong accents in courtyards or entry locations. Position at the bases of boulders for graceful, pleasing combinations.

Planting & Care—Plant any time from containers but best in fall or early spring. A location in full sun is important, as is good soil drainage. To keep plants looking neat, remove stems after seed pods have formed in late fall. As dead leaves develop at base of plant, cut or pull off to give leaf clusters a clean effect. Supply with low water after plants are established. Too much water will actually cause plant vigor and flowering to decrease. Separate clumps for transplanting after plants are three or four years old. Clumps pull apart easily; use a knife to sever roots. Allow separated clumps to dry in a shady location for several days to seal cuts before planting. Transplants are more easily established during warm periods of the year and should be planted at the same soil level as the original planting.

Native to Texas and northern Mexico

Yucca-like perennial; blooms in spring and summer

Adapted to SCC, SCI, SCLD, SCMHD, NCC, CACV, AZLD, AZMHD, NMMHD, SNV, TXEP, TXTPR

Grows to 6 feet or more, spreading 3 to 4 feet wide; flower stalks grow 4 to 5 feet high

Accepts most any well-draining soil

Low water use

Plant in full sun; accepts partial shade

Heuchera — Coralbells, Alumroot

Flowers of *Heuchera* open as tiny fairy bells of pink, white, coral and red on slender succulent stalks that unfurl from late spring through summer. Native to North America, *Heuchera* forms clumps of evergreen leaves 6 to 8 inches high. Flower stalks reach 1 to 1-1/2 feet high. They are lovely as cut flowers, adding airy clouds of color. Hummingbirds are attracted to the flowers.

Recommended Species—*H. maxima*, native to the Southern California Channel Islands of Anacapa, Santa Cruz and Santa Rosa, is well adapted to coastal gardens and shady areas in inland valleys. Plants grow in clumps from 1 to 2 feet across. Stem clusters 1-1/2 to 2-1/2 feet high bear small, greenish white to creamy white flowers. *H. micrantha* 'Palace Purple' is a recent introduction from England. It has a unique appearance with attention-grabbing reddish bronze foliage. Small, pinkish white flowers 15 to 18 inches high bloom during summer months. *H. sanguinea* is native to cool, shady areas in the mountains of southeastern Arizona and Mexico. Growth is mounding with heart-shaped, geranium-like leaves that support loose clusters of pink to bright red, bell-like flowers on tall, slender stems. 'Chatterbox' has deep pink flowers; 'Pluie de feu' blooms are cherry red; 'Rosamundi' has coral flowers. Plants reach to 1-1/2 feet high. In hot-summer climates, protect from the intense sun by growing in shade of trees or as an underplanting beneath tall-growing shrubs. 'Santa Ana Cardinal' is a vigorous hybrid developed at the Rancho Santa Ana Botanic Garden in Claremont, California, and is one of the best for warm regions. Flower colors range from white to red.

Planting & Care—Plant from seed in place or set out plants from containers in early spring. Soil should be slightly acid and kept moist. Remove flowers as they fade to promote longer bloom. Divide mature plants in late winter or early spring during cool weather.

Native to North America

Perennial; blooms late spring into summer

Adapted to SCC, SCI, SCLD, SCMHD, NCC, CACV, AZLD, AZMHD

Grows 1 to 2 feet high, spreading 2 to 3 feet wide

Provide slightly acid, fertile, loamy, well-draining soil

Moderate to low water use

Plant in shade in desert and inland valleys; sun to partial shade on coast

Above: *Hemerocallis,* daylily, produces flowers in clusters at the ends of branches. A wide variety of colors are available, mostly in shades of yellow, pink and near-white.

Above right: *Heuchera* 'Santa Ana Cardinal' is a vigorous hybrid developed at the Rancho Santa Ana Botanic Garden in Claremont, California. It is one of the best for warm, dry regions.

Lampranthus filicaulis, Redondo creeper, has fine-textured, creeping foliage just 3 to 4 inches high. Hot pink flowers cover the plant in the spring.

Far left: *Carpobrotus edulis* is a fast-growing, coarse-textured ice plant that works well as a slope cover. Flowers are light yellow to pink and bloom in spring.

Left: *Iberis sempervirens,* perennial candytuft, forms low mounds of glossy, dark green leaves that look beautiful in rock gardens, as edgings or spilling over raised beds.

A wide selection of ice plants and cacti cover this slope near San Diego, creating a spectacular springtime scene.

Iberis sempervirens — Perennial Candytuft

Native to southern Europe

Perennial; blooms early spring to summer and sporadically through the year in mild-climate regions

Adapted to all regions of the arid West, but best SCC, SCI, NCC, CACV

Grows 9 to 12 inches high, spreads 24 inches wide

Provide with well-draining, fertile soil

Moderate to high water use, depending on soil type and exposure

Plant in full sun along coast; provide afternoon shade inland

Perennial candytuft forms low mounds of glossy, dark green leaves that look beautiful in rock gardens, as edgings or spilling over raised beds. Use plants next to walkways or plant in front of shrubs. In the warmer reaches of its hardiness zones, this evergreen plant forms a dense, low clump that keeps its good looks year-round. In cold-winter areas it will look scraggly by winter's end. Shear back then, and new growth will come on quickly in spring. Densely packed, pure white flowers also appear in early spring.

Recommended Varieties— 'Snowflake' grows less than 1 foot high and spreads to about 2 feet wide. 'Autumn Snow' blooms both spring and fall, growing 9 to 12 inches high. 'Purity' has a long spring-blooming season with large flowers on neat mounds.

Well adapted to rock gardens or edging along borders. Attracts bees.

Planting & Care—Sow seeds of the species in spring or fall for flowers the following year. In hot-summer regions, plant from containers in fall to establish before high temperatures come on. In cool coastal regions, plant in spring. Grow in fertile, well-draining soil for best results. Candytuft will tolerate some shade. Shear back after first bloom to encourage a second flush of flowers. Propagate by taking 2-inch stem cuttings from nonflowering shoots during summer, or divide in spring after blooming.

Ice Plants

Native and introduced perennial ground covers

Bloom spring through summer, depending on species

Well adapted to coastal climates; several kinds adapted to inland valleys and desert regions

Mature sizes are variable; see descriptions

Tolerate most any soil type

Low to moderate water use

Plant in full sun

Sorting out the many flowering plants labeled as ice plants can be somewhat confusing. At one time they were classified as *Mesembryanthemum* but are now subdivided into the classifications described here. When botanical names are used, the differences between plants become more apparent and make it easier to select the correct plant for your use and climate.

Use ice plant for erosion control on steep slopes, in rock gardens, for bright flower colors and as an underplanting for taller plants. The high moisture content of the leaves makes ice plants suitable as fire-retardant plants. The following perennial ice plants are described in some detail, since they are water-efficient plants and valuable landscape additions from coast to desert.

Aptenia cordifolia 'Red Apple' is a fast-growing low, ground-hugging plant. It spreads to 2 feet wide with trailing, bright green, succulent leaves. This is a warm-weather performer. During late spring and summer, red, 1-inch flowers appear on top of the plant, making it a favorite filler for small areas, in rock gardens, on slopes and in containers. In hottest desert regions, locate in afternoon or filtered shade. Avoid placing under trees where leaves may fall onto plants—they become difficult to rake out. Also avoid western exposures where temperatures can reach 110F or more. Provide moderate water in all situations; avoid watering in the middle of the day. Often grown as an annual in cold-climate areas. Easily grown from cuttings; also available in flats or pots at nurseries.

Carpobrotus chilensis is native to slopes of coastal sand dunes. It has 3-sided, fleshy, succulent leaves. Mature plant size is 12 to 18 inches high and wide-spreading. Rose-purple flowers 2 inches across bloom in summer. The coarse texture of the foliage makes this a plant best relegated to distant viewing. It's a good binder for gentle slopes, but too steep a grade may cause plantings to slip due to their own weight with heavy rains or irrigation. Propagates readily from 6- to 12-inch cuttings. Spreads quickly; space cuttings 12 to 18 inches apart.

Cephalophyllum speciosum 'Red Spike', red ice plant, develops a clumping form with spiky, bronze-red leaves to 5 inches high and to 18 inches wide. The 2-inch, cerise-red flowers bloom abundantly during the winter months. Plants normally tolerate drought, except in low-elevation deserts, where some moisture is required to prevent damping-off fungus disease. 'Red Spike' is actually better adapted to 2,000- to 3,000-foot elevations. Hardy to 20F.

Delosperma 'Alba', white trailing ice plant, has a low, spreading growth habit topped off with small white flowers that bloom in summer. It is ideal for coastal plantings in rock gardens and borders in full sun, yet when given low water and afternoon shade, plants generally thrive in inland valleys and low-elevation desert regions.

Drosanthemum floribundum, rosea ice plant, has leaves covered in spots that produce an effect of glistening ice crystals. Plants grow to just 6 inches high and spread wide and fast. The pale pink, 3/4-inch flowers produce a carpet of bloom in late spring and early summer. Locate plants in full sun in rockscapes or planters, where the graceful, soft branches can drape and trail. Along the coast, plants are low-water users. In other regions moderate irrigation is required to keep plants looking healthy. This is a fine erosion control plant that will grow on steep slopes. It also has fire-retardant qualities. As an added bonus, rabbits don't like it, unlike other ice plants.

Lampranthus aurantiacus is almost subshrub in size at 15 inches high and 18 inches wide. Three-sided succulent leaves to 1 inch long set the stage for bright orange flowers that bloom from February into May. Two other superior selections are 'Glaucus' with bright yellow flowers and 'Sunman' with golden yellow flowers.

L. filicaulis, Redondo creeper, has fine-textured, creeping foliage just 3 to 4 inches high. Small pink flowers bloom in the spring. This is an ideal ground cover for small areas. Low water use along the coast; moderate other areas.

L. spectabilis, trailing ice plant, has gray-green foliage spreading 1-1/2 to 3 feet wide. Flowers of this ice plant are among the most striking, and plants are blanketed in flowers ranging from rose-pink, pink, red and purple during the spring months. After flowering, cut back fruit capsules to help plants renew their foliage.

All *Lampranthus* species are best adapted to the coast but will grow in inland valleys. Plant in full sun and provide with low water.

Malephora crocea has smooth, gray-green, trailing leaves to 6 inches high. Orange or salmon flowers bloom heaviest during the spring months and produce scattered blooms the balance of the year. Plants are ideal for large sunny areas and for erosion control, and they will tolerate heat and wind. This is also the most cold-hardy ice plant, tolerating temperatures to 10F, making it useful in colder inland regions. Low water use.

Planting & Care—Ice plants grow readily from cuttings, as well as from flats or containers available at nurseries. Rooted cuttings can be planted almost any time, but spring, summer or early fall are best. Grows well in almost any soil. Mature ice plants are known for their ability to thrive on little water. After new plants are established, cut back on watering to low to moderate, especially during summer months, to reduce chances of fungus disease.

Climate Adaptation Key

SCC:	**S. Calif. Coastal**
SCI:	**S. Calif. Inland**
SCLD:	**S. Calif. Low Deserts**
SCMHD:	**S. Calif. Medium/ High Deserts**
NCC:	**N. Calif. Coastal**
CACV:	**Calif. Central Valley**
AZLD:	**Arizona Low Desert**
AZMHD:	**Arizona Medium/High Deserts**
NMMHD:	**New Mexico Medium/High Deserts**
SNV:	**Southern Nevada**
TXHP:	**Texas High Plains**
TXEP:	**Texas Edwards Plateau**
TXRRP:	**Texas Red Rolling Plains**
TXTPR:	**Texas Trans-Pecos Region**
CWR:	**Cold-Winter Regions**

Iris — *Iris*

Native to many regions; most in Northern Temperate Zone

Perennial; blooms in spring and early summer

Adapted to all regions of the arid West; *I. douglasiana* to SCC, SCI, NCC, CACV

Grows 1 to 3 feet high, spreading in clumps 1 to 2 feet wide (varies with species)

Provide with well-draining soil; some species prefer slightly acid soil

Moderate water use before and during bloom; low other times

Plant in full sun; in hot-summer regions plant in eastern exposure or beneath trees providing filtered shade

In mythology, Iris is the goddess of the rainbow. The name is well applied, because all colors of the spectrum except true red are represented in this genus. Irises can be organized into several groups: bearded *Iris germanica*, Japanese *I. ensata* (formerly *I. kaempferi*), Siberian, Spuria and many selections of species irises.

The tall, bearded irises are some of the best-known and most-loved garden plants. Long slender leaves shaped like fans rise stemless from knobby rhizomes, followed by branching flowering stalks, each bearing several flowers. Flowers might be all one color—*self.* They also come in combinations, with the three upright petals or *standards* being a different shade or color from the three spreading or down-curving petals, called *falls.* Markings, frills or ruffles sometimes adorn the petal edges. Flowers come mid- to late spring. Some bearded irises rebloom in fall.

Japanese irises are the aristocrats of this group, with large, elegant, flat flowers, sometimes 6 to 9 inches across, that seem to float above the narrow green leaves. Japanese irises are not as hardy as tall, bearded kinds and require moist, slightly acid soil. Colors are more limited than the bearded types—shades of blue, purple, yellow and white.

Siberian irises have airy, delicate flowers with horizontal falls and upright standards held above narrow grassy leaves. They also thrive in moist and fertile soil. Both Japanese and Siberians bloom later—in early summer.

Recommended Varieties—Tall Bearded: 'Sapphire Hills' is a good blue variety. Any of the Dykes Medal Winners are also good choices. Some of these include 'Victoria Falls', 'Beverly Sills', 'Song of Norway', 'Vanity', 'Pacific Panorama', 'Pink Taffeta' and 'Debby Rairdon'.

Japanese: Look for any in the Higo strain as excellent choices, with large flowers in shades of blue, purple, lavender and white.

Siberian: 'White Swirl', 'Blue Burgee', 'Caesar' (violet-purple) and 'Caesar's Brother' (blue-black), 'Flight of Butterflies' (blue standards, white falls with purple veining) and 'Orville Fay' (deep blue).

Species: *I. douglasiana,* Douglas iris, is well adapted to the West and is native along the California coast from Santa Barbara County north to southern Oregon. Plants also grow in inland valley regions. Evergreen plants form clumps to 2 feet wide. Creeping rhizomes are much smaller than tall bearded iris. Dark green leaves are 1/2 to 3/4 inch wide and 1 to 2 feet long. Flowers bloom in spring and come in shades of deep purple to blue, lavender, white and yellow. Accepts most any soil; prefers slightly acid organic soil.

Planting & Care—Plant from rhizomes in late summer to early fall. With existing plantings, make divisions of firm, healthy rhizomes with three fans of leaves. Trim roots and leaves to 6 inches long. Plant tall bearded rhizomes on a mound in a shallow hole so rhizome top is just at ground level. Cover roots and bottom with soil but do not bury rhizome top: try to plant one-half of rhizome above soil, one-half beneath. Set Japanese and Siberian types 2 inches below ground level. Space rhizomes 15 to 18 inches apart unless an immediate mass effect is wanted, in which case set 10 inches apart. Tall bearded irises do best in full sun except in hot desert and inland regions, where they'll do better with afternoon shade. Provide regular moisture before and during bloom; reduce to low water after bloom and until growth resumes again in spring.

Keep planting area free of weeds. Because rhizomes and roots are near the soil surface, pull weeds by hand. To discourage borers, keep planting area clean. Cut leaves back to six inches in fall and pull off old leaves in late winter. If borer damage is evident, discard rhizome, or cut away damaged portion and replant. Soft rot causes clumps to die out in the center; rhizomes become mushy and foul-smelling. Dig and discard affected plants. To prevent, avoid excessive water and fertilizer.

Justicia spicigera, Mexican honeysuckle, has bright orange, tubular flowers that bloom in spring. Plants grow to 3 feet high and as wide. Growth is more luxuriant in filtered shade such as beneath canopy trees.

Iris douglasiana, Douglas iris, is native along the California coast from Santa Barbara County north to southern Oregon. Plants are also adapted to grow in warm, inland regions.

Justicia — Chuperosa

Native to the U.S. Southwest and Mexico

Perennial or subshrub; blooms late winter to spring

Adapted to SCLD, NCC, AZLD

Grows 2 to 6 feet high and 4 to 5 feet wide

Provide with well-draining soil

High to low water use

Plant in full sun; *J. spicigera* is more lush with some shade

Once one has observed the brilliant, red to orange, funnel-shaped flowers of chuperosa in its native Southwest, there is a strong impulse to find a place in the garden for one or more of these colorful plants. They are especially adept in helping create a natural wildlife habitat. The tight, interwoven, pale-green leaves and low-growing branches provide thick undergrowth shelter for birds and small animals, and hummingbirds are especially fond of the prolific flowers. With the exception of *Justicia brandegeana*, these species are well adapted to warm inland valleys and low- and middle-elevation desert regions of the West.

Justicia brandegeana (Belaperone guttata), shrimp plant, grows 2 to 3 feet high in a rounded, shrub-like form. Leaves are soft green. Spike-like, pinkish, copper flowers droop from ends of branches almost year-round. Moderate to high water use; best located among other high-water-use plants, such as in a mini-oasis. Well adapted to coastal and temperate inland regions. Provide afternoon shade in warmest areas. Does better in soil improved with organic matter. Plants are cold-tender.

J. californica, chuperosa, puts on a show of bright red flowers during late winter, summer and again in fall when planted in a sunny location. Plants grow with a free-form habit 4 to 6 feet high with an equal spread. Chuperosa is indigenous to the edges of the Colorado Desert. Cold tender. Low water use.

J. spicigera, Mexican honeysuckle, has bright orange, tubular flowers that bloom in spring. Plant form is well-rounded to 3 feet high and as wide, with pale green leaves. Growth is more luxuriant in filtered shade. Moderate to low water use.

Planting & Care—Plant from containers in fall or spring. Summer planting is possible if you pay careful attention to watering. To renew growth as plants age and become woody, thin out interior and reduce perimeter growth by about one-third, retaining natural form.

Kniphofia uvaria — Red-Hot Poker, Poker Plant

Native to South Africa

Perennial; blooms through summer

Adapted to SCC, SCI, SCLD, NCC, CACV

Grows 2 to 4 feet high, spreads 1-1/2 to 2 feet wide

Provide with fertile, well-draining, sandy loam

Moderate water use

Plant in full sun

Kniphofia uvaria is a real attention-grabber. Tall stalks topped with elongated clusters of densely packed, tubular flowers in powerful colors have earned this summer bloomer its descriptive common name of red-hot poker. In July, flowers open in vibrant orange, red, yellow and cream, some in dynamic color combinations. Leaves are bright green and grassy and persist through the winter.

Use *Kniphofia* as a focal point in the garden. Effective companions include *Euryops, Helianthus* and *Rudbeckia*. Be aware, however, that its flower colors tend to clash with magenta and pink. It's also effective in clumps as specimens and planted with shrubs. For an effective combination try planting behind the gray-leaved, yellow-flowering dusty miller. It's also long lasting as a cut flower. Plants grow to 4 feet high, but the thick stems don't need staking. A good plant for seaside gardens, and one that is highly attractive to hummingbirds.

Recommended Varieties—'Shenandoah' and 'Springtime' have yellow and orange flowers, and reach 3-1/2 feet and more. 'Pfitzeri' is smaller, just over 2 feet high, with orange blooms in July and August.

Planting & Care—Sow seeds in spring for flowers the third year. Or set crowns 2 to 3 inches deep and 1-1/2 to 3 feet apart in rich, well-worked soil. Supply moderate water while plants are blooming, then taper to low water during winter. In cold-winter areas plant in a sheltered spot. To protect against winter cold, tie foliage up over crowns and cover with mulch. *Kniphofia* is a heavy feeder. Enrich soil before planting, then feed every spring with a fertilizer high in phosphorus. Remove old flower stalks after bloom season has passed for neat appearance. Make root divisions of existing plantings in early spring.

Lantana montevidensis — Trailing Lantana

Originally from South America, trailing lavender lantana has become an increasingly valued addition to water-conserving landscapes in the arid West. Attributes include vigorous growth and 1-inch, lavender-shaded flowers that literally cover the plants continuously throughout much of the year except for periods of frost. Even lightly frosted foliage turns a colorful purple hue.

Plant on slopes for erosion control, as a ground cover, in natural gardens tucked in among boulders, as a foreground to perennial beds or allow to drape over a wall or edge of a container. The undulating, mounding growth habit complements taller plants such as *Encelia, Hemerocallis, Euryops* and *Salvia* species. Trailing lavender lantana at the base of *Salvia greggii,* red salvia, makes a particularly attractive combination.

Recommended Varieties—Two trailing forms with similar growth habits are 'Spreading Sunset' and 'Spreading Sunshine', both of which have yellow flowers. Plants are more prostrate than the species, and combine well with tall background shrubs.

Planting & Care—Plant from flats or containers almost any time, but do avoid planting during winter months. Space plants at least 2 to 3 feet apart for extensive spreading growth, which can reach 3 to 6 feet. Provide deep, spaced irrigations. Gradually taper off irrigation in fall to harden off plants for cold temperatures. As the season begins to warm in early spring, cut back older plants to 6 to 12 inches into hard wood to renew growth and encourage future flowering. Prune to control invasive growth around other perennials or small shrubs.

Native to South America

Perennial ground cover; blooms all year in frost-free areas; spring through fall in other regions

Adapted to SCC, SCI, SCLD, NCC, CACV, AZLD

Grows 2 to 3 feet high, spreads 3 to 6 feet wide

Accepts most soils, good drainage important for deep rooting

Low to moderate water use

Plant in full sun only; heat-tolerant

Lavandula species — Lavender

The lavender or blue flowers and aromatic, gray-green leaves of lavender provide interest year-round, giving stability to the garden. The fragrant flowers are prized for indoor arrangements and can be used fresh or dried. When combined with a wide range of companion plants such as *Rosmarinus, Santolina, Salvia, Verbena* and *Leucophyllum* species, you can create plant groupings with similar low moisture needs, as well as blend leaf textures and color.

Lavandula angustifolia, English lavender, is easiest to grow, and grows to a compact 3 to 4 feet high and as wide. The flowering period runs from July through August, with 1-1/2- to 2-foot spikes that produce a rich fragrance. Dwarf forms are available, such as 'Munstead', which grows to 1-1/2 feet high and as wide. It is excellent as a neat, controlled foreground plant in the perennial border or in rock gardens. Flowers are deep blue-lavender and bloom as early as late May to June, lasting until July. Leaf color is darker gray-green and growth is more compact than *L. dentata.* Hardy to 0F.

L. dentata, French lavender, is distinguished by its narrow, 1-1/2-inch, gray-green, square-toothed leaves. In addition, it has short, lavender-purple flower spikes and petal-like bracts. Flowers bloom over a long period, especially in mild-winter gardens. Plants grow to 3 feet high. Hardy to 15F.

Planting & Care—Plant from containers in fall or early spring in full sun. Accepts just about any well-draining soil. Provide with moderate water after plants are established. Cut back flowers after bloom period has passed. Rejuvenate old plants that have become ragged by cutting branches back, but retain the natural form.

Native to the Mediterranean

Perennial; blooms in summer and fall

Adapted to all regions of the arid West, except coldest CWR

Grows 1-1/2 to 4 feet high, spreads 3 to 4 feet wide

Provide with well-draining soil

Moderate water use

Plant in full sun

Right: *Kniphofia* is an attention-grabber in the garden. Tall stalks topped with elongated clusters of densely packed, tubular flowers in powerful colors have earned this summer bloomer the descriptive name of red-hot poker.

Far right: *Liatris* is a wonderful, low-maintenance perennial that provides exclamation points of rose-pink, magenta or white. Spikelike flowers bloom from late summer into late fall.

A colorful garden is created with low-growing *Hemerocallis,* daylily, and upright *Kniphofia,* red-hot poker, with *Bauhinia variegata,* orchid tree, in background.

Lavandula, lavender, makes an interesting and colorful slope cover in combination with *Bougainvillea.*

Far left: *Lilium* species, lily, is among the most beautiful and elegant garden plants. By combining different types, you can enjoy blooms from summer to fall.

Left: Although lilies make lovely cut flowers, cutting them robs the plant of its ability to produce food for growth. Grow some plants for cutting only, and plan to replace them periodically. Shown is Asian lily.

Leonotis leonurus — Lionstail

Native to South Africa

—

Perennial; blooms summer and into fall

—

Adapted to all regions of the arid West, except coldest areas

—

Grows 3 to 6 feet high, spreads to 3 to 4 feet wide

—

Provide with well-draining soil

—

Low to moderate water use

—

Plant in full sun

—

The deep orange color of lionstail flowers is unique among old-fashioned, low-water-use perennials. This old-time favorite has a shrubby growth habit and strong branching structure to 3 to 6 feet high. Opposite serrated leaves 2 to 5 inches long on hairy stems support the tubular flowers that appear in dense whorls at the bases of leaves.

Flowering begins in summer and lasts into fall. More flowers are produced when flowering stems are selectively pruned as flowers come and go in their bloom cycles.

Position plants in clusters at the rear of flower borders or along a fence or wall. The orange flower color of lionstail is especially attractive combined with yellow-flowering Mexican sunflower or black-eyed Susan, which have similar moisture needs. In addition, the lush growth of lionstail helps mask the bareness of the tall, naked sunflower stalks.

Planting & Care—Plant from containers in the fall, if possible, but spring and summer plantings also fare well. Before planting, pre-moisten soil and water rootball in container thoroughly to get plants off to a good start. Tolerant of most soil types and able to sustain growth with minimum water after establishment. When spacing plants, allow for wide-spreading growth—to 3 to 4 feet. In cooler, high-elevation regions, cut plants back severely in late fall. In more temperate areas, such as along the coast and in sheltered locations inland, thin and prune in late winter to encourage new growth. In regions with strong winds, provide protection to prevent the soft flowering branches from being damaged.

Liatris — Blazing Star, Gayfeather

Native to North America

—

Perennial; blooms in summer

—

Adapted to all regions of the arid West

—

Grows 1-1/2 to 5 feet high, spreads 2 feet wide

—

Provide with most any well-draining soil

—

Moderate water use before and during flowering, low use other times

—

Plant in full sun most areas; provide afternoon shade in hot-summer regions

—

Liatris species are wonderful, low-maintenance perennials that provide exclamation points of rose-pink, magenta or white. The 6- to 9-inch spikes bloom from late summer into late fall. Color during this period is most appreciated, since this is the time most flowering perennials begin to go into dormancy. The stiff stems have thin grassy leaves below the flower clusters, which open from the top downward. The flower stems grow 2 to 5 feet high and are long lasting as cut flowers in arrangements. A mature plant may produce a dozen or more flowering wands.

Include in the perennial border or in a wildflower or natural garden. 'Kobold' can be used in the rock garden. Once established, this North American native tolerates dry conditions. *Liatris* also attracts bees and butterflies.

Recommended Species—*L. scariosa alba* 'White Spire' grows to 3 feet, has flowers of pure white.
L. spicata 'Kobold' is a dwarf, growing only to about 1-1/2 feet, with flowers of deep rose-pink.

Planting & Care—Divide and plant in spring or fall, or sow seeds indoors in pots in early fall for spring planting. Set plants 12 to 18 inches apart; 12 inches apart if planting in groups or masses. Provide with well-draining soil in full sun; filtered shade in hot climates is desirable. Moderate moisture before and during flowering produces better and longer-lasting blooms. Plants go dormant in the winter, yet recover well by spring. Gayfeather is long lasting and becomes a reliable part of the garden for many years.

Lilium — Lily

Undisputedly, lilies are among the most beautiful and elegant garden plants. There are many different types—Asian, trumpet, American, Aurelian, Turk's cap (martagon), Oriental, *candidum* and regal. Flowers are upfacing, outfacing or downfacing, reflexed, open and trumpet, spotted or unspotted, but never *plain*. And many of them are fragrant. By combining different types, you can enjoy blooms from June to September in a wide range of colors. Although lilies make lovely cut flowers, cutting them robs the plant of its food-producing equipment. Grow some plants for cutting only in a separate location, and plan to replace plants periodically.

June & July Blooming:
'Enchantment' bears 6-inch, deep red flowers on 3-foot stems. 'Regale Strain' has large trumpet flowers, white inside, dark outside, and fragrant. Grows to 4 feet high. 'Sentinel Strain' has white flowers on 5-foot stems.

July & August Blooming:
'Connecticut Yankee' grows 4 to 6 feet high with orange, 6-inch, recurved, down-facing flowers. 'Moonlight Strain' has large, fragrant, green-yellow flowers on 4- to 6-foot stems.

August & September Blooming:
'Rubrum' is an old-fashioned favorite with recurved, down-facing, spotted white and deep pink flowers. Grows to 5 feet high. 'Stargazer' has fragrant, deep, rose-red flowers with white edges on 3-foot stems.

Planting & Care—When buying lilies, it's important to obtain virus-free bulbs. Buy the largest bulbs you can afford. Plant as soon as bulbs become available in garden centers in early fall. Plant in deep, loose, fertile loam that has good drainage and high organic content. Set small bulbs 6 to 8 inches apart; larger ones 10 to 12 inches. Madonna, Turk's cap (martagon), and American bulbs should be set 2 inches below soil. Other types develop roots both at the base and along the stem, so set them deeper, with several inches of soil over the bulb crown. Press bulbs firmly into soil to eliminate air pockets.

Native to Northern Hemisphere, China, Japan, Europe

Perennial bulb; blooms in summer

Adapted to all regions of the arid West (avoid extreme wind)

Grows 3 to 6 feet high, spreads 1 to 1-1/2 feet wide

Provide with deep, fertile, well-draining, slightly acid soil

Moderate water use

Plant in full sun

Limonium perezii — Sea Lavender

Sea lavender is a striking plant, grown for its large leaves and profuse flowers that bloom in clusters. Each summer, the rich-hued purple flowers grow to 2 to 3 feet high, and are excellent tucked among shrubs or to create lushness in the foreground of the border. It is well adapted to the Southern California coast, and has naturalized among the rocky cliffs in selected regions. Flowers are also used fresh or are long lasting when dried in bouquets.

Limonium latifolium produces smooth, large, 10-inch leaves. Plants grow to 2-1/2 feet high and as wide. They provide a dramatic setting for the white and bluish, airy clusters of flowers that literally cover the plant during the summer months. Use in rock gardens, perennial borders and in the foreground to taller shrubs as low-growing foreground clusters. Grow in sun or partial shade in gardens from coastal climate to inland valleys.

Planting & Care—Start with nursery-grown plants or take root divisions and set out in fall or early spring. Plants accept extremes of coastal winds and ocean influence. Cold hardy to 25F. Provide with most any well-draining, light, sandy soil. Water use is low along the coast, moderate in interior valleys and desert regions. In coastal and inland valleys, a sunny location is ideal. Locate where plants will receive some afternoon shade in regions with intense sun.

Native to the Canary Islands

Perennial; blooms over long season from late spring into fall

Adapted to SCC, SCI, SCLD, NCC, CACV

Grows 2 to 3 feet high, spreads to 3 feet wide

Provide with most any well-draining soil

Low to moderate water use

Plant in full sun most areas; provide afternoon shade in hot-summer regions

Right: *Limonium perezii,* sea lavender, is grown for its large leaves and profuse flowers that bloom in clusters late spring to summer. It is well adapted to the Southern California coastal region.

Below left: *Linum perenne lewisii* is a California native that grows 1 to 2 feet high. The wiry stems are leafless, showing off the profuse, light blue flower clusters.

Below right: *Lobelia cardinalis,* cardinal flower, is native to higher elevations of the U.S. Southwest. It is known for the brilliant scarlet flowers that bloom on top of its 4-foot-high stems.

Linum — Flax

Three species of flax are well adapted to arid gardens in the West. All are low-water users and accept full sun. Their upright growth habits make them choice plants for the perennial border. Place them in the middle of the border, behind the lower-growing selections.

Each of the following species produces five-petaled, shallow-cupped flowers: every flower lasts only one day. Plants bloom for a long period—from late spring through summer and into fall.

Linum flavum, golden flax, is compact, 12 to 15 inches high. Growth is erect and can become woody at base of plants. Golden yellow flowers to 1 inch wide bloom in clusters through April into June.
L. grandiflorum 'Rubrum' is an annual with bright, crimson-red flowers. When sown in among perennials, it creates a sparkling accent. Sow seed in full sun. Flowers profusely from March until April.
L. narbonense has flowering stems to 2 feet high on lush, 18- to 24-inch high plants. Glistening azure-blue flowers highlighted with a white eye are 2 inches in diameter, blooming during summer. Plants tolerate heat as well as dry sterile soils.
L. perenne, perennial blue flax, grows 1 to 2 feet high. The wiry stems are leafless, allowing the light blue flower clusters to dominate. Flowers are most prolific from May through September. The California native *L. p. lewisii* is similar in appearance but has a more robust growth habit. It does best along the coast.

Planting & Care—All species are easy to grow from seed. Plant during early fall in warm regions in well-draining soil; wait until spring to plant in cooler regions. Supply moderate moisture while seeds or cuttings are beginning to establish, then reduce to low water at maturity. Reseeds readily to maintain plantings. To propagate, take basal cuttings in spring; plants are difficult to divide.

Native to southern Europe and the Mediterranean region

Perennial; blooms in summer and fall

Adapted to all regions of the arid West

Grows 1 to 2 feet high, spreading 1 to 2 feet wide

Provide with deep, well-draining soil

Low water use

Plant in full sun

Lobelia — Cardinal Flower

The *Lobelia* species described here once enjoyed great popularity. They are easy-care plants that add bright color to the garden as long as their need for constantly moist soil is met. Plants grow with branching, stiffly upright stems covered with lance-shaped, toothed leaves 3 to 5 inches long. Stems are topped with wands of brilliant red or blue flowers that are highly attractive to hummingbirds.

Lobelia species look best planted in groups with wildflowers or in low, moist, protected locations beneath trees or along watersides. They are usually short-lived but given the right conditions will self-sow. They accept full sun if regular and abundant moisture is available.

Recommended Species—*L. cardinalis,* cardinal flower, is native to higher elevations of the U.S. Southwest. Brilliant scarlet flowers on 3- to 4-foot stems bloom from late July to September. Plants are erect with serrated, dark, reddish bronze leaves.
L. laxiflora is a native of New Mexico. It grows to 2 feet high and 1-1/2 feet wide. Stems are covered with narrow leaves, supporting the tubular, orange-red flowers that bloom from June to August. Plants are hardy and will accept low water.
L. siphilitica, great blue lobelia or blue cardinal flower, is somewhat shorter, growing 2 to 3 feet high, with deep blue flowers that are more densely packed than *L. cardinalis.* Great blue lobelia is also easier to grow than its red cousin, and it tolerates more heat. Native to eastern U.S.

Planting & Care—If plants don't self-sow, sow fresh seed in fall or spring after *stratifying* them. (See page 140.) Plant in moderately rich soil in bright shade. *Lobelia* seem to do best when left to fend for themselves. Apply a thick layer of organic mulch around plants to protect them through winter and in summer to help keep soil moist. Existing plants can be divided in spring. *L. cardinalis* can be propagated by stem layering.

Native to various regions of the U.S.

Perennial; blooms in summer

Adapted to all regions of the arid West

Grows 2 to 4 feet high, spreads 1-1/2 feet wide

Provide with well-draining, moisture-retentive soil

High water use in fast-draining soils; moderate in other soils

Plant in partial shade; accepts sun with more water

Lupinus — Lupine

Native to U.S. Southwest

Perennial; blooms early spring to early summer

Adapted to all regions of the arid West

Grows 1 to 4 feet high, spreads 1-1/2 to 2 feet wide

Provide with deep, well-draining soil

Moderate water use

Plant in full sun to partial shade

The magnificent flower spikes of lupine can reach up to 2 feet long. Planted in masses, they look like so many multi-hued candelabra. The Russell hybrids of *L. polyphyllus* are considered the most desirable by many gardeners, but are difficult to grow in warm dry climates. Russell hybrids reach 3 to 4 feet high, and offer the widest variety of colors as well as the largest, fattest flower spikes. However, Russell hybrids do not tolerate summer heat and will thrive only in the cool and humid climates, such as areas of the Pacific Northwest.

Recommended Species—Lupines for the arid West include:
In California's Mojave Desert, *L. odoratus* blooms in April and May, the same period as California poppy, *Eschscholzia californica.*
In Texas, *L. plattensis,* with its bluish purple flowers, prefers sand-dune conditions. Sow seed in the fall months for flowers the following spring.
L. sparsiflorus, arroyo lupine, puts on a show with violet-purple flowers during January through May.
L. texensis, Texas bluebonnet, is an annual, but it deserves special mention. To truly experience the Texas landscape, one should visit when the bluebonnets are in bloom—a 2- to 4-week period during March and April. Plants grow to 1 foot high and as wide, topped by plumes of dark blue flowers.

Planting & Care—Lupines need plenty of moisture and do not transplant well. Start from seed, sowing outdoors in place where plants are to grow. Sow in fall or early spring as weather begins to warm, moistening soil before sowing. Place in groups, spacing plants 1-1/2 feet apart, in sun or partial shade. Soil should be rich, well draining and deeply worked. Remove spent flowers regularly, unless growing seed for sowing. After first flush of bloom, cut plants back to the ground to promote a second flowering. Mulch in winter. Propagate by taking stem cuttings with small piece of root or crown attached.

Lychnis — Maltese Cross, Catchfly

Native to northern Russia, central Asia

Perennial; blooms in early summer

Adapted to SCI, SCLD, SCMHD, NCC, CACV, AZLD, AZMHD, NMMHD, SNV, TXTPR, CWR

Grows 1-1/2 to 3 feet high, spreads 2 to 3 feet wide

Provide with light, well-draining soil

Low water use

Plant in full sun; partial shade in hot-summer regions

Lychnis is an easy-to-grow plant for the perennial border, and as long-lasting cut flowers. Blossoms of the perennial species in this genus vary from the round, deep, rosy pink blossoms of *L. coronaria* to the red-orange, five-petaled, pinwheel-shaped flowers of *L. chalcedonica.* Leaves also are variable.

Recommended Species—*L. x arkwrightii* is an attractive hybrid between *L. chalcedonica* and *L. x haageana.* It has brilliant orange flowers and deep green leaves that are purple on the undersides. Plants grow to 1-1/2 feet high.
L. chalcedonica, Maltese cross, bears scarlet flowers in dense heads from early to midsummer. Individual florets are 1 inch wide. Plants grow 2-1/2 to 3 feet high. Leaves and stems are slightly hairy.
L. coronaria has vivid, rose-purple flowers and oblong leaves covered with woolly white hairs. Plants grow 1-1/2 to 2 feet high.
L. viscaria, German catchfly, is the hardiest and longest-lived of the genus, with reddish purple flowers in clusters on 1- to 1-1/2 foot stems in early summer. There are several named varieties in white and shades of red-pink.

Planting & Care—Single-flowered and nonhybrid types can be grown from seed sown in spring, and take two years to flower. Plant in organic but well-draining soil in full sun, or in partial shade in hot areas. Keep soil fairly dry, and stake taller varieties as necessary. Propagate by division in either spring or fall. In fact, dividing every three or four years keeps plants vigorous.

Lythrum — Purple Loosestrife

Lythrum is one of the easiest perennials to grow and does not need (or want) much care after it is established. Although most books and catalogs advise a constantly moist soil, plants do well in ordinary soil with moderate water. Gardeners in some parts of the upper Midwest complain that *Lythrum* is taking over wetlands by self-sowing. On drier ground and in heat- and drought-prone regions of the arid West, it stays put and is not as prone to be self-sowing. In addition, the named cultivars do not tend to be as invasive as *L. salicaria*. Plants bloom reliably and over a long period late in the season, when most other perennials have completed their bloom cycles.

Lythrum forms a bushy plant 2 to 4 feet high, with narrow, lance-shaped, dark green leaves and purple or rosy pink flowers on spikes. Use as single specimen in the background of the perennial border, or plant in masses among shrubs or in meadow or wildflower gardens.

Recommended Species—*L. salicaria* reseeds freely in moist environments, but this is not a problem in low-rainfall areas. Plants grow 2 to 4 feet high, with red-purple flowers on erect stems.

Sterile varieties include 'Firecandle', rose-red, growing to 3 feet, flowering mid to late summer; 'Morden's Gleam', red-pink, 3- to 4-foot plants; 'Robert', growing to only 2 feet, with rose-red flowers; and 'The Beacon', with flowers nearly red on 2-1/2 foot plants. *L. virgatum* is a smaller plant with darker green leaves. 'Dropmore Purple' has rich violet-purple flower spikes; 'Morden's Pink' (sterile) has deep pink blossoms produced midsummer to fall.

Planting & Care—Sow seed in fall or spring in ordinary soil that is not overly rich. Space plants 1-1/2 to 2 feet apart. After the flowering season has passed, cut back to basal growth to renew plants and for more flowers the following spring. Divide existing plants regularly, about every three years, to maintain vigor of planting bed.

Native to Europe and Asia

Perennial; blooms late summer and into fall

Adapted to all regions of the arid West

Grows 2 to 4 feet high, spreads 1 to 3 feet wide

Provide with ordinary garden soil

Moderate water use

Plant in full sun to partial shade

Melampodium leucanthum — Blackfoot Daisy

Blackfoot daisy is a great little flowering plant and has become a valued garden perennial in the arid West. It is easy to grow and has an extra-long flowering season that extends from March to November. The 1-inch, white, daisy-like flowers with yellow centers cover plants that grow 6 to 12 inches high and as wide. Leaves are an attractive, soft gray-green. In sunny garden locations, flowers release a pleasing scent reminiscent of wild honey.

Blackfoot daisy was introduced to home landscapes in Arizona and other Southwest desert regions several years ago. Plants now grace borders, perennial beds and boulder groupings and are used as a small-area ground cover. Companion plants in naturalized drainage swale gardens include *Penstemon* species and *Salvia greggii.*

Planting & Care—Nursery-grown plants are becoming available in containers. However, if container plants are not available, sow seed in the fall to produce flowering plants by the following spring. Provide with well-drained soil. In their natural environment among rocky areas, plants grow much smaller, 6 to 8 inches high. With additional water, plant size and flowers increase. Adapts well to moderate moisture once established due to deep taproots. Plants often become dormant in cold-winter regions. If plants begin to look unkempt, cut back in fall for fresh, new growth the following spring.

Native to U.S. Southwest and Mexico

Perennial; blooms during spring—the same time as Texas bluebonnet—and continues into fall

Adapted to SCI, SCLD, SCMHD, CACV, AZLD, AZMHD, NMMHD, SNV, TXHP, TXRRP, TXTPR

Grows to 1 foot high, spreads 1 foot wide or more

Provide with well-draining soil

Moderate to low water use once established, water deeply to promote deep taproot growth

Plant in full sun; accepts partial shade in afternoon

Above: *Lupinus polyphyllus* Russell hybrids are considered the most desirable lupines by many gardeners. Be aware they are difficult to grow in hot, dry climates.

Above right: *Lythrum* is one of the easiest perennials to grow and does not need much care after it is established. When given too much water, plants can become invasive. Avoid this problem by growing sterile varieties such as 'The Beacon', shown here.

Monarda didyma, beebalm, is not a refined plant, but what it lacks in grace it makes up in vibrant flower colors that attract butterflies and hummingbirds.

Lychnis chalcedonica, Maltese cross, bears scarlet flowers from early to midsummer. Plants grow 2-1/2 to 3 feet high.

Far left: *Melampodium leucanthum,* blackfoot daisy, has become a valued perennial in the arid West. It is easy to grow and has a long flowering season that extends from spring through fall.

Left: *Mimulus cardinalis,* scarlet monkey flower, is native to Oregon, California, Nevada and Arizona. Plants accept heat if located in lightly shaded areas and given regular water in well-draining soil.

Mimulus — Monkey Flower

Native to the West and Southwest

Perennial; blooms spring to summer

Adapted to SCC, SCI, SCLD, NCC, CACV, AZLD, AZMHD

Grows 1 to 3 feet high, spreads 2 to 3 feet wide

Provide with well-draining soil high in organic content

Moderate to high water use

Plant in full sun along the coast; provide partial shade in hot desert regions

This is a large group of soft-wooded, shrubby, evergreen perennials. Also known as *Diplicus,* monkey flower provides a great display of flowers over a longer time and in a greater array of colors than many other native plants. Tubular, often freckled, lipped flowers are borne singly in the axils of leaves. They bloom over a long period in late spring, lasting into late summer. Leaves are oblong and sharply toothed, growing 1 to 3 inches long in pairs along the stems.

Recommended Species—*Mimulus cardinalis,* scarlet monkey flower, is native to Oregon, California, Nevada and Arizona. This perennial grows 1 to 1-1/2 feet high and spreads to 3 feet wide with velvety, scarlet blooms. Flowers are profuse for a long period from April through October. Leaves typically come in pairs and are narrow, glossy green and often sticky. Plants accept heat if located in shaded areas and given regular water in well-draining soil. Excellent in the mini-oasis.
M. longiflorus (Diplicus longiflorus) is more shrublike, growing 2 to 3 feet high. Flowers are cream to orange-yellow in color. It is native to coastal regions of Southern California.
M. puniceus is native to Orange, Riverside and San Diego counties in Southern California. It hybridizes with *M. longiflorus* and *M. aurantiacus australis.* Their blooming season is late spring and into summer.

Use plants in tree-shaded garden areas, around ponds, in containers and in the mini-oasis garden. Monkey flower is also a favorite of hummingbirds.

Planting & Care—Sow seed in the fall or set out container-grown plants in spring. After the first flush of flowers early in the season, prune flower stems and unruly growth, which will cause the plant to produce more flowers. Under the best conditions, flowering may continue most of the year. Increase plantings by taking cuttings in early spring and plant in moist sand. Transplant when cuttings are well rooted—usually after several months.

Mirabilis — Four O'clock

Native to Peru, tropical Americas

Perennial; blooms in midsummer into fall

Adapted to SCC, SCI, SCLD, SCMHD, NCC, CACV, AZLD, AZMHD, NMMHD, SNV

Grows 2 to 4 feet high, spreads 4 to 6 feet wide

Provide with deep, well-draining soil

Moderate water use (tubers store water)

Plant in full sun

Mirabilis jalapa, four o'clock, is a time-honored perennial known for its ability to thrive with neglect. Plants wait until midsummer to flower, but then seem to make up for lost time by blooming well into fall. Flowers come in a wide range of colors from white, salmon, pink and lavender to yellow. The multiheaded flowerbuds develop and open late in the day, thus the common name of four o'clock. Plants grow 3 to 4 feet high with an equal spread. Leaves are deep green, 2 inches wide and up to 5 inches long, creating a lush, shrublike appearance.

M. multiflora is a magenta-flowering perennial that provides color from April through September. Mature size is to 2 feet high, spreading 4 to 6 feet wide. The deep, fleshy root system stores moisture, allowing plants to survive periods of drought. Leaves drop with cold temperatures, but plants recover quickly in spring.

Due to their luxuriant growth habit, plants work well as a background for other flowering perennials. They also blend in with other perennials as colorful fillers, such as between clusters of flowering tobacco, daylilies and gayfeather.

Planting & Care—Sow seed in place in a sunny location during fall. Thin seedlings to 3 to 4 feet apart to allow for mature spread. Once established, plants adapt to deep, infrequent watering. Little pruning or thinning is required, except for cutting back plants while they are winter-dormant to renew the following year.

Monarda didyma — Beebalm, Bergamot, Oswego Tea

Beebalm is not a refined plant, but what it lacks in grace it makes up in vibrant flower colors that attract butterflies and hummingbirds. Plants have square-shaped stems and aromatic, toothed, opposite leaves alternating in pairs, characteristic of the mint family. Small, long, tubular flowers in shaggy, dense heads appear on top of hollow, brittle, erect stems 2-1/2 to 4 feet high in summer. Native to North America, plants were used by the Oswego Indians to make tea. Leaves have a distinctive scent reminiscent of basil and mint.

Recommended Varieties—'Alba' has large white flowers. 'Cambridge Scarlet' has brilliant red flowers on 2-1/2- to 3-foot stems. 'Croftway Pink' flowers are rosy pink on 2-1/2 foot stems.

Planting & Care—Divide regularly each spring, or start new plants from seed in spring. Space new transplants 15 to 18 inches on center to allow for spread. *Monarda* tolerates partial shade and actually prefers it in the hottest climates. When plants are about 12 inches tall, support with wire hoop, stakes and string or brushy twigs stuck in the ground to help keep flowers upright.

Susceptible to rust disease. To prevent, space plants well apart from one another and remove debris from planting area. Avoid watering at night and keep moisture off the foliage. Drip or trickle irrigation helps keep foliage dry. Plants also tend to be short-lived in hot, dry climates, so be prepared to replace plants as they age.

Native to North America

Perennial; blooms in summer

Adapted to all regions of the arid West, but best in SCC

Grows 2 to 4 feet high, with equal spread

Accepts ordinary garden soil; does better in soil improved with organic matter

Moderate water use in summer, low water use otherwise

Plant in full sun; provide afternoon shade in hot-summer regions

Nepeta — Catnip, Catmint

N. cataria, catnip, has gray, hairy leaves that look attractive tumbling down among boulders in the rock garden or draping over walls or borders of raised beds. It is also an excellent ground cover for small areas. Space plants 18 to 24 inches on center for continuous cover. The aromatic foliage delights humans, and, of course, cats. Bushy plants with small, crenellated leaves bear lavender-blue flowers in late spring or early summer.

Locate plants where you can touch the leaves and enjoy their fragrance. Makes a fine cut flower for casual arrangements and bouquets. The soft gray of the leaves is a good color harmonizer, combining well with more brilliantly colored flowers. Combine with *Dianthus deltoides* 'Brilliant' and tulips for a knockout color combination.

Recommended Species—*N. x faassenii* 'Blue Wonder' forms neat, bushy plants to 2 feet high and flowers over a long season. 'Dropmore' has an upright habit, bearing lavender-blue flowers on 12-inch plants. *N. mussinii* grows 18 inches high and spreads 18 inches wide. It is sometimes confused with *N. x faassenii*, but growth is looser and more sprawling. Plants are extremely hardy—to -35F.

Planting & Care—Plants are generally available in containers for fall or spring planting. Plant in full sun, in sandy, infertile soil. Shear back after first flowering to promote a second flowering later in the year. Don't shear again until late winter or early spring, just before new growth begins to show. If cats damage plantings, selectively prune damaged stems to repair. To propagate, take cuttings of nonflowering shoots in midsummer, or divide in spring or fall.

Native to Iran

Perennial; blooms early and late summer

Adapted to all regions of the arid West

Grows 1 to 2 feet high, spreads 1 to 2 feet wide

Provide with well-draining soil

Moderate to low water use

Plant in full sun

Nierembergia hippomanica violacea Dwarf Cupflower

Native to Argentina

Perennial; blooms in summer

Adapted to all regions of the arid West

Grows 6 to 12 inches high, spreads 12 to 15 inches wide

Provide with fertile, well-draining soil

Moderate water use

Plant in full sun along coast and inland valleys; provide afternoon shade in hot-summer areas

Dwarf cupflower is excellent in the border or perennial bed, providing cool colors in rich blue to violet and white. Flowers are 1 inch long, bell-shaped, and cover the compact plants that grow to 1 foot high. The dark green leaves are stiff and narrow, about 1/2 inch long. The small, compact growth habit makes it a fine plant for rock gardens, for edging a border or walk, or among boulder beds.

Dwarf cupflower is grown as an annual in areas where temperatures drop below zero. In temperate regions, such as along the coast, the slightly cooler summer temperatures are often enough to allow plants to live over from one season to the next.

Planting & Care—Sow seed in place during fall for bloom the following spring. Container plants are also available in warm-summer regions for planting in fall. Do not overwater plants in summer; maintain regular moisture until plants are established, then cut back to moderate water use. Avoid planting too close to taller, more vigorous and spreading annuals and perennials. Trim straggly branches to maintain neat appearance. Also trim back after flowering season to revitalize plants so they'll produce new growth the following spring.

Oenothera Evening Primrose, Sundrops

Native to U.S. and Mexico

Perennial; blooms late spring and summer

Adapted to SCI, SCLD, SCMHD, NCC, CACV, AZLD, AZMHD, NMMHD, SNV, TXHP, TXEP, TXRRP

Grows 9 inches to 2 feet high, spreads 2 to 3 feet wide

Provide with fertile, well-draining soil

Low water use

Plant in full sun

These easy-to-grow perennials have blossoms that open only during the day, or only at night, depending on the species. Flowers are often yellow, sometimes white or pale pink. They have four petals in an open, buttercup shape, with a cluster of fluffy yellow stamens at the center. *Calyxes,* the sepals underneath the petals, are often bright red and showy. Plants have a basal rosette of leaves; flowering stems are sometimes erect, sometimes lazy. *Oenothera* spreads by underground runners and will quickly colonize.

Recommended Species—*Oenothera berlandieri,* Mexican evening primrose, flowers from late spring into summer with rose-pink, 1-1/2-inch flowers on stems 10 to 12 inches high. Once established, moisture needs are minimal. Plants can be invasive and overgrow smaller, less aggressive plants. Native to Mexico and Texas.
O. caespitosa, white evening primrose, also known as tufted evening primrose, is native to the U.S. Southwest. It has a unique, rounded growth habit with long, sword-shaped, gray-green leaves. Plants grow in clumps less than 1 foot high and to 3 feet wide. White flowers 4 inches in diameter open in the evening hours and close early the next morning. Plants bloom on and off all year but are most profuse during spring and fall. Cold-hardy to 5F. Low-water users; if overwatered in the summer, plant can decline due to rot. Plants reseed readily. A location in full sun and well-draining soil are important. Native to New Mexico, and the Rocky Mountains in Colorado.
O. missourensis grows to 9 inches tall, spreading about 2 feet, bearing bright yellow, showy, 4-inch, evening-blooming flowers from summer into autumn. This is a trailing plant, best for the front of the border. Native to the southern United States.
O. speciosa is a day-flowering plant growing 1 to 2 feet high with coarse brown stems. Flowers are white, fading to pink as they age.
O. stubbei, Baja evening primrose, has yellow flowers 2-1/2 inches wide that

Above: *Nepeta x faassenii* 'Blue Wonder' forms neat, bushy plants to 2 feet high and flowers over a long season. Here it works well in a formal herb garden.

Far left: *Oenothera caespitosa,* white evening primrose, has a unique, rounded growth habit with long, sword-shaped, gray-green leaves.

Left: *Oenothera berlandieri,* Mexican evening primrose, flowers from late spring into summer with rose-pink, 1-1/2-inch flowers on stems 10 to 12 inches high.

Oenothera, continued

Oenothera berlandieri

rise 8 inches above the dark green leaves. Plantings at the University of Arizona in Tucson and at the Boyce Thompson Arboretum at Superior, Arizona, have successfully endured high summer heat and drought. Well adapted to other Southwest desert areas. Native to Baja California.

Most *Oenothera* species look their best when interplanted among shrubs or in a natural garden setting between rocks and boulders. In these settings growth can be rampant, go through unattractive dormancy and not affect the overall garden scene. It's also an ideal ground cover in the wildlife habitat garden.

Planting & Care—Plants are available at nurseries in containers for fall or early spring planting. Or sow seed in spring or fall. Grow in moderately rich, well-draining soil in full sun, spacing 8 inches apart for upright growers, 12 inches for spreading types. Fertilize plants annually and keep planting beds free of weeds. Occasionally, worm infestations will move through plantings. Plants recover quickly and grow with renewed vigor. Divide existing plantings in early spring or take stem cuttings in late summer.

Papaver — Oriental Poppy, Iceland Poppy

Native to Southwest Asia

Perennial; blooms in early spring to summer

Adapted to SCI, SCMHD, NCC, CACV, AZMHD, NMMHD, SNV, TXEP

Grows 2 to 4 feet high, spreads 1-1/2 to 2 feet wide

Provide with moderately fertile, well-draining soil

Moderate water use; reduce moisture from mid-July to September when plants are dormant; low water use during winter

Plant in full sun for best flower show

The tissue-like flowers of *Papaver orientale,* Oriental poppy, provide brilliant splashes of color early in the season. They bloom the same time as iris, and when placed together, create dramatic displays.

In fall, Oriental poppies form a basal rosette of hairy, lobed leaves that live over winter, then send up flowering stems 2 to 4 feet tall. After flowering the plants go dormant, disappearing completely from mid-July until September. For this reason, don't mass poppies together in the border or you will have large holes while they are absent. Flowers come in shades of red, orange, pink and white, and can be as much as 6 inches or more across. Excellent as cut flowers. Sear end of stem with flame after cutting, and place immediately in water for longest-lasting blooms.

Recommended Varieties—These are just a few of the many cultivars of *P. orientale* available: 'Barr's White' has purple-black markings at base. 'Bonfire' is a brilliant, orange-red with crinkled, crepe-like petals. 'Carnival' has orange-red petals with white at the base. 'May Curtis' is watermelon pink. 'Pinnacle' has white petals with red edges. 'Warlord' is one of the best, with deep crimson flowers.
P. nudicaule, Iceland poppy, is a perennial grown as an annual in mild-winter regions. It produces thin flower stalks that support satiny flowers up to 3 inches in diameter. Flower colors are similar to Oriental poppy. Plant in fall for flowers in the following spring.

Planting & Care—Plant Oriental poppies only when they're dormant, in August or September. Set each crown 3 inches deep in well-prepared, moderately fertile, well-draining soil. Water regularly, but keep soil on the dry side in winter. Poppies are best left undivided and undisturbed. Because of their tall stems, it may be necessary to stake plants in windy areas. Do not remove leaves until they completely dry; they manufacture food that is stored by plant for next season.

Penstemon — Beard-Tongue

Penstemon is a high-quality plant that deserves to be more widely grown. The many species available make excellent choices for the border, wild garden, prairie garden, meadow and rock garden. This large genus of North American natives can be found from the Great Plains west and south. Many species are not widely adapted, but there are penstemons for almost every climate, from high, cool and mountainous, to temperate, to hot and dry desert regions. Both deciduous and evergreen species are available.

Plants form a basal rosette of lance-shaped or ovate leaves. In late spring or early summer they send up stems that carry the tubular, flared flowers. Flower colors include vibrant shades of red, white, blue, purple and yellow. All attract hummingbirds.

Combine penstemon with other low- to moderate-water-use plants. *Justicia* species and *Hesperaloe parviflora* are two plants that provide color later in the year, after penstemon has ceased blooming.

Recommended Species—Hundreds of species are native to the United States. These listed here are a small selection of those that are more readiliy available. Contact native-plant specialists for a more complete list.
P. barbatus varieties include 'Prairie Fire', orange-red flowers from midsummer to frost on 1-1/2 to 2-foot plants; 'Rose Elf', clear pink flowers; 'Elfin Pink', to just 12 inches high; 'Mesa', flowers are deep lavender on 20-inch plants. All are cold hardy to 25F.
P. eatonii, firecracker penstemon, is a favorite species. Long, narrow, scarlet flowers are supported by 2-foot-high stems. Adapted throughout the arid West.
P. heterophyllus purdyi 'Blue Bedder' has rose-lavender to blue spikelike flowers. Plants grow 1 to 2 feet high and as wide. Bloom period is April into July. Grows along coast and in inland valleys; adapted elsewhere.
P. palmeri, pink wild snapdragon, also known as Palmer's penstemon, develops flower spikes 5 to 6 feet high that are highly fragrant. Large white blossoms are tinged with lilac or pink. Blooms in early summer. Provide low to moderate water; excessive water causes flower stalks to droop.
P. parryi, Parry's penstemon, flowers in early spring. It is an exceptional species with spikes to 2 feet high topped with pink tubular blooms.

P. wrightii, a native of Texas, is similar to *P. parryi,* but its flower color is a unique, intense, pinkish red.

Planting & Care—Penstemons grow easily from seed, which should be sown in spring. Plants are also becoming available in containers at plant nurseries, and should be set out in fall or spring. Well-draining soil is necessary. Poorly drained soil, especially through winter, encourages crown rot. Space plants 12 to 18 inches apart. Many of the species are low-water users once established. Extending irrigation (but avoiding excessive water) in late spring helps prolong the flowering season. Divide existing plants in early fall, or take stem cuttings in summer or fall.

Native to the western U.S.

Perennial; blooms from spring to summer

Adapted to all regions of the arid West

Grows 1 to 6 feet high, spreads 1 to 3 feet wide

Provide with light, well-draining soil

Low to moderate water use

Plant in full sun; provide filtered shade in low-elevation deserts

Right: *Papaver orientale,* Oriental poppy, provide bright splashes of color early in the season. Also see full-page photo, page 128.

Far right: *Papaver nudicaule,* Iceland poppy, produces blooms similar to Oriental poppy except flowers often have black centers.

Below: *Penstemon parryi,* Parry's penstemon, flowers in early spring, here in combination with *Encelia farinosa,* brittle bush.

Far left: *Platycodon grandiflorus,* balloonflower, is a reliable, old-fashioned perennial. Flowers appear as swollen hollow buds like small balloons and open into star-shaped, saucerlike flowers.

Left: *Phlox subulata,* creeping phlox or moss pink, is one of the first perennials to bloom in spring, carpeting the ground in vibrant hues of white, pink, rose and lavender.

Primula species, primrose, are traditional favorites for the shaded border and adapt well to a mini-oasis garden or in containers. Tubular flowers in an extensive range of colors bloom on top of tall, slender, leafless stalks.

Perovskia atriplicifolia — Russian Sage

Native to Russia

Subshrub; blooms in summer

Adapted to SCI, SCLD, SCMHD, NCC, CACV, AZLD, AZMHD, NMMHD, SNV, TXHP, TXEP, TXRRP, TXTPR, CWR

Grows 3 to 4 feet high, spreads 3 to 5 feet wide

Provide with well-draining, ordinary soil

Low to moderate water use

Plant in full sun to partial shade

Perovskia is an aromatic subshrub whose airy, feathery branches lend lightness to the landscape. It is one of the easiest perennials to grow, blooming over a long period. It adds a delicate, lavender-blue color to the garden, as well as being attractive in indoor bouquets.

This is an easy-care plant, that is not bothered by pests or diseases. Plants grow 3 to 4 feet high with many-branching woody stems and adapt quite well to revegetation projects. Small, toothed, gray-green leaves are coated with tiny hairs; flowers are presented much like diminutive spikes of lavender.

Plants that relate well with Russian sage, as well as having similar moisture requirements, include *Rosmarinus, Salvia, Teucrium, Encelia* and *Ericameria* species.

Planting & Care—Plant from containers in full sun during spring or fall, spacing 3 to 4 feet apart. This allows plants to develop their natural form without crowding. *Perovskia* thrives on lean, gritty, well-draining rather poor soil. Provide drainage to heavy soils by adding sand or organic matter. Trim tips and spent flowering wood as the season progresses to encourage reblooming. During winter dormancy, prune plants 6 to 12 inches above ground level, maintaining natural growth habit, to stimulate new spring growth. Propagate by cuttings.

Phlox — Phlox

Native to North America

Perennial; blooms spring or summer

Adapted to all regions of the arid West except SCC

Grows 1 to 3 feet high, spreads 1 to 2 feet wide

Provide with deeply worked, rich, well-draining soil

Moderate water use

Plant in full sun to light shade

Phlox, in its various forms provides colorful flower clusters through much of the gardening year. *Phlox subulata,* creeping phlox or moss pink, is one of the first perennials to bloom in spring, carpeting the ground in vibrant hues of white, pink, rose and lavender. *P. stolonifera* is another ground-covering phlox that flowers later in spring. *P. divaricata,* woodland phlox, bears delicate flowers of blue or white in late spring. *P. paniculata* produces a large number of fragrant flowers from midsummer until late summer. A wide range of colors are available, and many types have a darker or contrasting eye at the blossoms' centers. *P. maculata* has smaller flowerheads than *P. paniculata,* but plants are mildew resistant.

Recommended Species—*P. maculata* 'Alpha' has rose-pink flowers with darker eyes. 'Omega' has white flowers with distinct violet eyes. Both bloom July through September on 2-1/2-foot plants. 'Miss Lingard' is an old favorite white form that flowers in June and July. It is sometimes sold as *P. carolina.* *P. paniculata* 'Fairy's Petticoat' has large heads of shell-pink flowers with darker eyes. 'Orange Perfection' has salmon-orange flowers on 2- to 3-foot plants. 'Caroline Vandenberg' blooms are lavender-blue on 3-foot plants.

Tall forms work well in the middle foreground of perennial beds and borders. The ground-covering types are good in borders, rock gardens, raised beds and slopes. Excellent in mass plantings for large areas, or among shrubs or perennials in small spaces.

Planting & Care—Plant container plants in fall or early spring in fertile, deeply worked loam in full sun, spacing plants 2 feet apart. As plants take on some size in spring, thin to three to four vigorous shoots. Keep plants well-watered and feed with a low-nitrogen fertilizer. Remove spent flowerheads to groom plants and to prevent seeding. To propagate summer or garden phlox (*P. maculata* and *P. paniculata* varieties), divide every few years in spring or fall, or take root cuttings in fall.

Platycodon grandiflorus — Balloon Flower

Platycodon is a reliable, old-fashioned perennial that, once established, will be a steady performer for many years. Plants grow 1 to 3 feet high, with gray-green, ovate leaves. Swollen hollow buds like small balloons open into star-shaped, flattened, saucer-like flowers in shades of pink, blue and white.

The thick, fleshy roots need good soil drainage and resent disturbance, so locate them in a permanent planting bed where they will not have to be moved. For the best visual effect, plant in clusters of three or more.

Recommended Species—There is one species in this genus, but it has several good cultivars. 'Albus' has white flowers on bushy, compact plants growing to 15 inches. 'Shell Pink' has large pink cups veined with deeper pink. It grows to 2 feet high and keeps its color better if planted in light shade. 'Apoyama' is a 6-inch dwarf with mauve-blue flowers; 'Mariesii' grows to 15 inches with blue flowers.

Planting & Care—Easy to grow from seed; sow in place in spring. Flowers will be produced after two years. Space 12 to 15 inches apart in light, sandy, well-draining soil in full sun or partial shade, depending on where you live. Stake taller varieties, or support with hoops. Plants go completely dormant in winter and emerge slowly in spring. Because you can't see plants, you must be careful not to dig or cultivate the roots. Mark locations in fall before the foliage withers and dissipates. Remove spent flowers to prolong flowering season. Divide existing plants in spring.

Native to Japan, eastern Asia

Perennial; blooms June to August

Adapted to all regions of the arid West

Grows 1 to 3 feet high, spreads 1 to 3 feet wide

Provide with improved, well-draining soil

Moderate water use

Plant in full sun along coast; partial shade inland

Primula — Primrose

A primrose garden can take on the look of a carnival, with white, shades of pink, blue, red, apricot and purple—some with white eyes. The color range is so great it's worth a trip to the nursery to select the colors you like. Primroses are old favorites for the shaded border and adapt well to today's mini-oasis garden. Plants form a rosette of oblong or tongue-shaped leaves of substance that are fleshy and wrinkled. Tubular flowers appear on tall, slender, leafless stalks.

Recommended Species—*P. auricula* forms rosettes of leathery evergreen leaves. In spring, flower stems reach 6 to 8 inches high. Flowers have white eyes and are available in a wide range of colors. Good for rock gardens in semishade.

P. denticulata, Himalayan primrose, has round, dense flowerheads in shades of purple, rosy purple or white, all with yellow eyes. The flower bud forms in fall and sits at the soil surface until spring, when its thick stalk elongates to 1 foot. Grow in soil with excellent drainage and provide winter protection.

P. japonica prefers deep, rich soil or waterside conditions in shade. Flowers look like small candelabra in shades of magenta, pink, rose-red or white, and appear arranged loosely on stalks in late spring to early summer.

P. malacoides, fairy primrose, is dainty yet prolific, with many flower colors. It adds a delicate, refined touch to the shaded border.

Planting & Care—Plant from containers in fall or early spring in rich, moist, well-draining soil. Space plants 8 inches apart. Plants look best if given a location protected from wind and sun. The auriculas and Himalayan primroses should have a gritty, fast-draining soil. Subject to spider mites, which thrive in hot, dry situations. A mild infestation can be controlled with frequent spraying with a stream of water from the garden hose. Divide existing plants in spring.

Native to European Alps, western China

Perennial; blooms in spring

Adapted to SCC, SCI, SCLD, NCC, CACV, AZLD, SNV

Grows to 12 inches high, spreads 12 to 15 inches wide

Provide with organic-rich soil

Moderate water use with enriched soil

Plant in bright shade

Psilostrophe — Paperflower

Native to the U.S. Southwest

Perennial; blooms during spring into fall

Adapted to SCI, SCLD, SCMHD, CACV, AZLD, AZMHD, NMMHD, SNV, TXEP, TXRRP, TXTPR

Grows 1 to 2 feet high, spreads as wide

Accepts most soils; good drainage is important

Low to moderate water use

Plant in full sun or partial shade

Paperflower shows its refreshing flowers over a long period from spring to fall and often year-round. Miniature yellow, sunflower-like blooms 1 inch wide cover the low, 1-1/2- to 2-foot mounding plants. Basal branch growth is dense but with sparse foliage. Flowers practically cover plants during periods of peak bloom.

Psilostrophe cooperi is native to Utah, western New Mexico, Arizona, Southern California and northwestern Mexico. Plants are naturally adapted to hot, low-rainfall regions. In the deserts of the Southwest, paperflower is largely unnoticed, and deserves wider garden use. It is worth noting that when plants are allowed to dry out for several months and then watered deeply, masses of flowers come on for another show of color.

P. tagetina, Texas paperflower, may be less well known than *P. cooperi,* but it is blessed with a long flowering season from February into October. The well-rounded, 1- to 1-1/2-foot plants are literally covered with 1-inch yellow flowers. When flowers are at the papery white or tan stage, you can cut and use them as long-lived dried flowers. Moderate water will maintain plants through the long flowering season. A deep taproot gives plants an increased water supply during periods without irrigation.

Either species is effective as a low foreground or border plant. They blend well with many of the gray-foliaged plants that grow in arid gardens, requiring only low water use and little or no maintenance.

Planting & Care—Seeds germinate readily, and plants, especially *P. cooperi,* are sometimes available in containers at specialty nurseries. Seed-grown plants may take a year or so before flowering. Plant in full sun in well-draining soil. After each blooming period and when flowers have faded to a tan, papery texture, shear them off to stimulate growth of new flowering stems.

Romneya coulteri — Matilija Poppy

Native to California

Perennial; blooms in summer

Adapted to SCC, SCI, SCLD, NCC, CACV

Grows to 8 feet high, spreading 8 to 10 feet wide

Provide with well-draining soil

Moderate water use to establish, then low water for mature plants

Plant in full sun

Matilija poppy is certainly one of the most spectacular and valued of all native California plants. Plants greeted the Spanish missionaries and soldiers as they traveled northward along the California coast over 400 years ago. Its natural distribution provides a clue to preferred culture in garden areas: canyon beds and sandy washes in coastal California from Santa Barbara County south to San Diego County and Baja California at elevations from near sea level to 2,000 feet.

Plants are vigorous, woody-based perennials, growing 6 to 8 feet high and spreading 8 to 10 feet wide. Due to its size and rough-hewn good looks, it is not recommended for the small garden or for continuous up-close viewing. However, in larger areas on slopes and on deep lots, a distant view of the immense, crepe-like flowers that grow 4 to 9 inches across is something to behold. Near the plants the pleasant fragrance of the flowers is substantial. Flowers bloom most abundantly in early to midsummer, then after a short summer vacation bloom again in the fall. This varies according to location. High moisture content of plants makes them fire-retardant.

Two larger flowering kinds are 'White Cloud' and 'Butterfly'. Cut flowers will last 3 to 5 days if stems are cauterized before immersing them in water.

Planting & Care—Plants are usually available in containers at specialized nurseries. Difficult to start from seed. Plants will not tolerate soggy or poorly drained soil. Plants can become unsightly after bloom period. Cut back to near ground level in the late fall for vigorous regrowth. The most efficient propagation method is to remove suckers from older plants and replant. Or take 2-1/2-inch-long root cuttings in November or December. Plant cuttings in a mix of well-moistened and blended loam, peat moss and leaf mold. Place cuttings in the soil in horizontal position. Surround with sand to provide drainage.

Perovskia atriplicifolia, Russian sage, is an easy-to-grow, aromatic subshrub. Its airy, feathery branches lend lightness to the landscape.

Romneya coulteri, matilija poppy, is one of the most spectacular and valued of all native California plants. Plants grow 6 to 8 feet high and spread 8 to 10 feet wide.

The immense, crepelike flowers of *Romneya coulteri,* matilija poppy, grow 4 to 9 inches across.

Rosmarinus officinalis — Rosemary

Native to the Mediterranean

Perennial ground cover; blooms in late winter and spring

Adapted to all areas of the arid West except CWR

Grows 2 to 5 feet high, spreads 4 to 6 feet wide

Provide with well-draining soil

Low to moderate water use

Plant in full sun; tolerates high heat

Rosmarinus officinalis 'Prostratus' is the ground-hugging form of rosemary, and it is more commonly grown in the arid West than the species. It has many uses in the garden, performing well as a cascading ground cover on slopes, draped over a wall, as an alternative for a non-traffic lawn area or in the foreground for a flower bed. The gray-green leaves create a dense, 2-foot-high plant and can spread 4 to 6 feet in diameter. Bright blue flowers that attract bees cover the aromatic foliage late winter to early spring.

R. officinalis has an upright, shrub-like growth habit, reaching 3 to 5 feet high and as wide. It blends well with many of the gray-foliaged plants found in the natural garden, such as *Leucophyllum, Salvia* and *Cassia* species. In addition to providing shades of gray-green to the garden, rosemary's soft texture allows it to blend well with many shrubs and ground covers. Flowers are darker blue than 'Prostratus'.

Planting & Care—Set out from containers in fall or early spring. Accepts most any well-drained soil. Rosemary enjoys high heat, so plant in full sun in all areas. Water needs are low to moderate once established. Avoid fertilizing and giving plants too much water; it causes growth to become rank. To maintain a low, flowing, plant form, cut plants back to hard wood, reducing foliage build-up in center of plant. Prune to maintain natural plant form. Do this every year or two in late winter, prior to the strong surge of early spring growth. Don't let several years pass before pruning, or keeping the plant's natural appearance will be more difficult to achieve.

Rudbeckia — Coneflower, Black-Eyed Susan

Native to North America

Perennial; blooms in summer and fall

Adapted to all regions of the arid West; best with heat

Grows 2-1/2 to 7 feet high, spreads 2 to 3 feet wide

Provide with ordinary garden soil

Moderate to low water use

Plant in full sun

Black-eyed Susan is a cheerful and familiar sight in meadows from the Northeast to the Central States, and increasingly in the warm Southwest. Coarse hairy leaves give rise to many-branching flower stalks. Flowerheads have yellow ray flowers with a fuzzy brown cone in the center. *Rudbeckia* blends well with other low-maintenance perennials such as ornamental grasses, *Yucca* species and *Echinacea.*

Recommended Species—*R. fulgida* 'Goldsturm' is the best of the genus, with deep yellow flowers 3 to 4 inches wide and almost black cones. Plants grow to 2-1/2 feet high. This long-lived plant blooms August to frost.
R. hirta, gloriosa daisy, begins forming buds for its summer and late fall flowering season at the same time many other perennials are ending their flower show in late spring. However, plants have been known to bloom early in spring in frost-free areas when grown in a warm microclimate. Flowers are 5 to 7 inches across, in bright yellow, orange and russet. Plants grow to 3 to 4 feet high. Two smaller selections can be used in foreground plantings: 'Marmalade' to 2 feet high, and 'Goldilocks', 1-1/2 feet high.
R. laciniata, the "Golden Glow" of grandmother's garden, grows to a whopping 7 feet. It can be invasive, but it is still loved for its prolific, 2- to 3-inch double flowers. 'Goldquelle' (sometimes listed as *R. nitida*), is a tamer plant that stays put, growing to a more modest 2-1/2 feet. It flowers July through September.

Planting & Care—Plant seed in place or set out nursery-grown plants in early spring in cold-winter areas; in fall in mild climates. Set 2 to 3 feet apart in soil that is not too fertile. Plants given fertile soil and ample water can grow rampant. Deadhead spent flowers to encourage continued blooms during summer. Cut back spent flower stalks to basal growth and clean up old leaves in late fall. Divide every three years in spring or fall.

Ruellia — Ruellia

The blue to violet, petunia-like flowers of *Ruellia* species provide dependable color during summer and occasionally through the rest of the year. About 250 species grow in Africa, South America and Asia. *R. peninsularis,* ruellia, is native to the Sonoran Desert and adapts well to climates and soils of the low-elevation deserts of California and Arizona. Leaves are 1 inch long, gray-green and dense enough to serve as a natural hedge or background to 3 feet high. Plants seldom need pruning except for an occasional thinning to stimulate new growth. Clusters of three to five plants can create stability in gardens as companions to taller shrubs such as *Penstemon, Yucca* and *Encelia* species. Once established, plants require low water, and will recover quickly with low water even after periods of drought. Grow best in full sun; flowering is reduced in filtered shade.

Recommended Species—*R. californica* is a free spirit in the garden, popping up in the most unexpected places. Plants spread when the small black seeds ripen and scatter with the wind. Lavender, 1-1/2 to 2-inch blooms last for a day or two. Foliage growth is sparse on 18-inch stems; however, plants have the ability to blend with other plants without being intrusive. Plant from containers in spring. Moisture needs are in the low to moderate range once established. After the flowering season, trim back to 1 foot above ground level. With the arrival of warm weather, the growth and bloom cycle begins again.
R. nudiflora, violet ruellia, is common throughout Texas except in the Panhandle region. It reaches 2 feet high and as wide. Flowers 2 inches wide in rich violet to lavender hues bloom for over a month in spring and again in the fall. Plants go dormant in winter, but regrow vigorously in spring. Provide with well-draining soil and partial shade. Accepts moderate moisture.

Planting & Care—See individual species descriptions.

Native to Africa, Asia, South America and U.S. Southwest

Perennial; blooms in summer

Adapted to SCI, SCLD, CACV, AZLD, AZMHD, TXEP, TXTPR

Grows 2 to 4 feet high, spreads 2 to 3 feet wide

Provide with well-draining soil

Moderate to low water use

Plant in full sun

Salvia — Sage

Planted in masses, perennial *Salvia* species provide a dense carpet of flowers in blue to purple to red flower colors from early spring to fall. Plants grow 2 to 4 feet high with erect flower spikes. Leaves are oblong and gray-green, with tiny hairs underneath. Sages are low-maintenance plants that give a long season of color, are good for cutting and drought-tolerant. They are not bothered by insects or disease. Use them in the border, combined with *Achillea, Rudbeckia, Penstemon, Kniphofia, Euryops, Rosmarinus* and *Hemerocallis.*

Recommended Species—*S. azurea grandiflora* (often listed as *S. pitcheri*) forms a shrub 3 to 4 feet high. Blue flowers open in late summer.
S. clevelandii, San Diego salvia, grows as a well-rounded plant to 3 to 4 feet high with smooth, gray-green leaves. Blue flowers that bloom from late spring to late summer have a delightful fragrance that is even more pronounced after the flowers are dry. Locate in full sun and in well-draining soil. Plants are well adapted to slope plantings and can even be used for revegetation. Hold back on water in the summer months once established. Selective pruning in early spring will improve plant appearance later in the season.
S. coccinea, scarlet Texas sage, goes dormant during the winter, then comes alive in spring. Flowers open white and change to red. Other flower colors include white and shades of blue with compact growth. Lush green foliage grows vigorously and can become unruly; trimming during the growing season will make plants bushier. Accepts partial shade as well as full sun. Tolerates most soils and performs well with low to moderate water.
S. farinacea, mealy-cup sage, is a perennial in mild-winter climates, an annual in colder areas. Growth is rapid to 2 to 3 feet high; the violet-blue spikes stand up well above the plant. 'Victoria' has dark blue flower spikes. Avoid pruning in summer; wait until fall to clean up straggly growth. Locate in sun or afternoon shade. Excessive overhead watering or too much rain can cause mildew.

Native to various regions; see individual descriptions

Perennial; blooms spring to fall

Adapted to all regions of the arid West except CWR

Grows 2 to 4 feet high, spreads 2 to 4 feet wide

Provide with ordinary, well-draining soil

Low water use

Plant in full sun to partial shade; see species descriptions

Rudbeckia hirta, gloriosa daisy, blooms during summer and late fall, at a time when many other perennials are ending their flower show.

Ruellia species is a dependable bloomer, producing blue to violet, petunialike flowers during summer and occasionally through the rest of the year.

Salvia greggii, red salvia, is a workhorse color plant in hot, dry regions.

Far left: *Salvia leucantha,* Mexican bush sage, grows gracefully to 3 to 4 feet high. Velvety purple flowers bloom from summer into early winter.

Left: *Santolina chamaecyparissus,* lavender cotton, produces profuse amounts of small, bright yellow flowers that contrast nicely with the fine-textured, gray-green foliage.

Salvia, continued

If plants become affected in winter, cut back to basal growth, and new spring growth will be mildew-free. Propagate by division in early spring.

S. greggii, red salvia, is a true star performer in hot, dry regions of the arid West. Introduced from Texas, this subshrub is a favorite in the perennial border, wildlife or natural garden, and as a mass planting. It is valued for both hardiness and long flowering season, which begins in early spring and lasts into winter. Red, tubular flowers are highly attractive to hummingbirds. Plants grow 2 to 4 feet high and thrive with low to moderate water. After each bloom period, trim away dead flower stems and new stems will regrow for repeat blooms. 'Sierra Linda' has magenta flowers that outperform the species in both color and flower production. It also accepts more heat.

Salvia greggii

S. leucantha, Mexican bush sage, is a favorite in natural gardens. Growth is graceful to 3 to 4 feet high, with vigorous arching stems covered with gray-green, crinkly leaves. Velvety purple flowers are gracefully arranged above the leaves, blooming from late summer into early winter. After flowering ends, prune and thin plants to about 1 foot above ground level. Plants will regrow the following spring. Low water use in sun or partial shade.

S. superba reaches 1-1/2 to 2-1/2 feet and flowers from early summer until frost. Several varieties are available, including 'East Friesland', 1-1/2 to 2 feet, with deep violet-purple flowers. 'May Night' is a compact plant, growing to 1-1/2 feet, with deep violet-blue flowers.

Planting & Care—Plant salvias in light, well-draining, gritty soil in full sun in fall or spring. Most species are available in containers at nurseries. Once established, they can tolerate dry soil. Seed-grown plants are variable. Stake or support tall-growing kinds. Cut off spent flower spikes as they appear to encourage new waves of flowers. High heat will reduce flower production in hot desert regions, but flowering resumes when temperatures cool.

Santolina

Lavender Cotton

Native to the Mediterranean

Perennial; blooms in summer among contrasting gray foliage

Adapted to all regions of the arid West; except CWR

Grows 1-1/2 to 2 feet high; spreads to 4 feet wide

Provide with most any well-draining soil

Low water use, avoid abundant water in summer along coast

Plant in full sun

These are reliable subshrubs that play many roles in western gardens. Two species of *Santolina* are used, often in combination plantings: *S. chamaecyparissus* and *S. virens.*

S. chamaecyparissus has small, bright yellow flowers that bloom in summer on unclipped plants. For a cleaner, less "shaggy" look, clip spent flowers. Useful as a ground cover, flower bed border, clumped in rock gardens and as foreground cover in shrub beds. Leaves are also aromatic.

S. virens is a green-foliaged companion, has narrower textured leaves, interesting in contrast to the small, cream-chartreuse flowers. Green lavender cotton establishes somewhat faster than its gray-leaved cousin.

Planting & Care—Plants are generally available in containers at nurseries. Fall and early spring plantings are ideal. If a solid ground cover is the goal, space at 3-foot centers. For border use or for a low, informal hedge, plant at 2-foot centers. Plants can be shaped after bloom into a soft, flowing pattern or as a formal hedge. This helps keep plants under control and helps prevent an open, sprawling habit from developing. Both plants are low-water users along the coast and in inland valleys. In the hotter, low-elevation desert areas, moderate water is required.

Scabiosa — Pincushion Flower

Pincushion flower is a traditional favorite and still remains a popular garden plant. It is an excellent cut flower, and, in fact, cutting flowers frequently for indoor use helps produce more blooms. The common name pincushion flower comes from the long stamens that protrude from the flat, mounding flowerheads. It is a low-maintenance plant, not recommended for specimen planting, but best when mixed with other flowering species. Flowers come in shades of blue, lavender and white—beautiful in a pastel color scheme. The plant forms a basal rosette of lance-shaped leaves; stem leaves are divided. The arching stems grow up to 2 feet long, contributing a light and airy feel to the garden.

Recommended Species—The following are selections of *S. caucasica:* 'Fama' grows to 2 feet, has true lavender flowers. 'Isaac House' hybrids are available in a range of colors from white and silver to shades of blue and lavender. Flowers reach 1-1/2 to 2 inches on 2-foot plants. 'Miss Willmott' has creamy white flowers. 'Blue Perfection' has lavender-blue flowers on 2-foot plants from early summer until late autumn.

Planting & Care—Divide existing plants in spring or sow seeds in place in spring or late summer. Spring-sown seed will produce flowers the following year. When dividing, leave the parent plant in place if possible, taking offshoots from near the base. Set 12 to 15 inches apart. Deadhead frequently to encourage more blooms. Staking may be needed when growth is lush and excessive.

Native to the Caucasus Mountains of Russia

Perennial; blooms in June until late fall or first frost

Adapted to SCC, NCC, CACV, AZMHD, NMMHD, CWR

Grows 1-1/2 to 2 feet high, spreads 1 to 2 feet wide

Provide with well-draining garden soil; accepts some alkalinity

Moderate water use; low water use during winter

Plant in full sun; best in areas of moderate summer heat

Sedum — Stonecrop

This large group of hardy succulents has a lot to offer: easy care, neat appearance, versatility, reliable bloom and plantings that increase easily. Bees and butterflies love *Sedum,* and plants stand up well to city conditions. They make excellent, long-lasting cut flowers and dry well. Low-growing sorts are well known as star performers in the rock garden, and can be used as an edging for borders and walks, as small-space ground covers and to tuck into crannies in rock walls. Taller types give subtle beauty in the border. Fleshy leaves are oval to round and often toothed. Plants form compact mounds.

Recommended Species—'Rosy Glow' has floppy stems 12 to 15 inches high. Lobed leaves are highly attractive, purplish gray; flowers are rosy red.
S. kamtschaticum forms a 4-inch mound of green, lobed leaves. Yellow starburst flowers bloom July until frost.
S. morganianum, donkey tail, produces long, pendulous, gray-green stems. Plants are striking in containers or when allowed to drape and trail. Does well along coast and in inland valleys. Provide afternoon shade in low-desert regions.
S. x rubrotinctum, pork and beans, has plump leaves that turn colorful shades of bronze. Growth is low and sprawling. Well adapted to coast and inland valleys.
S. spectabile 'Carmen' has soft rose flowerheads on 1-1/2-foot plants.
S. telephium 'Autumn Joy' is similar, with reddish pink flowers. It is one of the best *Sedum* species for color.

Planting & Care—Divide existing plants or sow seed in spring. Take stem cuttings in spring or summer. Space 18 inches apart in light, well-draining soil in full sun. Taller sorts such as *S. telephium* and *S. spectabile* need more room, about 2 feet between plants, for adequate spread. *S. spectabile* and *S. telephium* benefit from a hoop support—the large, flat flowerheads can get heavy and fall over. Plants go dormant in cold weather.

Native to many continents

Perennial; blooms spring to late summer

Adapted to all regions of the arid West; hardy to -35F

Grows 1 to 1-1/2 feet high, with an equal spread

Provide with well-draining, sandy soil

Low water use

Plant in full sun along coast; partial shade inland

Right: *Sedum x rubrotinctum,* pork and beans, has plump leaves that turn colorful shades of bronze. Growth is low and sprawling, which makes it excellent for a small-area ground cover.

Below: *Sedum* 'Autumn Joy' is one of the easiest perennials to grow, and looks good in the garden throughout the year. Soft, reddish pink flowers are attractive even when dried.

Below right: *Stachys byzantina,* lamb's-ears, is great in rock gardens, on slopes, at the front of the border or in spaces edging a walk. It is grown primarily for its touchable foliage, and many gardeners remove the mid-summer flowers as they appear to maintain a neat appearance.

Far left: *Tagetes lemonii,* lemon marigold, creates a colorful display during late fall and into winter in frost-free areas. The strongly aromatic foliage reminds one of a blend of marigold, mint and lemon.

Left: *Thalictrum aquilegifolium,* meadowrue, is an excellent plant for the woodland garden or lightly shaded border. Plants grow to 3 feet high, with purple-lilac flowers.

Trichostema lanatum, woolly blue curls, is native to coastal foothills from Santa Barbara south to San Diego. It has a special open and graceful quality, enhanced by its distinctive blue flowers on long curving stalks.

Stachys byzantina — Lamb's-Ears

Native to Turkey and southwest Asia

Foliage perennial; small flowers bloom in summer

Adapted to all regions of the arid West; hardy to -35F

Grows 1 to 1-1/2 feet high, spreads to 3 feet wide

Provide with well-draining garden soil

Low water use

Plant in full sun to light filtered shade

Lamb's-ears is a plant you instinctively want to touch. Gray-green leaves to 4 inches long are coated with white hairs, giving them a silvery appearance and a downy softness.

This is a carpeting plant, great in rock gardens, on slopes, at the front of the border or in spaces edging a walk. In midsummer, erect fleshy stems are covered with oddly shaped lavender-purple flowers that rise 1 foot or more high above the leaves. Bumblebees are attracted to the flowers. Lamb's-ears is grown mainly for its foliage, and many gardeners cut the flower stems off as they appear to maintain a neater appearance.

The unusual, soft, velvety foliage creates an attractive, dense cover that provides great contrast as an edging along walks and in borders for flower beds. Also effective placed in clumps in rock gardens.

Planting & Care—Grows easily from seed, or divide existing plants in early spring. Cover seed lightly with soil and keep moist. In fact, it's wise to divide every four years or so to keep plantings vigorous. Plants accept sun or light shade under high canopy trees. Good soil drainage is important. Excessive water can be harmful; drip irrigation at base of plant will keep moisture off foliage so they will maintain an unblemished appearance. Old plants get tattered-looking. Cut back flower stalks in fall to keep neat through winter. Remove shabby leaves before new growth begins in spring.

Tagetes — Lemon Marigold

Native to Arizona, Mexico, Guatemala

Perennial; blooms late summer to fall

Adapted to SCI, SCLD, NCC, CACV, AZLD, AZMHD

Grows 3 to 4 feet high, spreads to 3 feet wide

Provide with well-draining soil

Moderate to low water use

Plant in full sun

The daisy-like, golden-orange flowers of *Tagetes lemonii,* lemon marigold or mountain marigold, create a most colorful display during late fall and on into winter in frost-free areas. The refined, aromatic foliage reminds one of a blend of marigold, mint and lemon. The fragrance may be a little too strong for some but should not be a deterrent. In landscape situations, plants are well suited among Chihuahuan and Sonoran natives such as the fall-flowering purple and blue Texas rangers, blue and red salvias and *Dalea pulchra.* They create a grand bouquet in the perennial border or serve as colorful groupings planted in clusters.

Plants are long-lived and can grow to small shrub size—3 to 4 feet high. Foliage is damaged at 28F to 30F. If plants are damaged by cold, cut back frozen wood after danger of frost has passed to renew growth. Recovery will be rapid as the weather warms. Plantings respond well in most soils, and moisture requirements are minimal once established. Native to Arizona's higher elevation oak country.
T. lucida, licorice marigold, has dark green leaves to 2 inches long and 1/2 inch wide. Mature size is similar to lemon marigold, but growth is more erect. Plants grow 3 to 4 feet high and as wide. Flowers are profuse in the fall months, with yellow, daisy-like blooms. When leaves are brushed, they emit a scent similar to black licorice. Native to Mexico, Guatemala.

Planting & Care—Plant from containers in spring or summer. Locate in full sun for maximum growth and bloom. Color, texture and low water use make *Tagetes* valued garden plants. They do need attention to regular pruning or plants often sprawl. Trim and thin about one-third of the plant during late-spring growing season to strengthen branch development and promote strong vertical growth in time for fall flowers. No need for ample water or fertilizer. Either will create weak, floppy growth.

Teucrium chamaedrys — Germander

Prostrate germander performs well in all climate zones as a reliable subshrub or ground cover, and is often used as a substitute for small lawn areas. It also has a place as an edging in the foreground for perennials on slopes or as part of a natural garden, including among rocks and boulders. The low, ground-hugging habit of germander is well suited to earth berms, or as a colorful carpet at the base of accent plants such as *Cassia, Euryops* and *Yucca* species.

During the summer months, spikes of hairy, 3/4-inch, red, purple or occasional white flowers cover the plant. Plants normally grow 1 to 2 feet high. 'Prostratum' is even more dwarfish at 6 inches high, spreading to 3 feet wide. Flowers are attractive to bees.

Planting & Care—Plant from containers almost any time, but best time is fall or early spring. Space plants on 2-foot centers and at least 3 feet away from companion plants to allow for spread. Plants tolerate high heat, prefer full sun and grow best in well-drained soils. They accept low-water applications after establishing and will take moderate water if soil is well draining. In early spring, trim back old growth to encourage new growth. Cut back flower stems after summer flowering.

Native to Europe and southwest Asia

Perennial ground cover; blooms in summer

Adapted to all regions of the arid West

Grows 6 inches to 2 feet high, spreads 2 to 3 feet wide

Provide with almost any well-draining soil; tolerates poor rocky soil

Low to moderate water use

Plant in full sun

Thalictrum — Meadowrue

The airy meadowrues are excellent plants for the woodland garden or lightly shaded border. Leaves and plant structure resemble columbines. With graceful, wandlike stems and feathery bursts of flowers, they add a charming, make-believe quality to the garden. Plants look best when grown in groups of three or more. Even tall varieties do not need staking. Meadowrues make wonderful cut flowers. The cut foliage also brings an interesting accent to indoor arrangements.

Recommended Species—*T. aquilegifolium* grows to 3 feet high, has purple-lilac flowers. Look for 'Album', white flowers, 'Roseum', pink flowers, and 'Dwarf Purple', which grows to 2-1/2 feet high and as wide.
T. rochebrunianum 'Lavender Mist' grows 5 to 6 feet high. It bears deep lavender flowers with yellow stamens in July and August.
T. speciosissimum, dusty meadowrue, has fragrant yellow flowers in August on plants 4 to 6 feet high. Leaves are blue-gray.

Planting & Care—Sow seed in place in late summer or autumn. It's helpful to locate plants in a sheltered spot away from the wind. Space plants 1-1/2 to 2-1/2 feet apart in rich, deep, moisture-retentive soil. Divide in spring or fall. Protect fall-transplanted plants with a mulch over winter in cold regions.

Native to Asia and Europe

Perennial; blooms spring to early summer

Adapted to SCC, SCI, NCC, CACV

Grows 2-1/2 to 6 feet high, spreads 3 feet wide

Provide with moisture-retentive, loamy soil

Moderate water use

Plant in partial shade to full sun

Trichostema lanatum — Woolly Blue Curls

Native to coastal foothills from Santa Barbara south to San Diego

Perennial; blooms late spring into summer

Adapted to SCC, SCI, NCC, CACV

Grows 3 to 5 feet high, spreads 3 to 4 feet wide

Provide with well-draining soil

Moderate water use in fall, winter and spring; low water use during summer

Plant in full sun in all locations

There is a special open and graceful quality to woolly blue curls that is enhanced by its distinctive blue flowers on long curving stalks. In addition to the flowers that bloom from spring into early summer, the stalks are covered with soft, white, woollike hairs. The plant's full height with flowers and stems can reach 3 to 5 feet. Narrow, 1-1/2- to 2-inch leaves are green on top with white hairs on the undersides. The foliage is aromatic when brushed or bruised. Although native to Southern California's dry coastal foothills, its range includes inland valleys receiving moderating coastal influence. It is a fire-retardant plant useful for slope plantings in fire-prone areas.

Companion plants with similar moisture needs include germander, *Teucrium,* California brittle bush, *Encelia californica,* California fuchsia, *Zauschneria californica,* matilija poppy, *Romneya coulteri,* and yarrow, *Achillea millefolium.*

Planting & Care—Plants are difficult to start from seed, so it's best to plant from containers or root cuttings. Set out in fall or spring. Good soil drainage is important; slope plants are ideal. Provide with moderate amounts of water most of the year, but reduce summer watering while plants are dormant. As flowers complete their bloom cycle, cut back flower stems to encourage new growth for late summer and fall flowering. Keep plants attractive and in control with regular but selective pruning of soft wood.

Verbena — Verbena

Native to U.S. Southwest and South America

Perennial; blooms for a long period from spring to summer

Adapted to all regions of the arid West, where cold hardy (to 10F); best with summer heat

Grows to 1 foot high, spreads 2 to 3 feet wide

Provide with light, well-draining soil

Low to moderate water use

Plant in full sun; growth is rangy in shade

Verbena has a great tolerance to hot, sunny locations. Plants are vigorous and low-growing, making excellent ground covers. Plants are available in a range of flower colors. They are appropriate in natural garden designs, accepting low to moderate water.

Native to Arizona, *Verbena gooddingii* is widely adapted, thriving in west Texas, Utah, Nevada and California. It works well as a foreground cover at the base of low-growing shrubs, in narrow dividers, in mounded rock gardens and among boulders. It blends well with other perennials, and can control erosion on slopes. Plants grow 6 to 9 inches high and spread 2 to 3 feet wide. In mild climates, flowers appear throughout the year, up until the first good frost. The oval, deeply cut, textured leaves are also attractive.

V. 'Peaches and Cream' is an All-America Selection. Flowers are a unique apricot and cream.

V. peruviana grows rapidly to 2 to 3 feet wide and to 8 inches high. Flowers come in colors of red, pink, lavender and purple. It is cold-hardy to about 20F. Grown as an annual in cold areas.

V. tenuisecta, moss verbena, is native to South America. It has adapted well in the Southwest. It is a vigorous-growing perennial, its branches covered with clusters of lavender to purple flowers from early spring to fall. Becomes somewhat dormant in high heat and with temperatures below 28F. The finely divided, deep green leaves create a thick, ground-hugging mat to 1 foot high, spreading 2 to 3 feet wide.

Planting & Care—Plant from containers in fall or wait until spring when temperatures begin to warm. Important to locate in well-draining soil in full sun. Provide moderate to low water after established; over-watering can actually cause plants to flower less. Cut *V. tenuisecta* back severely in late winter for regrowth the following spring.

Above: *Verbena* species is one of the best perennials for hot, sunny locations. Here it combines with *Oenothera berlandieri,* Mexican evening primrose.

Far left: *Yucca* species are evergreen perennials that are especially dramatic placed at the bases of large boulders. Shown is *Yucca glauca,* soapweed yucca.

Left: *Zauschneria californica,* California fuchsia, is well adapted along the coast and desert regions of California and Arizona.

Veronica — Speedwell

Native to New Zealand

Perennial; blooms in summer

Adapted to SCC, SCI, NCC, CACV

Grows 1 to 2 feet high, spreads 18 inches wide

Provide with well-draining garden soil

Moderate water use

Plant in full sun along coast; partial shade in hot-summer regions

This large group of plants has much to offer the creative gardener. They are good choices for the border, rock garden or natural garden. All are easy-care plants that, once established, are tolerant of dry soils. Plants accept full sun but prefer afternoon or filtered shade in desert regions.

Speedwell is available in a large range of colors, including white, pink, blue, purple and even red. Low-growing forms create bushy, gray-green mounds of narrow leaves. Use them in the rock garden or for edging. Use taller types in the border. All have erect, vertical flower spikes that are long-lasting when cut early in the day.

Recommended Species—*V. alpina* 'Alba' is low growing, to 6 inches, with white flowers in early summer and intermittently thereafter.
V. incana, woolly speedwell, has woolly leaves and lilac flowers June to September. Plants grow to 6 inches high.
V. latifolia 'Crater Lake Blue' forms a dense, prostrate plant 6 to 12 inches tall, with 12-inch flower spikes of intense blue.
V. spicata 'Barcarolle' has flowers of rose-pink all summer long. 'Red Fox' has deep, red-rose flowers on 14-inch stems.

Planting & Care—Plants are available in containers at nurseries; plant in fall in hot-summer regions; in spring in other areas. Space plants 12 to 18 inches apart. Remove spent flowers to prolong bloom into fall. *V. alpina* can be sheared back after early summer bloom. Divide existing plants about every four years in spring or fall. Sow seed in spring or take stem cuttings in early summer; seed-grown plants are variable.

Watsonia — Watsonia

Native to South Africa

Perennial bulb; blooms late spring

Adapted to all regions of the arid West, but best in SCC, SCI, NCC, CACV, SCLD, AZLD

Grows 3 to 4 feet high, spreads 2 feet wide

Provide with well-draining soil

Moderate water use in fall, winter and spring; reduce summer watering to low

Plant in full sun ideal

Similar in appearance to gladiolas, watsonia is prolific in a number of ways. Flowers appear midway on flower stalks and bloom for over a month during late spring. Evergreen and deciduous forms are grown from corms, stemlike plant tissue that produces roots beneath and plant stems above.

Several of the best-known species include: *W. beatricis,* evergreen, with 3-inch-long, bright, apricot-red leaves on branched, 3-1/2-foot stems blooms during July and August.

W. pyramidata, a deciduous species, flowers in late spring into early summer with spikelike clusters on stems that reach 4 to 6 feet long. Rose-pink to rose-red leaves are gladiola-like, 2-1/2 feet long and 1 inch wide.

Watsonias provide great vertical color grouped among taller perennials such as *Heuchera* species, coral bells, and *Lobelia cardinalis.* Flowers are excellent for cutting for indoor use.

Planting & Care—Plant corms in early summer or fall. Established plants require moderate water during summer, low during the rest of the year. Fall and winter are prime growing periods. Plants prefer full sun and demand well-draining soil. Clean up spent foliage after bloom period. In mild climates, plants form clumps that can be left in place for years. If clumps do become crowded, lift and transplant clumps in summer after bloom and replant immediately. Keep new transplants moist through the summer.

Yucca — Adam's Needle, Spanish Bayonet

Yucca species are evergreen perennials that have the stature of small, spiny shrubs, adding a textural and architectural element to the landscape. They are low-maintenance plants, well adapted to dry climates of the West. They can be used effectively in place of shrubs or as foundation plants, accent plants or in clusters.

Plants form large rosettes of spiked, sword-like leaves that are medium green, variegated cream or yellow, bluish or gray-green. In summer, giant flower spikes rise to 5 feet high or more, opening into creamy, fragant flowers that are shaped like bells.

Recommended Species—*Y. angustifolia glauca*, soapweed, is the hardiest yucca. It grows to 3 feet and has slender gray leaves and greenish white flowers.
Y. baccata, broadleafed yucca, grows to 2 feet high. Flowers are reddish brown on the outside, white inside.
Y. filamentosa grows 2 to 5 feet high. Leaf edges have curly "strings" that have a subtle but pleasing effect. The variety 'Gold Sword' has leaves with green margins and yellow centers that are highly decorative.
Y. recurvifolia (also known as *Y. pendula*), produces soft and supple, gray-green leaves 2 to 3 feet long. Leaf tips are sharp but bend to the touch. Large white flower clusters are borne on stems 3 to 5 feet high during spring to early summer.
Y. rigida, blue yucca, grows at a moderate to fast rate to 12 feet high or more. Leaves to 3 feet long are powder blue with a yellow margin. Flowers are white and bloom in summer.

Planting & Care—Plant from containers in spring or in fall in mild-winter regions. Plant at the same depth as in the container; do not plant too deep. Space 4 to 6 feet apart in clumps. Plant in well-draining, infertile soil. Do not overwater. Propagate in spring by root division, offsets or seed. The easiest way to increase plantings is to remove infant plants (offsets).

Native to warm climates of U.S.

Perennial; blooms in summer

Adapted to all regions of the arid West

Mature size varies according to species. Refer to descriptions

Provide with light, well-draining soil

Low water use

Plant in full sun to partial shade

Zauschneria californica — California Fuchsia

This native subshrub is well adapted along the coast and in low-elevation deserts of California and Arizona. Plants remain evergreen in mild-winter climates where temperatures generally stay above 28F to 30F. Stems are somewhat arching with gray-green leaves and brilliant, scarlet, tubular-shaped flowers that are borne on terminal spikes. Flowers are highly attractive to hummingbirds. Ideal when used in a natural garden or wildlife habitat setting where its informal appearance and summer flowers add an understated elegance. Also suitable for slope plantings and revegetation projects.

California fuchsia seems to thrive in the most inhospitable habitats—in chaparral, on steep banks or disturbed slopes, even in sand dunes. Leaves of plants in low-elevation desert areas are often small and woolly compared with those at higher elevations or along the coast. Plants are well-suited for revegetation duty with companion plants such as four-wing salt bush, *Atriplex canescens*, and California brittle bush, *Encelia californica*.

Planting & Care—Set out plants from containers in the fall months. Mature plants reseed readily to extend plantings. In garden settings, space plants 4 to 6 feet apart due to their leggy growth habit. Pinching young growing shoots helps plants become more compact and manageable. Otherwise, maintenance is limited to an annual pruning in early spring. Drip irrigation is ideal watering method.

Native to California's coastal foothills

Perennial subshrub; blooms late summer and well into fall

Adapted to SCC, SCI, SCLD, NCC, CACV, AZLD, AZMHD, SNV

Grows 1 to 3 feet high, spreads 2 to 4 feet wide

Provide with most any kind of soil, from gravelly to clay

Low water use; decrease during summer in heavy soils

Plant in full sun

PLANTING AND CARE

The basics of planting and caring for flowering plants in the arid West are similar to those in temperate climates, but there are major differences. The variables that face each gardener such as soil type, wind, cold, heat and humidity are greater. These many factors affect how you approach garden care, particularly soil preparation and watering plants. This chapter includes the basics, but it will be your observations and experience in your own garden that are the ultimate guides to keeping your plants healthy.

Doing a little homework—selecting plants adapted to your region and providing the cultural conditions they need to thrive—prevents most problems from occurring. Adapted plants located in the right exposure and planted properly according to soil and water preferences are naturally healthier. This makes them look more attractive, and they become much more resistant to pests and diseases.

On a large scale, it helps to understand the natural progression.of the gardening seasons in your region, so you can time planting and maintenance in tune with them. Use a notebook or journal to record planting dates and methods, flowering periods, methods and times of weed control, times when plants were pruned, and so on. This will allow you to repeat your successes and avoid duplicating failures.

The vigor of native and adapted dry-climate plants is amazing. After they become established, they often thrive to such an extent that they even outgrow their normal height and spread. With a well-conceived natural garden design and proper plant selection, the result can be a rich tapestry of growth that requires less and less water and maintenance as each year passes.

A grouping of red and yellow *Papaver nudicaule*, Iceland poppy, puts on a springtime show. Seed was planted in this Phoenix garden in September to produce these flowers by mid-March.

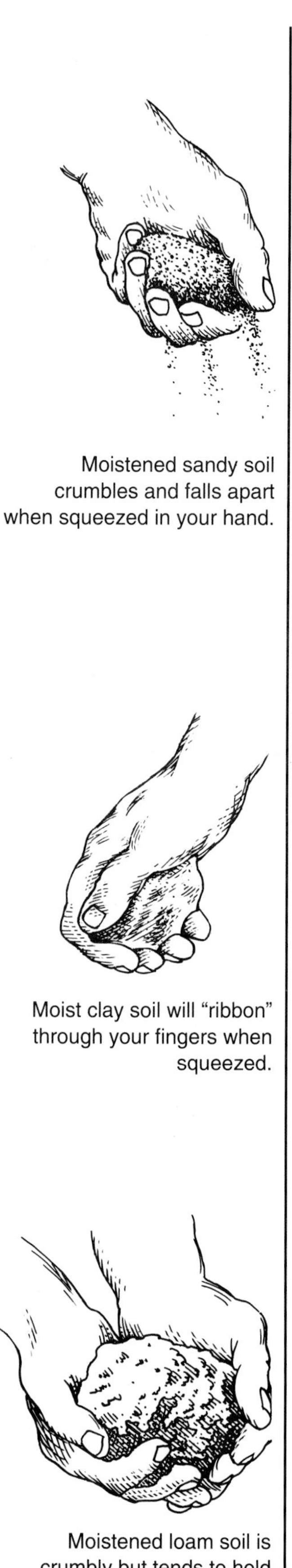

Moistened sandy soil crumbles and falls apart when squeezed in your hand.

Moist clay soil will "ribbon" through your fingers when squeezed.

Moistened loam soil is crumbly but tends to hold together in your hands.

Soils in the Arid West

One of the most-important aspects of growing flowering plants is providing them with the right soil. The question soon arises: should I improve the soil or leave it alone? Many plants native to arid regions do best in the natural, unimproved soil that exists on site. Other introduced plants (from non-arid regions of the world) or garden variety perennials prefer a highly organic soil. Unfortunately, many housing developments today are built on compacted soils that have been excavated and moved around, and are far from a natural state.

The majority of perennial plants stay in the same location year after year. If soil improvements are required, the time to do them is before planting. Coming back to the question of improving the soil, you have a choice whether to select plants to grow in the soil you have on site, or change the soil to suit the plants you want to grow. For example, if your soil is a slow-draining clay, the best choice might be selecting plants that will grow in these conditions, rather that trying to amend the soil.

If your soil is well-draining, you can grow the great majority of plants listed in this book. If in doubt, refer to the fact columns in the Galley of Flowering Plants on pages 36 to 127 to determine each plant's soil preference.

Soils in the West are also highly variable from one geographic region to the next, as well as from landscape to landscape on the same street. Most are low in organic matter. This is because natural vegetation is sparse in low-rainfall regions. Leaves, stems and other plant parts are not available in large quantities to decay and create organic material. The long periods of intense heat also cause organic matter to dissipate quickly. For many plants, especially those with shallow root systems, organic matter in the soil is beneficial, improving moisture and air retention in the root zone.

Soils in the arid West include heavy *clay soils,* such as those found in coastal California, or *sandy soils,* common to the desert regions of Southern California, Nevada, Arizona and New Mexico. Some regions are lucky to be blessed with *loam soils,* a balanced mixture of materials high in organic matter.

Sandy soils—These are composed of a high percentage of large particles and water drains through quickly. Moistened sandy soil will crumble and fall apart when squeezed in your hand. In desert regions the particulates that make up sandy soils cause them to blow easily in heavy winds. Nutrients, particularly nitrogen, are *leached*—washed down from plant roots—by this rapid drainage. Sandy soils absorb water at a rate of 2 inches or more per hour. They warm up more quickly in the spring compared to clay soils and are also the easiest to work with, allowing plant roots to develop freely.

Clay soils—Small, tightly compacted particles, heavy, dense and sticky when wet describe clay soils. If you squeeze moistened clay soil in your hand, it will "ribbon" through your fingers. Moisture moves through clay soils slowly. When you apply water, it tends to create puddles and pools rather quickly. Clay soils absorb water at a rate of less than 1/4 inch per hour. Do not dig or cultivate clay soil when it's wet or large clods will form when the soil dries. Clay soils can develop a crusting on the surface, which repels water. Roots grow slowly, and the considerable resistance makes it difficult for plants to develop a deep root zone.

Loam soils—These are ideal soils for plant growth. They are a balanced mixture of clay, sand and organic matter, and are generally well draining. Loam soil is crumbly or "friable" in your hand. Organic material in loam creates variable spaces among the soil particles, which help hold moisture and nutrients in the root zone longer to the benefit of plants. Loam soils absorb water at the rate of 1/4 inch to 2 inches per hour. They can crust over like clay soils, repelling water.

Granitized alluvial soils are less common, found at the bases of mountains and hills, and fanning out due to forces of water runoff. They are coarse, "young" soils, still in the process of breaking down from large particles to small ones. Alluvial soils drain well and roots penetrate if given plenty of moisture. When dry, they are difficult to work. These soils benefit from addition of organic matter to increase their moisture-holding capacity.

Problem Soils

Hardpan and *caliche* are serious problem soils in the West. Hardpan is generally found in heavy clay soil areas where the land has been farmed for long periods. Calcareous soils (caliche) are formed from mineral deposits that create cement-like layers—practically impenetrable if more than a few feet thick. The solution may be drastic—creating raised beds or drainage "chimneys" in planting holes with pickaxe, power auger or jackhammer. (See illustrations, opposite.) In fact, it's wise to check the depth and workability of the existing soil when shopping for a new home or property to avoid serious soil drainage problems.

Saline soils are also common on converted farmlands. Soils are salty due to years of irrigation to the same depth as well as regular use of salt-based fertilizers. Water supplied from the Colorado River is also high in salts. *Leaching out* saline soils by applying water slowly for several hours helps wash soil salts down and away from the plant's root zone. This is a common practice in many desert regions where soil salts are high.

Extremely rocky and boulder-strewn areas common in mountain areas may be intimidating from a preparation standpoint. Your choice may be to cultivate and amend soil between rocks and boulders to create a seedbed or planting bed. Some gardeners take advantage of boulders and use them in their landscape design. If you simply cannot till existing soil, an alternative is to truck in enough topsoil to build up a base about 12 inches deep for planting beds, or plant in containers.

Soil Nutrients

The most important nutrients for plant growth are nitrogen, phosphorus and potassium. If you purchase a packaged fertilizer, the ratios listed on the bag, such as 5-10-10, describe the percentages of nitrogen, phosphorus and potassium, respectively. Nitrogen is the nutrient that is usually lacking. Plants use a lot of nitrogen and it is leached out of the root zone, particularly in sandy soils. Phosphorus is often lacking in clay soils. It does not "move" in the soil, so it should be worked in before planting where it can be absorbed by the roots. Potassium is generally in good supply.

If your plants are not growing properly and you think it could be a nutrient problem, add compost or fertilizer. If things do not improve you can test your soil to find out what is out of balance. Most state cooperative extension services (California is an exception) perform soil testing. Private soil-testing labs will test your soil for a fee, or you can analyze your own soil with a test kit, available at nurseries or through mail-order catalogs.

A soil analysis will also measure the pH—the acidity-alkalinity—of the soil. The pH scale ranges from 3.5 (the most acid) to 9.5 (the most alkaline); 7 is neutral. Soils in the arid West tend to be more alkaline; soils in the East are more on the acid side of the scale. Most perennials prefer a soil that is near neutral.

Improving Soils

If you need to improve your soil, add organic matter. Well-aged animal manures, leaf mold, ground bark products and home-made compost are common amendments. Grape pomace compost, a by-product of commercial grape harvests, can be found in wine grape-growing regions. Shredded oat or alfalfa hay works well, particularly in sandy soils.

Enough material must be added to make a difference in the soil's texture. As a guide, about one-quarter of the soil in the planting bed should be organic matter. If you work a planting bed to a depth of about 6 inches, add a layer of organic matter about 2 inches deep over the area. Dig thoroughly into existing soil, blending it so there are no streaks or layers of material. Avoid an abrupt "begin and end" situation from improved soil to native soil. The soils should make a gradual transition from one to another so plant roots won't "stop" when the soil composition changes.

Organic matter mixed into sandy soils increases the nutrient- and water-

Provide drainage for individual plants through hardpan or caliche by making a "chimney" to well-draining soil below.

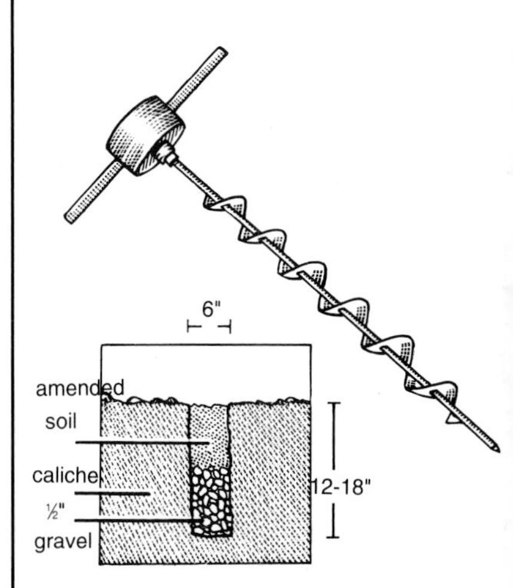

To provide drainage for a many plants in a planting bed, use a power auger or jackhammer to drill holes through hardpan or caliche.

Mix organic material into the top several inches of soil to improve drainage as well as the soil's ability to hold moisture and nutrients in the root zone.

A rototiller can save you time and energy when amending and preparing soil for a large planting area.

Maintain your compost pile at a height of about 3 to 5 feet. Alternate layers of materials for faster composting.

holding capacity. If your soil is sandy to the point of being a sand dune, it will blow around in high winds. Plant windbreaks or install a fence or wall to protect plants and to keep soil in place. Organic matter improves the drainage and workability of heavy clay soils.

As mentioned, not all plants require an improved soil. Some have natural adaptations that allow them to grow better in poor, sandy or rocky soils. Most plants adapted to arid regions do require good drainage, however. Before you prepare soil for planting, refer to the Gallery of Flowering Plants to learn each plant's soil preference.

Backyard Compost as Soil Amendment

Compost is decomposed organic matter high in nutrients. Fully decomposed compost looks much like rich, dark soil. A backyard compost pile serves a dual purpose. First, it recycles yard and kitchen waste that would only serve to speed the filling of public landfills. (In some communities, up to 20 percent of solid wastes are composed of leaves, trimmings and clippings.) Second, compost is a superior soil amendment or mulch for your plants.

If maintained properly, a compost pile will not cause odors or attract flies to bother you or your neighbors. Keep the pile neat with fencing or build a simple bin to contain it. Concrete blocks stacked together work well. Some gardeners make three bins: one to hold fresh, raw material, another for the composting process, and another for the finished product.

What You Can Compost—Leaves, grass clippings (allow them to dry before adding), weeds, trimmings, kitchen refuse such as fruit peelings, coffee grounds and vegetable leavings can all be used. To increase the volume and to add nitrogen to the pile, necessary for the decomposition process, add horse, goat, cow or chicken manure. Be aware that some manures add salts, particularly cattle and horse manure. If your soil tends to be saline, do not use them.

What You Shouldn't Compost—Avoid materials that compound the problems of western soils. These include salted foods and salt-laden plants such as tamarisk, as well as bones and eggshells—they add unwanted calcium. The same is true of wood and barbecue ashes; they tend to make soils more alkaline. Don't add foods cooked in oil or fat, or use meat scraps—they attract animal pests. Don't add poisonous plants such as oleander; eucalyptus leaves contain growth inhibitors. Bermudagrass and nutgrass can be be invasive. Also, don't use plants or lawn clippings sprayed with pesticides or herbicides.

The smaller the size of materials, the faster microorganisms can break them down. Avoid adding branches with a diameter larger than one inch. Use pruning shears or a machete to cut stalks and twigs into lengths of 6 inches or less. Better yet, shredding materials gives microorganisms more surface area to work on, accelerating the process.

Build your compost pile to at least 3 feet high. Don't go much over 5 feet high or the materials may compress and prevent oxygen from entering the pile—necessary for decomposition. If your compost pile produces a sour, ammonia odor, aerate the pile so it will receive more oxygen.

Alternate layers of materials, adding a 3- to 6-inch layer of fine-textured or finely chopped leaves or grass clippings, then another layer of coarse matter or animal manure. Maintain a ratio of approximately 20 to 1 (by weight) of green to dry (dead) mater-ial. Moisture is necessary for decomposition, so water each layer. Keep the pile moist but not wet. Cover the pile with a tarp or a thin layer of soil to help maintain moisture and reduce evaporation. Scattering a few handfuls of high-nitrogen fertilizer or cottonseed meal hastens the decomposition process.

A proper balance of ingredients and moisture will cause the pile to "cook," reaching temperatures in the pile's interior up to 160F. The pile will become noticeably smaller as the materials settle and decompose. After several weeks, move materials on the outside of the pile and mix them into the center for a more even decomposition. After three to four months (some materials can take longer), the compost should be ready to use. In addition to being a superior soil amendment, compost is an excellent mulch. Apply in layers over plant roots to cool the soil during summer, and reduce moisture loss through evaporation.

Weed Control

Advance planning to control weed growth is an important and an all-too-often-bypassed step in creating a flower garden. Eliminating or controlling weed growth creates a less competitive environment for seedlings and young container plants. Water and nutrients then benefit your flowers, not the weeds.

A simple preliminary plan of action will *prevent* weeds from taking over. If you can, prepare or treat planting areas (see following) several months prior to planting. Treat in late summer for fall planting and in late winter for spring planting. If weed seedheads are not removed, the cycle of heavy, annual weed growth continues. Remove weeds when you see them when they are young.

Major Weed Invasions—Follow this method of control if you've had serious problems with weeds in the past. It works on the principle that you rid the planting area of weeds by encouraging them to germinate and grow, then kill them all at once.

Using a shovel or rototiller, dig down about 6 to 8 inches, turning the soil over. Grade and level the soil, raking it smooth. Apply enough water so it will reach several inches deep. Now wait and watch the weeds grow. And grow. Continue light applications of water up to about 6 weeks, until weeds develop into young seedlings. (The rate of growth depends on warmth and day length.) Remove with a hoe or rake, or better yet, pull them, roots and all. Or till and water as above, then cover the proposed planting area with clear plastic, which "cooks" the weeds. Leave cover in place for several weeks, securing perimeter with rocks. The heat kills weeds and weed seeds near the soil surface.

Minor Weed Invasions—If your soil is generally free of weed seeds, follow this method. Do not rake or dig the soil, removing only weeds and debris in area to be planted. This of course does not allow you to improve the soil with amendments, as discussed on page 131. If you use this method, test your soil for good drainage beforehand.

Remove weeds as they appear, pulling by hand. The idea is to disturb the soil as little as possible. After the site has been cleared, you are ready to plant.

Planting

Perennials are available for purchase in containers at nurseries and occasionally bareroot (mostly from mail order companies). Many plants can be grown from seed; for some it is the best method. Bareroot plants are dormant. Their roots have no soil around them and plants are less likely to begin top growth before roots are established in soil. They are also less expensive, but the times they are available are often limited (winter months) because the dormant season in many regions of the arid West is short.

Container plants extend the planting season to practically year-round. In fact, most perennials are actively growing when they're purchased. You get a preview of what the plant and flower color will look like. Be aware many native and adapted low-water perennials look deceivingly scrawny in their containers. Don't judge their potential by a few stems and leaves of immature plants, but do be selective when purchasing plants. Avoid plants that are root-bound, with roots extending out the container bottom. Ideally, plants should have a robust, healthy appearance. As a rule, select a small plant with vigor rather than a large, less-robust specimen.

Fall is the preferred planting time in most regions of the arid West, with some exceptions. During fall the soil is still warm, promoting root growth, while air temperatures are moderate so new plants are not stressed by cold or heat. As fall progresses into winter and spring, the now-established roots are quick to respond to the warmer weather and produce healthy top growth. Even in mild-winter areas, gradually taper off irrigation frequency (but not amount applied) as winter approaches. This will *harden off* new tender growth so it will be less susceptible to damage from winter cold.

Spring is the second-best planting period. In hot-summer regions, plant as early in the season as possible so plants begin to establish before the heat comes on. In cold-winter regions, fall-planted plants will be susceptible to cold damage. Plant in spring after danger of frost has passed. In moderate coastal climates, planting can be done year-round, but more water is required

In most of the arid West, fall is for planting. Air temperatures are moderate and soil temperatures are warm, promoting root growth. Winter rains get plants off to a good start the following spring.

Minor weed infestations can be pulled by hand. The best time to do this is after a decent rain.

When using a garden hoe to remove weeds, disturb the soil as little as possible to reduce germination of weed seeds in the soil.

Planting from containers

Water plant a few hours or so before planting. Remove plant by turning upside down and gently tapping bottom of pot.

Dig a hole about twice as wide and as deep as the rootball. Plant should be situated at the same depth as it was in its container.

Fill soil around rootball and firm gently around roots. Water well. See the watering schedule for new plants, page 136.

to establish plants set out during late spring to summer due to the warmer temperatures.

If in doubt about the proper time to plant for your region, keep this simple rule in mind: Plant any time you can usually count on four weeks or more of mild weather. This will allow plants to be established before stress—in the form of either heat or cold—comes on.

Planting Step-by-Step

Plant on a cool, cloudy day. If you must plant on a sunny day, do it late in the afternoon. It is often a good idea to create your design (see pages 21 to 35) and dig planting holes *before* you purchase plants. This helps ensure that plants will be planted without delay: a gardener's eyes are often bigger than his planting shovel. In addition, preparing holes beforehand allows you to moisten soil deeply, providing a reservoir of moisture in the soil. Grade of planting beds should be located about 2 inches below surrounding paving or other hardscape.

Dig a hole twice as wide and as deep as the rootball. Make the hole with straight sides and loosen soil at bottom. Add water to the hole a day or two before planting. If the plant requires well-draining soil, test for drainage. Fill with water and allow to drain. Fill again. Water should drain in about three to four hours. If it hasn't, try another site, or create a drainage chimney. For mass plantings such as a flowerbed, a jackhammer or power auger can be used to create drainage channels. See the illustrations on page 131.

Remove plant gently from pot, loosening roots. If soil mass is rootbound, use a knife or pruning shears to slice the outside of the rootball and gently splay it open. Set in planting hole and add in soil around the rootball, gently pressing soil around roots. Water thoroughly to settle, and check planting depth. It should be the same as it was in its container. Build a soil basin to hold the water. Make it a few inches high and extend it just beyond the outer edge of the rootball. Be prepared to expand the basin as the plant grows.

Space plants far enough apart to allow them to develop to their mature size. See the Gallery of Flowering Plants listing for mature heights and widths. If you combine annuals with perennials, be aware that many annuals are vigorous growers, particularly spring to early summer. They can crowd and retard the growth of slower-developing perennials. Keep annuals at least 12 to 18 inches away from crowns of perennials.

If temperatures are warm, shade newly planted plants from the afternoon sun. Use evergreen branches, palm fronds, baskets or boards stuck in the soil. Keep soil moist around the rootballs of new plantings, gradually tapering off watering to follow a water-efficient irrigation program, such as described on page 136.

Planting Seed

When you're ready to sow seed directly in a small area, sow seed by hand. Because most seed is quite small, it's hard to tell where it is distributed. Mix one part seed with three parts of white sand, and you can see where the seed is applied. Water the soil surface to darken it before applying the seed-and-sand mixture. If you have qualms about seeding this way, practice with sand only in another area until you feel confident you are applying the seed evenly. Mechanical seed spreaders are handy if you are sowing seed over a large area. Certain fertilizer spreaders can also double as seed applicators. Follow the same steps for preparation as with the hand method. Rake into the soil, and cover with an organic mulch.

Water the seeded area directly after sowing with a sprinkler that emits a fine spray pattern. Avoid puddling to prevent erosion and washing of the soil, which will disturb the seeds. Germination periods for plants will vary greatly, from a few days to several weeks. Warm soil temperatures generally speed up germination.

Starting Seed Indoors—To grow certain plant species sometimes requires starting seeds indoors in a sunny window, setting out seedlings at the right season. This is not as common in hot regions of the West as in other parts of the country, due in part to our fall planting season. In addition, the great majority of plants in this book are available as plants in containers or pots at nurseries. If you decide to grow from seed, it is best to sow them in pots or trays filled with a packaged potting mix rather than soil from the garden. This prevents weed seeds from germinating with your perennial plants, and reduces the chances of damping-off disease from killing tiny seedlings.

Selecting Planting Sites

Picking a location for your perennial garden requires attention to two basic factors: Will the plants grow well in your chosen spot? And is the garden located where it's convenient to view its beauty, both indoors and out?

Most perennials require at least six hours of sun each day, but many plants also do well in shade. (The specific requirements for plants are provided in the Gallery of Flowering Plants, pages 36 to 127.) However, sunlight is highly variable, depending on your climate and the time of day plants are exposed to the sun. Morning sun (eastern exposure) is much less intense than afternoon sun (southern or western exposure). In addition, six hours of sunlight is not nearly as intense in a cool coastal region as in the sunny desert. Garden plants in Phoenix, Arizona, for example, are almost always appreciative of afternoon shade, or the shade supplied by a canopy tree.

The many small climates around your garden, *microclimates,* are planting opportunities. For example, if sunshine is lacking, a warm south wall, particularly if it's light in color, reflects heat. Paving also absorbs heat and radiates it at night to increase temperatures. An overabundance of heat can be tempered by planting shade in the form of trees or structures such as lath panels. For more information on microclimates, see pages 7 and 8.

Nearby trees and shrubs provide mixed blessings. They can produce desirable shade, turning a too-hot western exposure into a tolerable planting area. Then again, roots of many trees and shrubs invade your planting beds, stealing water and nutrients from your flowering plants. Be prepared to do battle, or compensate with additional moisture.

To determine if the area is sunny enough for the plants you want to grow, note how much sun falls on a proposed planting site during the growing season. After you've eliminated locations that are not suitable, select a spot that offers you, your family and visitors the best views.

Watering

The most important watering period for plants begins after planting. Newly planted perennials, even if they are low-water natives, require moist soil. Any prolonged dry period will prevent roots from developing deeply and uniformly, and plant growth and performance can be permanently affected. Even native plants that typically do not need regular water during summer should receive regular applications during this season to develop healthy and deep root systems.

Schedule daily irrigations for newly planted areas. If the weather is cloudy, skip a day or two. If it is windy, the upper 1 to 2 inches of soil or mulch can dry out very quickly. Apply water slowly in a basin around the plant's rootball. Do not sprinkle the soil, especially if it's windy. This wastes the water, increases evaporation and does not apply it evenly. Continue to monitor soil moisture by checking the soil regularly for several weeks. If plants are in a planting bed, inexpensive soaker hoses work well in saturating the soil around plant roots. Cover the hose with mulch to conceal it if the bright green color is bothersome.

The amount of water applied depends on soil type, exposure and prevailing weather. Daily waterings of new plants may last only a week or two along the coast, yet could be required for several weeks in hot, inland valley and desert areas.

If plants are located on slopes, water in intervals. This helps prevent soil erosion. Do this by watering for a determined period, such as 5 minutes, allowing water to soak into soil. Repeat later with another watering, and so on, until moisture has soaked deeply into the soil.

After plants adjust to planting and show growth, gradually space out waterings, perhaps to two or three applications per week. After young plants reach the ready-to-flower stage, provide deep-penetrating irrigation about once every week or so. Again, irrigations will be fewer along coastal areas and more frequent in the hot deserts and inland valleys. If heat increases to 85F or more, or if winds are excessive, check each day for moisture in the top several inches of soil and water if soil is dry.

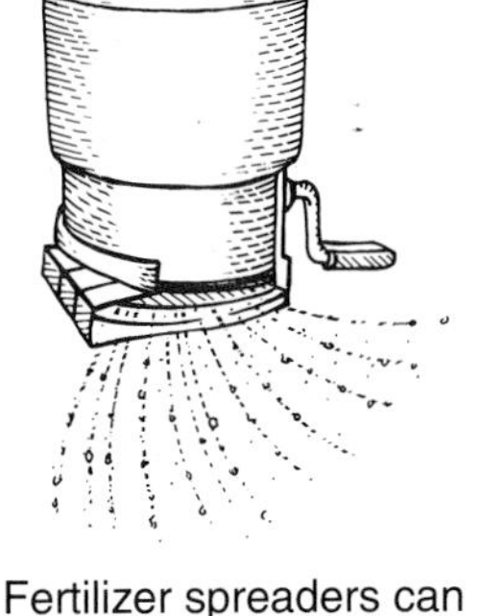

Fertilizer spreaders can double as seed spreaders when sowing seed over large areas.

After sowing, double-rake seed to help ensure good contact with the soil.

One method of starting seed indoors: Plant in pots in sterile soil mix. Water thoroughly and cover pots with plastic. The plastic will keep the soil moist. After seeds germinate, remove plastic.

Newly planted plants require regular water for several weeks after planting. In hottest regions, you may have to water once or twice a day, even more often when windy.

Use a shovel or trowel to dig down into the soil to see how deep the moisture is reaching. The top few inches of soil surface should be kept moist, but do not allow it to stay wet at any time. Most plants prefer the soil to dry out partially between waterings, which allows beneficial oxygen to reach plant roots. Windy conditions with high temperatures may mean you'll have to water once or even twice per day.

Developing an Efficient Irrigation Program

After plants are established, which usually means living through a complete summer season, you can begin a program of watering efficiently. Knowing the exact amount of water the many kinds of plants in your landscape require is difficult. Zoning plants by water requirements, called **hydrozoning,** groups plants with similar moisture requirements: high, moderate and low. This helps avoid overwatering or underwatering plants within the same area of the landscape. Zoning plants is necessary in designing and operating a drip irrigation system properly.

To develop your program, understand an important distinction between *duration* and *frequency.* Controlling the duration, how long each irrigation lasts, is important, because a long, slow irrigation allows water to soak the entire root zone. Frequency, how often you water, varies according to age of the plant, exposure, time of year, the extent of the root zone and soil type. The more shallow the root system, (as with new plants) the more frequent the irrigation. The rule, then, is to gradually *reduce* the frequency and *increase* the duration of irrigations. This will develop deep root systems, whether with new plants or to wean mature plants from a high-water diet.

It helps to know when your plants show the first signs of stress so you can quickly adjust watering schedules to prevent loss of growth, injury or even death. Here are some key points to help you water plants efficiently:

Know Your Soil Type—Soil type affects how deeply water goes into the soil, how quickly it gets into the root zone and how long it remains there. Most plants, but particularly those native to arid climates, require good soil drainage. Generally speaking, 1 inch of rain or irrigation in a sandy soil will go about 12 inches deep. For water to reach 3 feet deep, you'll need to apply water slowly for about 1-1/2 hours without runoff. Clay soils are dense and compact; 1 inch of water penetrates to only 4 or 5 inches. For water to reach 3 feet, for example, you'll need to irrigate slowly for about 4 hours. Loam soils, depending on the organic matter content, fall somewhere between these two extremes.

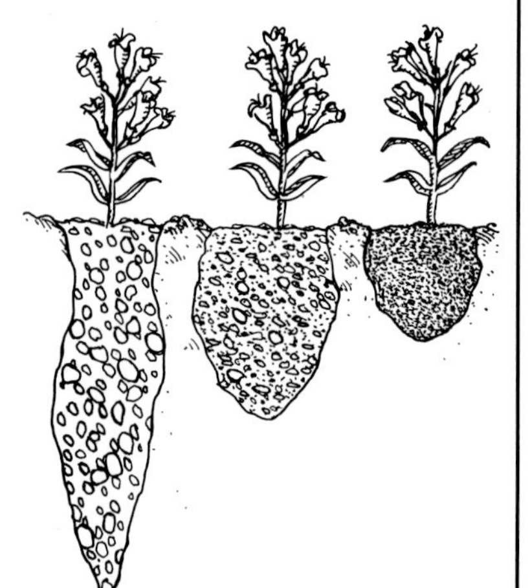

Soil type greatly affects the depth of water penetration. By comparison, from left: sandy soil, loam soil, clay soil.

Check for Soil Moisture—The depth of water penetration in your soil will help guide your watering schedule. Dig down after an irrigation to see how far moisture has penetrated. Or push a long, steel rod or screwdriver into irrigated soil. The rod stops penetrating when it reaches dry soil. A tool called a *soil sampler* will pull a narrow core of soil from the ground, showing the depth that moisture has penetrated. Doing this lets you see that the soil is dry and plants will soon need water—*before* they become water-stressed.

Know When Plants Show Signs of Water Need—Plants show when they need water by a change in leaf color from shiny to dull. Bright green leaves turn to blue or gray-green. Leaf tips turn brown. Drastic signs are when new plant growth wilts or droops, leaves curl and flowers fade quickly and drop prematurely. Older leaves turn brown and dry and fall off.

Encourage Deep-Rooting with Deep Watering—The depth to water depends on the plant. Roots of flowers such as annuals and some perennials reach 1 to 1-1/2 feet; small shrubs down to 3 feet. Trees reach to 5 feet or much more, depending on the species. Plant roots that go deep in the soil are better insulated against heat and cold, are anchored better against winds and have a greater reservoir from which to draw water when it is not provided on a regular basis. Shallow-rooted plants have none of these advantages. The upper soil layers dry out most quickly, and the first strong wind can knock plants over. Deep watering also washes damaging soil salts down and away from plant roots.

Put Water Where It's Needed—As plants grow, their roots grow and extend mostly out and down. The roots that absorb water—the feeder roots—tend to be concentrated at the outside edges of the plant's drip line—the area where rainwater drips off leaves to the ground. Extend a shallow watering basin almost to the trunk and to just beyond this imaginary line (just beyond the plant's canopy). This helps ensure plant roots are getting the most benefit from the moisture you're supplying.

Water When Evaporation Rates Are Low—Wind movement across plants not only disperses water elsewhere, it increases transpiration by moving water vapor away from the leaf surface rapidly. Low humidity also increases transpiration. In tandem with windy weather, water loss can be extensive. High heat such as that at midday during summer increases loss due to evaporation. Water during the cool times of day—evening or early morning—when there is little or no wind. During periods of hot, dry winds, construct temporary windbreaks around valuable plants to reduce moisture loss through transpiration.

Install Drip Irrigation—A drip irrigation system offers many benefits: Water is applied to the root zone of plants. Surrounding soil, walkways, and hardscapes such as patio surfaces do not receive your valuable water. Water is applied at the soil surface, so the wind is not able to blow the water away from plants. Drip avoids overwatering and water loss due to wasteful runoff, which often occurs with traditional sprinkler systems. Evaporation through sun and heat is lessened—much less than with hose-end sprinklers or hand-held waterings.

Drip saves time: no more evenings or mornings spent watering plant after plant, hoping you're supplying the right amount of water. (Chances are

Shallow watering, sprinkling the soil, helps produce shallow roots, causing plants to dry out quickly and suffer from stress.

Drip Irrigation

Drip irrigation is a system of watering where moisture is applied slowly and frequently to a small, confined area at the plant's root zone. It is a valuable tool in the arid West. When installed and used properly, drip irrigation can save 70 percent or more of your outdoor water use.

Many components and design options should be considered when developing your system. The basic components that you'll need include:

Controller—This is a timer that turns the system on and off for predetermined periods of time. Automatic, multi-programmable systems offer the most flexibility.

Valve—Often combined with a backflow preventer, automatic valves are designed to operate on low water pressure and volume. Some can operate as low as 6 gallons per hour, (gph). Those rated at 30 gph are best for most systems.

Filter—Sediment in the water can clog tiny emitters at the business end of the system. Filters with 150- to 200-mesh screen are recommended.

Pressure regulator—This prevents high water pressure from your hose bib from overloading and blowing up your drip lines.

Tubing—Professional landscapers prefer to use rigid PVC pipe installed underground. Flexible poly tubing, sold in 1/2-inch or 3/8-inch diameters, is easier to use but is also easy to damage. Some installers compromise and use PVC for main lines and run poly tubling from these.

Microtubing and emitters—Small, 1/4-inch-diameter tubing can be inserted into poly tubing to serve as distribution lines for a variety of mini-sprayers. Emitters can also be fitted into the poly line directly. For best results, use compression fittings.

To create a drip irrigation system, make a scale drawing of your planting plan, noting position of plants, their age and water requirements, and root depth. Include hardscape features such as sidewalks, patio paving and the like. Note the prevalent soil type and changes in elevation. Call your water company and find out your water pressure. The more details you include, the easier it will be to design an efficient system the first time around. Professional irrigation designers are also available to design a system for you for a fee.

With scale drawing and information in hand, visit an irrigation supply house. They will provide quality components and expert advice to help you install a long-lasting system.

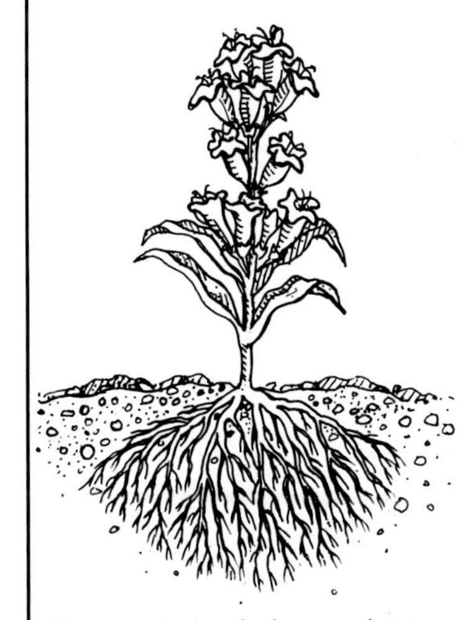

Deep watering helps produce deep roots. Plants have a greater reservior of moisture to draw upon, and the fragile root system is better insulated from hot or cold temperatures near the soil surface.

Mulch, at left side of plant, modifies soil temperatures. Temperature extremes are greater in upper layer of soil.

"Deadheading" blooms that are past their prime encourages plants to produce more flowers, and keeps them looking neat.

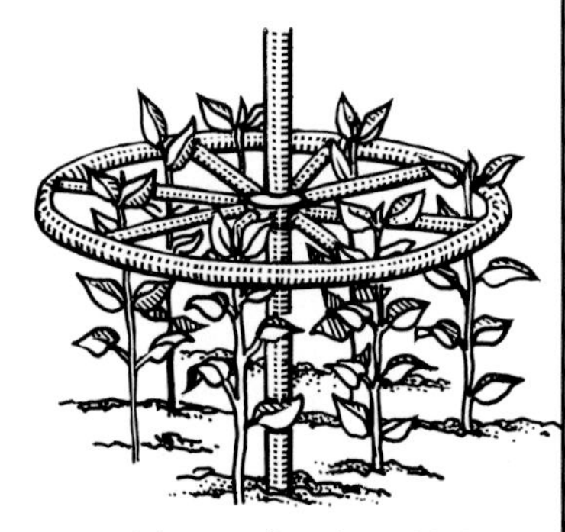

A large wire ring with inner compartments held horizontally on wire legs helps support clump-forming plants that tend to flop or splay out.

you're not.) It's as simple as turning on a spigot for a period of time, or if you have a timer (which is recommended), plants are watered automatically. Plants receive the right amount of water so they grow faster and are healthier. (It's also possible to slow plant growth after they're established by proper scheduling of water.) Water goes deep into the root zone of plants on a regular basis. Plants are not stressed due to dry soil and are given near-optimum amounts of water to grow to their potential. A drip system can be adjusted to suit the needs of your outdoor plants. By changing the emitter or gallonage of emitters delivering water to the many kinds of plants, you can regulate the water flow. For example, plants in containers must be watered much more frequently than established plants in the ground.

Practice Water Conservation—Check outdoor spigots for leaks, and don't water when it rains or during heavy winds. Turn off automatic sprinkers and irrigation systems if rain is forecast. Use a rain gauge to see how much rain has fallen on your landscape. When watering from a hose, use a watering nozzle with a shutoff valve. These spring-loaded devices allow you to shut off the water flow when you want—conserving water. Utilize rainwater runoff from the roof or gutters. Channel runoff to plants, or locate them near downspouts. Add a watering basin to catch the runoff, and plants will receive a good soaking with each substantial rain.

Fertilizing Plants

Some plants, particularly those native to dry regions of the world, do not require fertilizer to stay healthy. They actually grow better without it, especially fast-acting chemical or liquid fertilizers. These encourage rapid, excessive, soft growth that is more susceptible to disease and insect attack. However, sandy soils and other soils low in organic matter tend to need additional nitrogen due to their poorer nutrient content.

Slow-release fertilizers, in tablets, pellets or granular form, placed in the soil at the time of planting, are beneficial and recommended for most plants. They release nutrients slowly, stimulating the establishment of roots and new growth. These are effective when used in conjunction with drip irrigation, and to feed plants in containers. Some plants do not perform well with fertilizers. If in doubt, use one-fourth or less of the recommended application, and watch how plants respond.

Cold-hardy garden perennials can be fed twice a year—early in spring just prior to new growth and again in early summer. Water fertilizer in immediately after applying, and wash it off leaves. Applying compost as a mulch and digging it into the soil around plants will also supply some nutrients to plants. Organic fertilizers such as cottonseed meal or composted manure or slow-release fertilizers are less likely to overfertilize or burn plants. Additionally, animal manures as fertilizer also decompose to benefit the soil.

Mulching

Covering the bare ground around plants with a layer of material—usually organic—has many advantages. A 2- to 3-inch layer of mulch helps controls weeds that compete for moisture and nutrients. It also slows evaporation of soil moisture, moderates soil temperatures, spruces up the look of things and adds organic matter to the soil as it decays. Leaf mold, shredded leaves, straw, compost, pine needles, grass clippings and ground bark are common organic mulches. The region where you live will determine which materials are generally available.

Inorganic mulches such as rock, pea gravel and decomposed granite also conserve moisture and reduce weeds, but do not break down to improve the soil. They are often used as a ground covering around flowering perennials in place of lawn or living ground cover.

In mild-winter areas, apply mulch after temperatures warm in spring. This allows the soil to warm, which encourages plant growth. Apply a mulch *before* heat gets too intense to reduce moisture loss through evaporation and to modify the soil temperature around the root zone. Some growers recommend mulching a new planting bed before plants are planted to keep the mulching material out of the crown and leaves of new plants. If you try this, be sure plants are set at proper depth.

In extremely cold areas, a mulch can protect plant roots. Apply mulch to soil *after* it becomes frozen, so it will remain that way until the spring thaw. This way the soil does not alternate between freezing and thawing, which can literally "heave" plants from the soil, exposing their roots and killing them.

Pruning, Grooming and Staking

Many perennials and subshrubs benefit from being cut back after bloom. This induces plants to bloom again later in the season, or causes them to produce new vigorous growth for more flowers the following season. Use pruning shears to make cuts close to the remaining branch or stem. Make major cuts first to maintain the desired structure and form of the plant.

Some winter-dormant perennials and subshrubs such as *Rudbeckia, Helianthus* and many ornamental grasses can be pruned back close to the plant's basal growth late in fall or early winter. New growth will emerge the following spring. If plants are damaged by frost, wait until the following spring and remove dead wood after new growth begins.

If your goal is a natural garden appearance, avoid shearing plants. Rather, selectively thin excess interior growth and wayward branches. This way you can maintain the plant's natural form and still control its growth. Do not prune basal growth so the plant has a bare trunk. Allow branches to drape and trail to the ground. To reduce a plant's height, cut vertical growth down to and flush with a laterally growing stem or branch. To reduce a plant's width, cut side growth and lateral branches to upright-growing stems.

Certain species develop woody growth at the center of the plant, which greatly reduces flowers and fresh, healthy growth. Maintain a schedule of cutting plants back by one-third or more every year or two before the heavy wood has a chance to develop. *Rosmarinus, Santolina* and *Lavandula* are susceptible.

"Deadheading," removing flowers that are well past their prime, is an ongoing process during the blooming season for many flowering plants. It keeps plants looking their best, and the energy goes into more flower production that would otherwise be used to produce seed. Flowers with long stems should have the stems removed as well to maintain the plant's appearance. Plants that produce flower spikes, such as *Penstemon* and *Salvia,* should be cut back to the first set of leaves. This often causes the plant to produce a new wave of flowers where the leaves meet the stem.

Staking—Some perennials cannot stand up to wind and rain on their own and will sprawl over the planting bed. Providing stakes or other supports keeps plants upright, in control and looking attractive. The type of support used depends on the plant. Staking must be done early, before the plant shows signs of needing support, or the stalk or clump will be damaged by the next strong wind or rain. Staking early allows the plant to grow around the support and mask it with leaves. The underpinning should not be visible. The illustrations on page 138 and above right show some common methods of staking plants for beauty and protection.

Common Pests and Controls

Strong-growing, clean plants growing in well-draining soil seldom have serious problems with diseases or insects. In addition, a natural design or mixed border rarely suffers from pests or diseases due to the diversity of plant species. However, when plants are overfed or stressed by heat or drought, they become more susceptible to problems.

Insects—Typical insect pests include aphids, spider mites, slugs, snails, blister beetles, caterpillars and leaf miners. Using a photographer's handheld magnifying lens (10 to 14 power) is one way to inspect plants for pests, as well as diseases. As a guide, inspect plants every week, looking closely at undersides of leaves.

Pests such as aphids and spider mites can be largely controlled by hosing them off with a strong stream of water. Some gardeners spray them with a dilute solution of dish soap, 1/4 cup to 1 gallon of water. Caterpillars and beetles can be removed by hand. Serious infestations of caterpillars and other larvae can be controlled by using Bacillus thuringiensis (Bt). This is a bio-

For tall, columnar plants, support with one stake and tie stalks in two or three places. Use soft cloth, soft twine or twist-tie.

Whiteflies are tiny, mothlike insects that fly up in swarms when disturbed. Actual size is 1/16 inch.

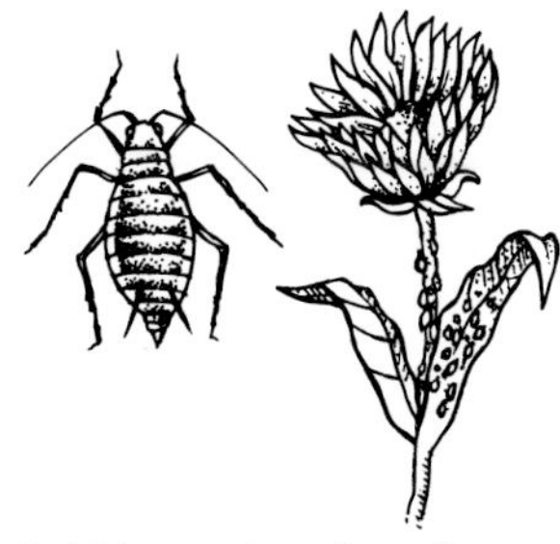

Aphids can be winged or wingless, as shown. They're found most frequently on new growth. Actual size is 1/16 inch.

Dividing Plants

Iris are propagated by their *rhizomes*— fleshy underground stems. Each new plant should have a fan of leaves and rhizome (roots). Set the rhizome underground, the fan of leaves above ground.

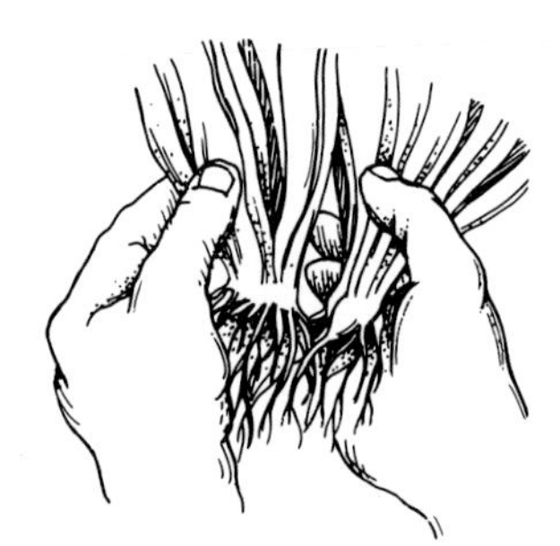

Most small plants can divided by pulling clumps apart. Replant the sections as new plants where needed.

Some plants form more solid root masses, but they can be pried apart. Here two garden forks are used back-to-back.

logical control that introduces a disease into the insect. Saucers of beer sunk flush with the ground level attract snails and slugs, which fall in and drown. Sprinkling diatomaceous earth on the soil surface also helps control them.

One of the benefits of a natural garden design is that it attracts birds, lizards and predatory insects such as ladybugs and praying mantids that will help control harmful insects. See page 29 for information on creating a wildlife garden.

Animal pests—Rabbits, gophers, ground squirrels, moles and deer may find your perennial plants a nice addition to their diets. Sturdy fencing will help keep the smaller critters from eating your plants.

Propagating Plants

Perennials can be propagated by several methods, including division, seed, stem or root cuttings and offsets. Some ways work better for specific plants, and many perennials can be increased by more than one method.

Division

This is a good way to increase many perennials, and, in fact, some plants should be divided to grow best. It is important to divide at the proper time. As a rule, divide spring-flowering plants in fall or directly after flowering. Divide fall-flowering plants in spring (early spring in mild winter and desert regions). The goal is to have several weeks of mild temperatures following the division to allow young plants to become reestablished.

Unless you have lots of ground to fill, don't keep every division. Replant pieces with strong roots and fat healthy growth points or stems. Some perennials get woody or die out in the center. When dividing these, replant only the vigorous outer pieces. Set new divisions at the same level they were growing at before. Water well, following basic guidelines for planting as discussed on page 133.

Seed

See page 134 for information on how to plant seed. If you collect seeds from your own plants, store them in a jar of dry sand, with a tight-fitting lid, and keep in the refrigerator. This will help keep seed fresh for better and quicker germination. Refrigerating seed is also a method of *stratifying* them. Doing this overcomes their natural dormancy, and gets them ready for germination.

With a few exceptions, seed collected from cultivated varieties, termed *cultivars,* seldom grow up to become as attractive and healthy as the donor plants from your garden. (Cultivars are designated in this book by being enclosed in single quote marks.) These cultivated varieties are hybrids of two species or special forms of a species, and have a mixed heritage, which usually results in inferior plants. However, seed grown from a species will grow true from seed, and look and perform the same as the parent plant.

Collecting Seed in the Wild—As a rule, don't do it. Many plants are now endangered due to loss of habitat, and collecting seed places even more pressure on the species to survive. To be sure you're not harming an endangered plant, purchase seed from a reputable dealer.

Cuttings

Some perennials can be propagated from pieces taken from stems or roots called *cuttings.* Take cuttings of stems from spring-flowering plants in midsummer. Plants that flower later in the year can have cuttings taken before flowering. Root cuttings are best taken in the fall when the parent plant is dormant. If done at other times, dig away some soil and take the cutting without lifting the plant. Cuttings taken in spring can be planted out in early fall. Later cuttings should be wintered over in a protected spot before planting out in the open the following spring.

Offsets

Perennials with bulbous root systems and the rhizomes of iris can be increased by separating offsets, which are immature bulbs or rhizomes. Plants are lifted from the ground, and small offsets are removed. They can then be planted at the appropriate time the same as new plants.

Irises are propagated by dividing rhizomes. After the bloom period has passed, dig up plants. If the rhizomes are massed, as shown in the illustration above left, divide the rhizomes so that each piece has both a fan of leaves and roots.

For More Information

Beautiful Gardens: A Guide to over 80 Botanical Gardens, Arboretums and More in Southern California and the Southwest Eric A. Johnson and Scott Millard
Ironwood Press, Tucson, AZ

Climate and Man
1941 Yearbook of Agriculture
U.S. Department of Agriculture

Complete Garden Guide to the Native Perennials of California
Glenn Keator
Chronicle Books, San Francisco, CA

Gardening in Dry Climates
Scott Millard
Ortho Books, San Ramon, CA

How to Grow the Wildflowers
Eric A. Johnson and Scott Millard
Ironwood Press, Tucson, AZ

Native Texas Plants
Sally Wasowski and Andy Wasowski
Gulf Publishing, Houston, TX

National Arboretum Book of Outstanding Garden Plants
Jacqueline Heriteau
Simon and Schuster, New York, NY

The Perennial Gardener
Fredrick McGourty
Houghton Mifflin Company, Boston, MA

Perennnials: How to Select, Grow & Enjoy
Pamela Harper & Frederick McGourty
Price Stern Sloan, Los Angeles , CA

Plants for Dry Climates
Mary Rose Duffield and Warren D. Jones
Price Stern Sloan, Los Angeles, CA

Southwestern Landscaping with Native Plants
Judith Phillips
Museum of New Mexico Press, Santa Fe, NM

Sunset Western Garden Book
Sunset Publishing, Menlo Park, CA

Taylor's Guide to Water-Saving Gardening
Houghton Mifflin Company, Boston, MA

Taylor's Guide to Gardening in the Southwest
Houghton Mifflin Company, Boston, MA

Trees and Shrubs for Dry California Landscapes
Bob Perry
Land Design Publishing, San Dimas, CA

Water-Conserving Plants & Landscapes for the Bay Area
Barrie Coate/East Bay Municipal Utility District
Alamo, CA

The Xeriscape Flower Gardener
Jim Knopf
Johnson Books, Boulder, CO

Index

entertaining vegetarians

celia brooks brown

entertaining vegetarians

photography by Jan Baldwin

whitecap

contents

foreword

"A vegetarian is not a person who lives on vegetables, any more than a Catholic is a person who lives on cats."—George Bernard Shaw

There are all sorts of reasons for giving up or cutting down on meat. For me, meat is something that has just never been appealing. I was nineteen when I moved to Britain from the U.S. in 1989, and back then I ate chicken occasionally, but I'd never eaten much other meat. I was no gourmet—I lived on canned soup, salads, and fast food. Boiling water and opening cans was the extent of my culinary skills. Not long after I arrived, there was a food scare in Britain. It put me off chicken, and I gave up meat for good.

Soon after giving up meat, I started to develop an interest in cooking. This is no coincidence. I knew I couldn't live on cans of beans and lumps of fatty cheese. As my mental perception of food became more acute—I started to see food as something other than just fuel—my sensory perception improved too. I was desperate to learn how to cook, so I could explore the creative process of using ingredients, tools, and all five senses to make something delicious. The greatest satisfaction of all, I found, was giving other people pleasure through eating what I prepared. I soon discovered that food that is cooked with passion evokes passion in the person eating it.

The whole realm of food is a healthy obsession for me, and it's not limited to cooking. So much of the fun and fascination lies in shopping for fresh, high-quality ingredients in specialty food stores. It also includes poring through books about food and filling my head with recipes, folklore, and culinary and social history. I'm also rather partial to stuffing my face.

My passion became a career in vegetarian cooking through catering, teaching, and writing. I'm certainly no vegetarian "evangelist." I merely hope to show people how easy and fun it can be to cook, and meat is simply not part of my repertoire. You must have what I call a "sensory relationship" with what you cook. If you can't engage every sense with your ingredients, what you cook just won't taste right. Even if I were to go through the mechanics of cooking a piece of meat, it would probably taste horrible.

My approach, in a nutshell, is this: Vegetarian cooking is more complex than simply throwing something under the broiler. It requires more thought, more construction. If you're not used to vegetarian cooking, try to think beyond the "meat and two vegetables" convention, in which vegetables play second fiddle. Try to create a balance of textures, colors, and flavors, and no one will notice the absence of meat.

Finally, when I tell people I'm vegetarian, the question that often follows is, "Do you eat fish?" OK, so vegetarians who eat fish are not technically vegetarians, but since when has the enjoyment of food been a technical business? I don't see it as hypocrisy to eat a bit of fish. People should be allowed to make their own decisions about what they put in their bodies and why. (That includes meat-eaters.) This modern breed of "pescetarians" are not rare, so I've included some fish recipes here for them, having done my best to recommend fish that is as eco-friendly as possible. This book is for every food lover, vegetarian or not. I hope you savor every page.

Celia Brooks Brown

how to use this book

—These days, what you decide to cook is as much determined by the event—a casual brunch party or perhaps a swanky cocktail dinner—as the time of year. So, I've grouped the recipes by the occasions they lend themselves to. At the beginning of each chapter is some advice and a few organizational tips, while in the middle I have suggested a menu for the occasion and given advice on planning, presentation, and drinks. All the recipes are designed for you to create a menu for everyone to enjoy, not just vegetarians, and I hope that some of the dishes will become part of your daily repertoire as well.

plan ahead—the golden rules of entertaining

Rule 1

A strong menu is the foundation of success:

Design a menu that's convenient to prepare in the time available.
Stick to seasonal ingredients.
Balance the color, flavor, and texture of every part of the meal.
Determine your budget—you can be generous without spending a fortune.
Think outside the appetizer-main-dessert box. Consider serving several small courses, or canapés followed by an extraordinary main course.
Consider the weather and how it affects what you want to eat—for example, cold soup on a hot day is magic.
Provide a little something to eat with alcoholic drinks, even if it's as simple as a bowl of nuts or olives.

Rule 2

Make life easy for yourself wherever possible:

Consider renting plates, cutlery, or even tables and chairs. Rental companies might even let you send everything back dirty for a small charge.
Consider your entertaining space—people inevitably gravitate to the kitchen at parties, but try to let the party actually happen well away from the working space.
Clean out your refrigerator—you can never have too much fridge space. Borrow space in your neighbor's fridge—as long as you invite them to the party! For a big event, rent a refrigerator.
Get your shopping out of the way the day before you start cooking.

Rope in as much human help as possible. Appoint or hire one helper for every ten guests.

If you've got lots of kids coming, provide a different menu for them, but don't knock yourself out cooking for them! Provide them with the stuff they'll like: chips, pizza, and sweets in individual packages as well as some of the simpler grown-up food.

If you are heating or cooking kids' food, don't forget to factor that in to oven and fridge space.

Rule 3

Remember the mundane but crucial details:

Get a big trash can ready. Buy plenty of garbage bags.

More and more people seem to have food intolerances these days. It is their responsibility to tell you ahead of time if they have special requirements. If they tell you once they've arrived and there's nothing for them to eat, don't feel bad—let them raid the kitchen.

Don't forget paper napkins—little ones for canapés, large ones for everything else, and at least two per person.

If it's cold outside, have a place where people can put their coats.

bar basics

If you're the cook, appoint someone else to be in charge of the bar.

Rough quantities of wine: Allow half a bottle of white wine and half a bottle of red wine per person. If you are serving champagne all night, allow three-fourths of a bottle per person.

If you can buy it "sale or return" from your wine merchant, opt for more.

Open nonsparkling wine and replace the corks before people arrive.

Save wine boxes for empty bottles. Recycle.

Consider renting glasses. Many liquor stores offer free glass rental, provided that you send them back clean. Some will inevitably break. For a big party, rent twice as many wineglasses as guests. People have one drink, put their glass down, then when they're ready for another, they forget where they put it or it's been cleared away, so they'll be needing another.

Provide tumblers as well as wineglasses for nonalcoholic drinks and cocktails.

Get one pillow-size bag of ice (about 25 lb. for every ten people).

Call an ice company that will deliver. Start chilling drinks at least two hours before the party.

Drinks chill faster in an ice bath (ice plus water) than on ice alone or in the fridge.

Don't clog your fridge with alcohol. Fill your bathtub with ice and water instead.

Provide lots of sparkling and plain mineral water.

For a big party, don't offer too many different drinks. Stick with wine and beer—or one fabulous cocktail.

Keep the nonalcoholic drinks simple. Provide a cordial such as elderflower or a pitcher of thawed concentrated juice for mixing with mineral water.

shopping & storage strategies

Make space in your fridge and in the kitchen for your ingredients before you shop.

Think quality. Buy the best of everything you can get.

If you come across a real bargain, you might consider altering the menu—but only if it's a fresh, high-quality ingredient. For instance, don't buy two-for-one strawberry cartons if they're looking past their best!

Organic food is usually superior, but it's more perishable. Inspect fresh produce carefully and use as soon as possible. Washed root vegetables will perish faster.

Organic eggs are always superior. Store in the fridge.

Ethnic food stores are treasure troves and can be an inspirational source of raw ingredients and special, unique desserts.

Support small businesses. Buy local produce whenever possible.

Salad greens and fresh herbs should be purchased no earlier than a day before your party.

Spray lettuce with water and store in the fridge, away from the fridge walls in order to avoid "fridge burn."

Bunches of fresh herbs should be washed and kept in a vase of water.

Never refrigerate basil or tomatoes. Keep berries in the fridge.

Take all fruit and vegetables out of any plastic packaging.

health matters

When you're entertaining, it's time to live a little. Indulgence is a good thing—in moderation. The fact is, healthy food makes you feel good—it boosts energy levels, strength, and vitality. On a day-to-day basis, everyone benefits from a healthy diet—that means low fat, lots of complex carbohydrates (like whole grains), fiber, a little protein, and plenty of fresh fruits and vegetables. I think the occasional naughty nibble is also essential for good spirits.

a vegetarian diet is a model diet

Research has shown that a vegetarian diet improves health, which is a great reason to eat vegetarian food on occasion or all the time. Vegetarians need to replace the nutrients that meat contains, in particular protein, iron, B vitamins, and selenium. Sources of these nutrients are abundant in an ideal vegetarian diet, which consists of a variety of foods including grains, beans, legumes, fruit, vegetables, nuts, seeds, and a small amount of fat. It's best not to rely on cheese as a source of protein—animal fat is saturated fat—although low-fat dairy products like yogurt are an important source of calcium. Eggs are packed with essential nutrients, but should also be eaten in moderation.

the entertainer's bag of tricks—Following is a list of useful ingredients to store in the kitchen so you're always prepared to cook with confidence, comfort, and finesse.

flavors for salty seasoning

Soy sauce—dark (fermented), light (unfermented)
Thai fish sauce—nam pla
Worcestershire sauce—traditional or vegetarian
Stock—high-quality vegetable stock powder or cubes

flavors for heat and spice

Chilies—fresh (store in freezer indefinitely or fridge until crinkly), dried (smoked and nonsmoked), cayenne pepper, mild chili powder; chili sauces: Thai, sweet chili, Tabasco, Jamaican hot; pickled chilies (sliced jalapeños, whole varieties); smoked Spanish paprika (pimenton)
Whole spices—black mustard seeds, pink peppercorns, fennel seeds, cumin seeds, coriander seeds, cardamom, fenugreek, saffron strands, whole nutmegs, cinnamon sticks, vanilla beans

flavors for depth, body, and accent

Oils and vinegars—extra-virgin olive oil; sesame, truffle, and walnut oils; aged balsamic and rice vinegars
Alcohol for cooking—Madeira, sherry, vermouth (substitute for white wine), mirin (Japanese cooking wine), port, brandy or cognac, rum
Fresh herbs—Italian parsley, basil, mint, sage, bay leaves, cilantro

flavors for a sweet tooth

Honey, pouring syrup, molasses, malt extract, rose water, orange blossom water, lemon curd
Pure unsweetened cocoa, 70 percent cocoa solids, semisweet chocolate, white chocolate

tasty morsels

Assorted olives, capers in vinegar or salt, capers, sun-dried or semidried tomatoes in oil (semidried usually store in the fridge), artichoke hearts in oil, pickled onions, pickled baby beet, cornichons and pickled cucumbers, dried cèpes, dried shiitake mushrooms, canned stuffed vine leaves, canned hummus
Nuts—(all shelled) pine nuts, peanuts, vacuum-packed chestnuts, hazelnuts, walnuts, pecans, pistachios, cashew nuts, almonds (whole blanched, slivered, ground), peanut butter
Seeds—(all hulled) sesame seeds, poppy seeds, pumpkin seeds, hemp seeds
Dried fruits—raisins, golden raisins, apricots, prunes, cranberries, figs, coconut

staples

Noodles and pasta—egg, rice, soba, and vermicelli noodles; linguine; pasta shapes; orzo pasta
Rice and other grains—basmati, risotto, whole-grain, and long-grain rice; couscous; bulgur wheat; quinoa grains
Legumes and canned vegetables—lentils, dried beans, canned beans of all sorts (including refried beans), artichoke hearts, roasted bell peppers, hearts of palm, roasted green chilies, water chestnuts

freezer essentials

Chopped and leaf spinach, peas, frozen berries, dough, ice cream, kaffir lime leaves, lemongrass, chilies, bread such as Turkish flatbread, tortillas, vodka, ice

1

canapés & cocktail bites

simple little bites with minimum fuss, to serve with drinks

Canapé is derived from a French word meaning "couch"—a tasty morsel reclining on an edible cushion before being popped in the mouth. The word has come to encompass all party nibbles—something tiny but delicious, to indulge the taste buds and buffer the effects of alcohol.

There's no doubt that hot, crispy nibbles are usually the most popular food to accompany drinks, but only if they're served as soon as they're cooked. This means that the cook is stuck in the kitchen and the grease is stuck to the cook (and the cook's fancy clothes). If you're still up for it, visit the freezer department of an Asian food store and you'll find tasty vegetarian spring rolls, dim sum, and wontons (read the labels to double-check for any hidden meat ingredients). Sink them into hot oil until golden, then serve with chili sauce.

If you're the cook and the host, however, rely on your best friend, the oven, to do the cooking while you see to other things. It's a good idea to carry a small kitchen timer with you if you leave things in the oven while the guests arrive. The smell of burned food is distinctive and embarrassing. Believe me, I've done it more than once.

The selection of canapés you choose should be a logical balance of hot and cold, and low on last-minute labor. Here are my guidelines on quantity (per guest):

Before-lunch canapés: 2–3 different canapés, 1–2 of each
As an appetizer: 3 different canapés, 1–2 of each
Early evening cocktail party: 6–8 different canapés, 1–2 of each
Canapés in place of an evening meal: 8 different canapés, 2–3 of each
Stick to the smaller quantity when providing canapés that are larger than one bite.

cucumber & herbed mascarpone bites

Here, the quintessentially English cucumber sandwich gets dressed up in a modern style and nibbled out of a carved bread bowl. Make up to four hours in advance.

ingredients

makes 36

1 large, round, rustic loaf of bread
9 oz. mascarpone cheese
4 heaping tablespoons finely chopped fresh herbs, such as dill, parsley, tarragon, and chives
grated zest of 1 lemon
salt and freshly ground black pepper
2–3 shakes Tabasco sauce
8 slices whole-wheat sandwich bread
½ cucumber, sliced paper-thin

method

To make the container, cut a circle out of the top of the loaf, leaving a border around the edge. Hollow out to form a "bread bowl," then cover with plastic wrap until ready to use.

Beat together the mascarpone cheese, herbs, lemon zest, salt, pepper, and Tabasco sauce, then spread evenly over two slices of bread. Place a layer of cucumber slices over the mixture on one slice, then top with the other slice of bread. Slice off the crusts, then cut each sandwich into nine little squares. Repeat with the remaining ingredients.

Fill the bread bowl with the sandwich bites, cover with plastic wrap, and keep in the refrigerator until ready to serve. (You may have enough bites to refill the bowl.)

spice-crusted baby potatoes with tamarind cream

These tiny potatoes, studded with crunchy spices, are always a treat. The dip has an element of surprise—the tamarind—that really gets people talking. Cherry-sized potatoes are ideal, as they can just be popped in the mouth.

ingredients

serves 20 as part of a canapé menu, 8–10 as finger food

2 lb. 4 oz. baby new potatoes, scrubbed
1 tablespoon coriander seeds
1 tablespoon cumin seeds
1/2 teaspoon ground turmeric
1/2 teaspoon cayenne pepper
1 teaspoon celery salt or sea salt
3 tablespoons olive oil
1 tablespoon wine vinegar

for the tamarind cream:

scant 1/2 cup crème fraîche or sour cream
scant 1/2 cup plain yogurt
2 tablespoons prepared tamarind, diluted to drizzling consistency if thick (see Top Tip below)

method

Preheat the oven to 425°F. Boil the potatoes in enough well-salted water to cover for 5 minutes, then drain and let cool. Dry them with a clean cloth.

Grind the coriander and cumin seeds in a mortar or spice grinder, then mix with the remaining spices and salt. Whisk together the oil, vinegar, and spices in a bowl. Place the potatoes in a large roasting pan, then pour the oil mixture on top and toss well to coat evenly. Roast them in the oven for about 15–20 minutes, until tender. Use tongs to remove the potatoes from the roasting pan and set aside until required. Reserve the toasted spices left in the pan.

For the tamarind cream, beat together the crème fraîche or sour cream and yogurt, then stir in the reserved spices. Scrape the cream mixture into a bowl and drizzle the tamarind on top. Serve with warm or cold potatoes. Use toothpicks if desired.

top tip

To prepare tamarind from pulp, briefly soak a hunk in boiling water, then press through a strainer (see photos above).

cranberry phyllo cigars

Sweet and sour cranberries combined with almonds, capers, and spice give these crispy nibbles an intriguing flavor. Is it sweet or is it savory? People have fun trying to guess just what goes into these Middle Eastern–inspired pastries.

ingredients

makes about 15

1/2 cup dried cranberries
1/2 cup ground almonds
1 tablespoon capers in vinegar, drained
1 tablespoon fresh oregano or marjoram, leaves stripped
1/2 teaspoon cumin seeds
4 small sheets phyllo pastry (approximately 6 1/4 x 12 in.)
2 tablespoons butter, melted

method

Preheat the oven to 425°F. Place the cranberries in a bowl and add enough boiling water to cover. Let soak for 15–20 minutes or until soft, then drain thoroughly. Place the reconstituted cranberries, ground almonds, capers, oregano or marjoram, and cumin seeds in a food processor or spice grinder and process until a purée results. Alternatively, chop everything very small and combine thoroughly.

Lightly grease a cookie sheet and line with parchment paper. Lay a sheet of phyllo pastry out horizontally on a clean, flat surface and brush all over with melted butter. Keep the rest of the pastry sheets covered with a damp towel. Along the bottom of the pastry, about 3/4 in. above the edge, arrange a long strip of the filling, about a pencil's width. Fold the bottom edge carefully over the filling, then roll the entire long sausage up tightly, moving along in sections, until rolled into a long cigar.

Using a knife or kitchen scissors, snip off the very ends of the cigar, then snip into baby cigars about 2 in. long. Place on the cookie sheet and brush generously with butter. Repeat with the remaining pastry.

Bake the cigars in the preheated oven for about 10–15 minutes, until golden all over. Serve warm or cold.

think ahead

Make the cigars up to the stage before cutting and baking a day in advance. Keep in the refrigerator, covered and not touching each other.

top tip

Vegans can use olive oil in place of butter. When serving, these cigars have a habit of sliding around on the plate, so they're best served on a bamboo mat or from a bowl.

eggplant, feta, & mint skewers

Charbroiled eggplants look great dressed in black stripes—but you could oven-broil them instead. Assemble the skewers up to four hours in advance.

ingredients

makes 20

1 long, thin eggplant, sliced as thinly as possible lengthwise into ten slices
olive oil, for brushing
3 1/2 oz. feta cheese, cut into approximately 3/4 in. cubes
20 large, fresh mint leaves
freshly ground black pepper
pomegranate molasses (page 71) or vintage balsamic vinegar, for drizzling

method

Place a ridged grill pan over high heat for 5 minutes or until very hot. Brush the eggplant slices with olive oil, then charbroil on both sides until translucent and striped with black. Let cool, then cut each slice into two long strips. Take one strip at a time and place a mint leaf on top, then tightly wrap both around a piece of feta. Secure with a bamboo skewer or cocktail stick and place on a large serving plate. Season to taste with black pepper, then drizzle with a little pomegranate molasses or a few drops of balsamic vinegar.

eggplant, feta, & mint skewers (left), cranberry phyllo cigars (right)

serving cocktails

—Cocktail parties have a lively energy—people are usually standing around, talking, so they often drink more quickly than usual. Consequently, it's important to keep the food flowing as well as the drinks, but try to pace it over the evening. If you're busy in the kitchen, nominate friends or family members to circulate with your creations, explaining exactly what's in each one in case the guests ask. Don't fuss around with too many garnishes—let the food speak for itself. Keep each canapé small, tidy, and bite size. Provide receptacles for used cocktail sticks, olive pits, empty shot glasses, etc., and don't send hot food out too hot.

shopping Asian food stores are always worth a visit for party paraphernalia like toothpicks, funky napkins, serving dishes and glasses, candles, nuts, and nibbles.

presentation For serving canapés use plates, bowls, lacquer trays, and bamboo steamer baskets. Assemble canapés on kitchen trays, then transfer to the serving dishes. Don't put too many canapés on at once: nobody ever wants the last, lone canapé.

drinks The best way to get a party going is for the host to serve one strong cocktail to everyone as they arrive. Try:

champagne cocktail Place a sugar lump in the glass and shake on a few drops of Angostura bitters, then add a dash of brandy and top up with champagne.

vodka martini Swirl vermouth in a glass, then discard to next. Top with ice-shaken or frozen neat vodka and an olive.

the menu

teriyaki almonds vegan

Shimmering clusters of glazed, toasted nuts are utterly irresistible. These are the ideal bar snack: salty, sweet, and crunchy. You don't have to limit yourself to almonds—pecans, cashews, and Brazil nuts are all fantastic as well, though if you mix them, bear in mind that they may not cook evenly.

ingredients

scant 2 cups blanched whole almonds
3 tablespoons olive oil
2 tablespoons dark soy sauce
2 tablespoons mirin (Japanese cooking wine) or sweet sherry
1/4 teaspoon cayenne pepper
1 tablespoon sesame seeds
1 tablespoon superfine sugar

method

Preheat the oven to 400°F. Spread the almonds out on a baking tray and toast in the preheated oven for 5 minutes, until pale golden. Reduce the oven temperature to 300°F.

Combine the remaining ingredients in a bowl and mix well. Add the toasted almonds and stir to coat evenly. Pour the mixture back onto the baking tray and cook in the oven for about 20–25 minutes, stirring every 5 minutes. The liquid will reduce in the oven, eventually becoming a thick, dark, sticky coating that glazes the nuts.

Let the nuts cool on the baking tray. Use a metal spatula to scrape the nuts and glaze off the tray. Break up any large clumps, but leave some in little clusters. Arrange in a bowl and serve, with napkins nearby.

avocado & semidried tomato crostini vegan

The semidried tomato is the new sun-dried—it's softer, brighter, and juicier—but good old sun-dried tomatoes are fine, too. The spicy avocado purée is best made no more than four hours before serving.

ingredients

makes 20

olive oil, for brushing
20 (1/2 in. thick) slices of very thin baguette or ciabatta
1 large or 2 small perfectly ripe avocados, pitted and peeled
juice of 1 lime
1 garlic clove, crushed
1 teaspoon ground cumin
1/2 teaspoon hot chili powder, or to taste
salt and freshly ground black pepper
20 pieces semidried tomato in oil, drained (or use sun-dried)
fresh chives, cut into 3/4 in. lengths

method

To make the crostini, preheat the oven to 350°F. Brush a cookie sheet with olive oil, then place the bread slices on the sheet and drizzle lightly with olive oil. Bake in the preheated oven for about 10 minutes, until light golden and thoroughly crisp. Let cool, then keep in an airtight container until ready to use.

To make the avocado purée, mash the avocado with a potato masher until smooth, then mash in the lime juice, garlic, cumin, chili, salt, and pepper. Cover with plastic wrap and keep in the refrigerator until ready to use.

To assemble each canapé, place a small spoonful of avocado purée on each piece of bread. It looks best if not smoothed down too much. Place a semidried tomato on top and finish with a piece of chive.

artichoke toasties (top), eggplant & olive truffles (bottom)

artichoke toasties

People can never seem to get enough of these warm, crisp, and cheesy tartlets. They're ludicrously easy to make, so make more than you think you'll need. Using a high-quality loaf of bread for the bottom layer is a waste of money and effort—regular white sandwich bread is the key to their simplicity.

ingredients

makes 24

12 slices white sandwich bread
soft butter, for spreading
14 oz. can artichoke hearts, drained and chopped
2 oz. fresh Parmesan cheese, finely grated
2 fresh, fleshy, mild green chilies, seeded and finely chopped
3 heaping tablespoons mayonnaise
a pinch of salt
freshly ground black pepper

method

Preheat the oven to 425°F. Using a 2 in. wide glass tumbler or cookie cutter, cut two circles of bread out of each slice. Butter one side fairly generously and press butter-side down in a shallow nonstick muffin pan, flattening the entire surface with your fingertips.

Mix together the remaining ingredients, then place a spoonful of the mixture into each bread case, smoothing down the top evenly. Bake in the preheated oven for 12–15 minutes, until golden and crisp. Let cool briefly before slipping out of the pan. Serve warm.

eggplant & olive truffles

These look rather like little meatballs, though they practically float off the plate with lightness. Try to serve them as soon as possible out of the oven—like most hot snacks, their appeal is immediate. Once let loose on the guests, they won't have a hope of hanging around. The mixture can be made up to one day in advance.

ingredients

makes 24

1 large eggplant, approximately 1 lb. 2 oz.
2 tablespoons olive oil
1/2 cup pine nuts
20 Kalamata olives, pitted and chopped
4 tablespoons dry bread crumbs
6 tablespoons freshly grated Parmesan cheese, plus 2 tablespoons for sprinkling
2 tablespoons chopped fresh parsley
1 plump garlic clove, crushed
1 organic egg, beaten
butter, for greasing

to garnish (optional):
fresh parsley leaves
Parmesan cheese shavings

method

Preheat the oven to 450°F. Cut the eggplant in half lengthwise and brush with olive oil. Roast in the preheated oven for about 30 minutes, until golden and completely soft. Let cool, peel off the skin and discard, then chop the flesh finely. Reduce the oven temperature to 400°F.

Mix the eggplant flesh, pine nuts, olives, bread crumbs, Parmesan cheese, parsley, garlic, and egg together in a bowl, then let rest for 10–15 minutes.

Liberally grease a large cookie sheet. Form the mixture into bite-size balls and place on the sheet, then top each one with a pinch of grated Parmesan cheese.

Bake in the oven for 15–20 minutes, until golden and puffed up. Serve hot, with a few parsley leaves and Parmesan shavings sprinkled over the platter, if desired.

2

feed the masses

big bowls and platters that go a long way

Cooking for a crowd usually means it's celebration time—a wedding, a big birthday, a graduation. For these occasions, sandwiches just won't do! Food is the life of the party, and if you're the cook, it can seem a little daunting, but it's also a lot of fun and immensely satisfying. Don't rely on a miracle; if you plan the menu sensibly and stay organized, everything will run as smooth as honey.

A stunning yet simple buffet is the best tactic for feeding crowds of people. Design a buffet with no more than four or five large dishes that can be eaten with a fork. They should have bold visual impact, presenting a contrast of textures, colors, and flavors. Choose one or two delicious nibbles to keep people happy before the buffet begins, but avoid anything that's complicated to make. Stick to one or two big desserts. Provide a backup of a giant cheese and bread tray. Bear in mind that hungry people are greedy at buffets and may take more than their fair share.

The irony of feeding the masses is that it takes almost the same amount of time to cook for 100 as it does for 1,000. Good food has to be fresh—so by nature it's ephemeral. The actual cooking can't be going on for much more than three days prior to the event. Solution? Delegation! Take on more pairs of hands than you think you need. Conserve energy and have the groceries delivered if you can. Assign one of the desserts to a friend or a local bakery, and buy prepackaged things such as petits fours and tart shells.

Finally, as the marathon begins, start with a well-rested body. Make a list of every task that needs to be done and check them off as you go. Take plenty of breaks—get some fresh air. Top tip: Drink water constantly, and don't forget to eat. You need to be firing on all cylinders!

Now, on your marks, get set...

tortellini skewers with herb oil

When cooking for large numbers, the smart entertainer will occasionally rely on a few items that are prepared by the pros (or by machine)—and this is a good example. Those hours of labor making homemade tortellini can be put to much better use. Delicious fresh pasta is widely available in major supermarkets, though if you can afford to be a little extravagant, get the tortellini made fresh at an Italian deli. These are perfect on a finger buffet; they're tempting, easy to eat, and quite substantial.

ingredients

makes 24 skewers
48 cheese-filled tortellini
$10\frac{1}{2}$ oz. mozzarella di bufala, *torn into coarse chunks*
24 high-quality pitted olives
12 sun-dried tomatoes in oil, each cut into two strips
for the oil:
approximately 20 fresh basil leaves
approximately 20 fresh Italian parsley leaves
$\frac{1}{3}$ cup extra-virgin olive oil

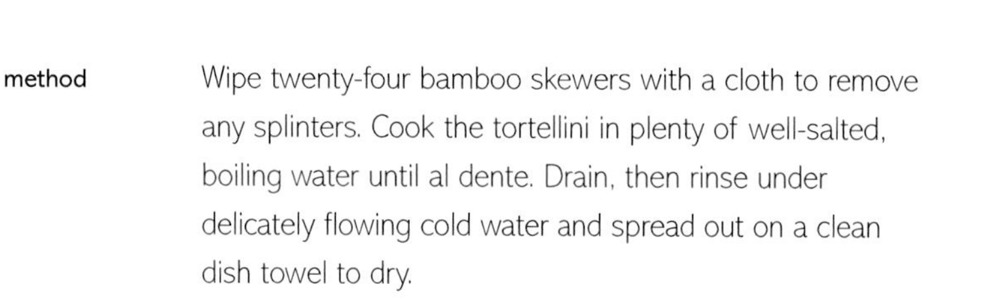

method

Wipe twenty-four bamboo skewers with a cloth to remove any splinters. Cook the tortellini in plenty of well-salted, boiling water until al dente. Drain, then rinse under delicately flowing cold water and spread out on a clean dish towel to dry.

Pair up a piece of cheese with an olive and wrap a strip of sun-dried tomato around them. Thread one tortellini onto a bamboo skewer, followed by the tomato-cheese-olive wrap, and finishing with a tortellini close to the end of the skewer. (If you're feeling lazy or rushed, thread them on as haphazardly as you like—they'll still taste scrumptious.) Keep the finished skewers covered in plastic wrap and chill in the refrigerator as soon as possible. Return to room temperature before serving.

To make the herb oil, blend the herbs and oil in a blender or spice grinder until fairly smooth. Arrange the skewers on a platter and drizzle with the herb oil just before serving.

think ahead

Assemble the skewers up to four hours in advance.

top tip

Buy more tortellini than you need, as some might fall apart in the cooking. Be careful not to overcook—they need to be really al dente. If you can't find buffalo milk mozzarella, use cow's, though not that rubbery pizza variety; settle for cubes of creamy Havarti or fontina instead.

serve with

These fit best into a buffet with a Mediterranean feel.

deluxe crudités

This sesame dip is the only dip I ever make. I am always asked to divulge the recipe, and people are amazed how something so simple could taste so divine. Even the person who loathes raw vegetables will manage to eat some with this stuff. The dip is best eaten on the day of preparation, as the sesame seeds tend to become soggy.

ingredients

serves 8–10

for the sesame dip:

1/4 cup sesame seeds
generous 1/2 cup strained plain or thick and creamy yogurt
generous 1/2 cup mayonnaise
3 tablespoons dark soy sauce

for the crudités (choose a selection of 4–5 items):

boiled baby new potatoes
blanched asparagus spears
Belgian endive leaves
trimmed radishes, a tiny bit of the top left intact
raw sugar snap peas
celery stalks from the heart, some leaves left on
baby carrots, trimmed
bite-size broccoli florets
bite-size cauliflower florets
sliced fennel

method

To make the dip, heat a dry skillet over moderate heat. Add the sesame seeds and toast, stirring until they are popping and lightly browned. Transfer to a bowl and let cool completely.

Combine the sesame seeds with the yogurt, mayonnaise, and soy sauce and mix very thoroughly. Transfer to a dipping bowl. Arrange the vegetables of your choice on a platter in individual clusters and serve with the sesame dip.

hot fennel salt

vegan—A good complement to the creamy dip, this tastes particularly good with cherry tomatoes and cucumbers. It's potent stuff—a dab is all you need.

ingredients

1 tablespoon rock salt; 8 peppercorns; 1 teaspoon fennel seeds; 1 teaspoon coriander seeds; 1 small dried chili or 1/2 teaspoon chili powder

method

Mix all the ingredients together in a spice grinder or use a mortar and pestle to work into a coarse powder. Transfer to a small, shallow bowl and serve.

green charbroiled antipasti platter

This blooming platter of succulent vegetables and marinated fresh mozzarella is magnetic—you can make a silly quantity and it's still guaranteed to vanish. You'll need one of those fabulous cast-iron ridged grill pans for this, ideally a large one that fits over two burners. A smoke-filled kitchen is inevitable (open the windows), but it's the smoke that works the magic on the vegetables. Alternatively, use an outdoor grill. Any vegetable responds well to this treatment, but root vegetables should be boiled first.

ingredients

serves 8–10

14 oz. green beans, trimmed
4 large or 8 small heads of Belgian endive, halved lengthwise
4 fennel bulbs, trimmed and cut into thick slices
2 heads of broccoli, stem peeled, cut into long pieces
4 tablespoons olive oil, plus a little extra-virgin olive oil for drizzling
salt and freshly ground black pepper
juice of 1–2 lemons
1 lb. 2 oz. mozzarella di bufala, *torn into thick shreds*
2 garlic cloves
1 teaspoon coarse sea salt
a handful of fresh Italian parsley, chopped
1 bunch of fresh basil, leaves torn

method

Heat a ridged grill pan over high heat for 10 minutes while you get started preparing the vegetables. Place one type of vegetable in a mixing bowl and drizzle lightly with olive oil, then use your hands to coat them all over. Cook one type of vegetable at a time until tender and nicely charred.

Once cooked, return each type of vegetable to the mixing bowl and season with salt and black pepper. Squeeze lemon juice over the beans, Belgian endive, and fennel while still hot. Avoid squeezing lemon juice over the broccoli as it may discolor. Let the vegetables cool, then store in plastic zip-seal bags in the refrigerator until required.

Place the torn mozzarella cheese in a large bowl. Pound the garlic with the salt in a mortar. Pound in the parsley until coarsely combined. Whisk in the olive oil and basil. Add the marinade to the mozzarella pieces and stir carefully, then chill in the refrigerator for at least 1 hour. Arrange the charred vegetables on a platter with the marinated mozzarella and serve immediately.

think ahead

This platter can be made up to one day in advance. Store the cooled vegetables in separate zip-seal plastic bags.

top tip

Buffalo mozzarella, made from buffalo's milk, is a luxury and is ideal for this recipe. If unavailable, use fresh cow's milk mozzarella, but not pizza mozzarella. Fresh mozzarella is very vulnerable to spoilage; keep it in the refrigerator until the last moment before combining with the marinade, then refrigerate until ready to serve.

serve with

Salad greens and plenty of fresh, crusty bread.

a celebration buffet—A beautifully arranged buffet table will inspire lots of "oohs" and "aahs," which is so gratifying. Set it up so that it flows in one direction—left to right is the most logical. Start with a pile of plates at the top end, alongside cutlery wrapped in napkins. Don't squash the food platters up too much—give them room to breathe. Place the dish you anticipate being the most popular at the end of the buffet, which will discourage greed. Don't forget serving spoons, and use medium, not giant, ones.

For loose salad greens, instead of making a separate dressing, just drizzle some good-quality balsamic vinegar and olive oil directly on the greens and toss well with salt and black pepper.

shopping If there's anything you can get delivered, go for it. Get all shopping out of the way the day before the celebration. If you're cooking over more than one day, try to buy everything in one shopping trip before you get started, but take any perishable items into consideration—look after fresh herbs and vegetables, and pack any dairy or other chilled items in the same bag. Use boxes to pack your food, making it easier to see what you have than when using a lot of bags.

presentation If your budget can handle it, consider renting nice dishes and platters, then sending them back dirty for a small fee.

drinks If you give people a choice between white wine and champagne, you can guess which one you'll run out of first! If you must limit your supply of bubbly, serve it alone first, then switch to wine. Get champagne flutes as well as wine goblets.

the menu

broccoli & lemon orzo **vegan**

Orzo is rice-shaped pasta with a toothsome bite. Here's a bright, citrus pasta salad that sings with fresh, green flavor. It's filling yet light, a meal in itself or a delicious accompaniment, making it an ideal buffet or potluck dish.

ingredients

serves 8–10

grated zest of 4 lemons
generous 3/4 cup fresh lemon juice (approximately 4 lemons)
4 shallots, finely sliced
salt and freshly ground black pepper
1 teaspoon superfine sugar
1/3 cup olive oil
1 large head of broccoli (approximately 1 lb. 2 oz.), cut into small florets, stem chopped
3 1/2 oz. snow peas, trimmed
1 lb. 2 oz. orzo
2 oz. pumpkin seeds
3 1/2 oz. raw sugar snap peas, sliced
a large handful of fresh Italian parsley, leaves stripped
20 semidried tomatoes in oil or 10 sun-dried tomatoes in oil, drained and cut into strips

method

Preheat the oven to 400°F. Bring a large pan of water to a boil and salt it well.

Place the lemon zest and juice in a bowl, add the shallots, salt, pepper, and sugar, then whisk in the olive oil. Set aside until required. (The shallots should soak in the dressing for a few minutes to become mild and soft.)

Blanch the broccoli and snow peas in the boiling water for 2 minutes. Remove with a perforated spoon or a strainer and plunge into a bowl of ice-cold water. Drain when the vegetables are cold.

Add the orzo to the pan and cook, stirring frequently, for 6–8 minutes or until al dente. Drain the orzo and rinse under cold running water until cool. Drain thoroughly and place in a large mixing bowl. Stir in the lemon shallot dressing. Set aside until required.

Place the pumpkin seeds on a cookie sheet and toast in the preheated oven for 5 minutes, until golden. Let cool.

Add the sugar snap peas, parsley, and semidried or sun-dried tomatoes to the bowl of orzo and mix thoroughly. Just before serving, stir in the broccoli, snow peas, and toasted pumpkin seeds.

think ahead

This dish can be made up to a day in advance, reserving the broccoli, snow peas, and pumpkin seeds to stir in just before serving.

sugarbeans vegan

Feeding the masses is made a lot easier by including these luscious legumes on the menu. They can be made ages in advance and only get better as the days go by. Like a really good chutney, they need time to mature, allowing the high quantity of sugar and vinegar to work their magic. They're also very cheap to make in quantity. Water chestnuts are the surprise ingredient in this salad, providing a welcome crunch against all those sweet, creamy beans.

ingredients

serves 10–12

for the salad:

1 lb. 2 oz. mixed dried beans
7 oz. green beans or string beans, cut into bite-size pieces
2 (8 oz.) cans water chestnuts, drained
1 green bell pepper, cut into bite-size pieces
1 red onion, sliced very finely

for the marinade:

1/2 cup balsamic vinegar
scant 1/2 cup superfine sugar
3 garlic cloves, crushed
2 teaspoons salt
freshly ground black pepper
1/2 cup olive oil

method

Soak the dried beans in plenty of cold water overnight, then drain and boil them in fresh water. Let them bubble furiously for 10 minutes, then simmer for 50 minutes, until tender but not falling apart too much. Alternatively, follow the package instructions. Do taste each type of bean to be sure they are all tender enough. Drain thoroughly.

Bring another small pan of water to a boil. Blanch the green beans for 2 minutes, drain, and rinse under cold running water or in a bowl of ice-cold water.

Meanwhile, prepare the marinade by whisking together all the ingredients except the olive oil. Beat in the olive oil gradually to emulsify.

Empty the drained cooked beans into a wide, shallow dish and pour the marinade over them while they are still hot. Let cool, then add the blanched green beans, water chestnuts, green bell pepper, and red onion. Stir thoroughly. Cover with plastic wrap and let chill in the refrigerator for at least 24 hours, preferably longer, stirring now and then. The salad will keep for several days in the refrigerator.

think ahead

This recipe should be made at least three days in advance and can be made up to four days in advance.

top tip

This recipe multiplies well, but portions decrease as the number of guests goes up. As part of a buffet containing several cold salads, I have fed 150 on eight times the recipe. For convenience, buy dried beans already packaged as mixed. The marinade can be made in a blender, but whisk in the oil by hand or else the dressing will appear unappetizingly cloudy.

seven-vegetable tagine vegan

Seven is for luck, and this tagine has never failed me. It's a riot of color and a symphony of flavor. Practically speaking, it's a caterer's dream. Roast the vegetables with whole spices until sweet and tender, then stir into a rich sauce. Walk away and leave it overnight to flourish . . . then all that's left to do is reheat and devour.

ingredients

serves 8–10

10½ oz. sweet potato, peeled and cut into chunks
10½ oz. carrots, peeled and cut into chunks
10½ oz. parsnips or celery root, peeled and cut into chunks
1 red and 1 yellow bell pepper, cut into chunks
1 large fennel bulb, cut into chunks
1 large red onion, cut into chunks
2 medium zucchini, cut into chunks
3 tablespoons olive oil
1 tablespoon cumin seeds
1 tablespoon fennel seeds
salt and freshly ground black pepper

for the sauce:

4 garlic cloves, chopped
3 tablespoons olive oil
14 oz. can chopped tomatoes
14 oz. can chickpeas, drained
1 cup full-bodied red wine
zest and juice of 1 orange
2 cinnamon sticks
12 pitted prunes, halved if large

to serve:

Parsley & Saffron Couscous *(see below)*
harissa (hot chili paste; optional)
thick yogurt (omit for vegans)

method

Preheat the oven to 425°F. Place all the vegetables in a roasting pan and coat with the olive oil, whole cumin and fennel seeds, salt, and pepper. Roast in the preheated oven for about 30 minutes, until soft and caramelized, stirring once or twice.

Meanwhile, to make the sauce, cook the garlic in olive oil. Add the remaining ingredients and simmer until thick. Remove from the heat and combine with the roasted vegetables. If you feel it is too thick, add a little water to achieve the desired consistency. Cover and let stand in a cool place overnight. Reheat until piping hot and serve with freshly cooked couscous, harissa, and yogurt.

parsley & saffron couscous vegan—Ideal with the tagine; great on its own.

ingredients

serves 8–10; *½ cup large golden raisins; 1 lb. 2 oz. couscous; 2 teaspoons saffron threads; 1 teaspoon salt; 1 cup whole almonds, toasted; 2 large handfuls of fresh Italian parsley leaves, left whole; grated zest and juice of 3 lemons; 6 tablespoons olive oil; freshly ground black pepper*

method

Place the golden raisins in a bowl and soak in boiling water for 15–20 minutes, then drain and set aside. Combine the dry couscous, saffron, and salt in a large bowl and stir well. Pour in just enough boiling water to cover. Let swell for 5 minutes, then fluff thoroughly with a fork, separating each grain. Place the remaining ingredients in a large bowl and mix thoroughly with the soaked golden raisins and couscous. Season as necessary and serve immediately.

giant cheese & spinach pie

Here it is—the ultimate spanakopita recipe, which my friend Cathy Lowis has passed on from her Greek mother. This classic phyllo pie is an utterly perfect entertaining recipe—big, bold, and easy to multiply, it always succeeds in appealing to everyone and is usually the favorite dish of the meal. This version has a clever twist with a handful of rice.

ingredients

serve 10–12

for the filling:

2 tablespoons olive oil
6 scallions, white and green parts, chopped
1 lb. 10 oz. fresh spinach, washed and trimmed, or frozen leaf spinach
1 1/2 cups cottage cheese, drained of any excess whey
2 cups crumbled feta cheese
3 tablespoons chopped fresh dill
3 tablespoons chopped fresh parsley
1 tablespoon uncooked long-grain rice
salt and freshly ground black pepper

for the pie dough:

14 large sheets of phyllo pastry
6 tablespoons olive oil
1 1/2 sticks butter (6 oz.), melted

method

Preheat the oven to 350°F. To make the filling, heat the oil in a large pan over low to moderate heat. Add the scallions and cook until translucent and soft. Stir in the spinach and cook until just wilted. (If using frozen spinach, cook until heated through.) Drain in a colander and press out as much moisture as possible. Let cool, then place on a clean cloth, gather up the sides, and squeeze the excess moisture out of the spinach. Chop coarsely.

Combine the spinach with the remaining filling ingredients in a bowl and mix very thoroughly. Taste for seasoning—you may only need to add pepper, as the feta is salty enough.

Unwrap the phyllo pastry and, if necessary, cut to fit the bottom of a large, deep, rectangular baking pan or casserole dish. Cover the pastry with a barely damp cloth to prevent it from drying out and becoming brittle. Combine the olive oil and melted butter, then brush the butter mixture all over the baking pan or casserole dish. Place one layer of phyllo pastry on the bottom, brush with the melted butter mixture, top with another layer of phyllo pastry, brush with butter, and so on, forming seven layers. Spoon all of the filling on top, spreading it out evenly.

Continue layering the phyllo pastry on top of the filling, again forming seven layers. Brush the top with the melted butter mixture and then, using a very sharp knife, cut the phyllo pastry into serving-size diamond shapes (cut vertically down the center and then diagonally across) or squares.

Bake the pie in the preheated oven for 45 minutes to 1 hour, until sizzling, deep golden, and crisp right through each of the phyllo layers. Cut again along the original slits before serving.

think ahead The filling can be made two days in advance. The whole cooked pie can be frozen, thawed, and reheated.

top tip The filling has a tendency to be on the wet side, but by throwing in a handful of uncooked rice, any excess moisture is absorbed and the bottom stays quite crisp.

serve with Salad and bread; Sugarbeans (page 38)

roasted asparagus & marbled egg platter

This is a particular favorite around Easter, when there is a lot to celebrate, including the start of the asparagus season! The extraordinary method of cooking eggs originates from an ancient Jewish recipe. Making the marbled eggs has become an absolute ritual for me every year, partly because of the fun of it, as well as the romance of the symbolism—fertility and rebirth. I usually slice and caramelize the leftover peeled onions and make soup or a savory tart.

ingredients

serves 12

12 yellow onions (not red or white)
12 organic eggs
3 tablespoons sunflower or corn oil
4–5 bunches of asparagus spears, trimmed
olive oil, for drizzling
salt and freshly ground black pepper

method

To make the marbled eggs, first peel the onions, reserving every bit of papery skin. Make a layer of onion skins in a pan and place the eggs on top, then cover with more onion skins, tucking them in between the eggs. Fill the pan with enough water to cover the eggs by at least 3/4 in. depth. Add the sunflower oil and bring to a boil, then reduce to a simmer.

After about 30 minutes, lift the eggs out with a perforated spoon and whack gently with another spoon to crack the shells. Return to the onion dye bath and simmer very gently for 5–6 hours, topping up the water as necessary, though the oil will go some way toward preventing evaporation. Let the eggs cool in the liquid, then drain and peel to reveal a beautifully marbled surface. Keep in the refrigerator until ready to serve.

Preheat the oven to 425°F. To cook the asparagus, place the prepared spears in a roasting pan, drizzle over enough olive oil to just coat the surface, and use your hands to coat evenly. Roast the asparagus in the preheated oven for 10–15 minutes or until done to your taste—ideally until tender but maintaining a little bit of bite. Season to taste with salt and black pepper, then serve warm or cold with the marbled eggs.

think ahead The eggs can be cooked up to two days in advance and the asparagus up to four hours in advance.

top tip Snap off the bottom of the asparagus spears—they will break above the woody end, ensuring tenderness.

serve with Sesame dip from the Deluxe Crudités, page 31

3

small courses

fantastic appetizers or components of a feast

The spiritual home of the small course is the entire sun-drenched, olive-rich region of the Mediterranean. From tapas to meze, little dishes made of exquisite ingredients are designed to get the appetite stimulated on lazy evenings in the sunshine with a chilled glass of wine. Many of these traditional dishes are by default vegetarian—the fertility of the Mediterranean bears such a lush selection of ingredients. Prepared simply, the intention is to enhance the natural beauty of the key ingredient. Throughout the Mediterranean, they really know a thing or two when it comes to enjoying life through food.

In modern times, we aim to eat with a light and healthy approach as often as possible. We embrace the food of the Mediterranean for its healthy olive oil and vitamin-rich qualities as much as for its sunny flavors. We can also embrace the custom of exciting the appetite and keeping it aroused with every small course, rather than extinguishing it with a big, heavy one. This is a rich tradition in Asia as well; at street markets you can enjoy "little eats"—hopping from stall to stall, trying a little bit at each one. It's a far more interesting way to eat, and when you are entertaining, it's an exciting way to cook.

All the recipes in this chapter can be enjoyed as the opening of a fantastic meal, as the components of a feast of little dishes, or simply on their own as a light meal. They can all be served from one platter or bowl, or as individual treats. If you are feeding many, you might wish to prepare individual dishes and have them waiting on the table before the meal begins. Every host should want to spoil the guests, but be judicious with multiple courses and space them out sensibly—that way every bite will be appreciated.

spiced baby eggplants with minted yogurt

Indian cooks are fond of stuffing baby eggplants, and these are cooked in the style of southern India, filling the house with a rich curry fragrance. Choose teardrop-shaped eggplants, about 2½ in. long, and cook them up to six hours in advance, combining with the sauce just before serving.

ingredients

serves 4–6

1 lb. 2 oz. baby eggplants
1 ¼ cups vegetable stock

for the spice oil:

5 tablespoons sunflower or corn oil
2 teaspoons black mustard seeds
4 garlic cloves, finely chopped
2–3 fresh red chilies, finely chopped
1 teaspoon ground turmeric
2 teaspoons cumin seeds
½ teaspoon fenugreek seeds (optional)
½ teaspoon salt

for the sauce:

generous ⅓ cup thick yogurt
a handful of fresh mint, chopped
juice of 1 lime
salt and freshly ground black pepper

method

First make the spice oil. Heat the oil in a nonstick skillet over moderate to high heat. Add the mustard seeds and when they start to pop, stir in the remaining ingredients. Immediately take the skillet off the heat and pour the oil into a cold ceramic bowl. Let the oil cool. Wipe the cooled skillet with paper towels, leaving a light slick of oil.

Meanwhile, prepare the eggplants. Grip by the stem end and lay on a cutting board, then, using a very sharp knife, slice the flesh from top to bottom, leaving the stem intact, making three or four thin slices. Alternatively, cut them into fourths, again leaving the stem intact.

When the spice oil is cool, use a teaspoon to apply a little oil and spice in between each layer of the sliced eggplants. Secure each one at the bottom with a toothpick or wooden skewer. Arrange them in the reheated skillet and cook over moderate heat until lightly colored on one side, then turn over and color the other side. Pour in the vegetable stock, cover, and reduce the heat to a simmer. Cook for about 10–15 minutes, until very soft—when prodded with a skewer they should offer no resistance. Remove the lid and increase the heat slightly, and reduce any remaining juices to a thick glaze that just coats the bottom of the pan.

To make the sauce, combine all the ingredients, then spread the sauce on a plate, place the eggplants on top, and drizzle any pan juices over them. Serve warm or cold.

raw thai salad in a pappadam shell vegan

This salad is all crunch and perfume—it really gets the appetite stirring, while being exceptionally light. I created it for a friend's summer wedding. The colorful salads were waiting at each place setting, forming part of the decoration as the guests came into the lavishly floral wedding tent. It's simple enough to produce in large quantities easily, but also works well for a smaller, less formal affair.

ingredients

serves 8–10

for the dressing:

1/3 cup corn syrup
2 tablespoons lime juice
1/4 cup light soy sauce
2 garlic cloves
2–3 small, fresh red chilies, sliced
3 lemongrass sticks, sliced (optional)
4 kaffir lime leaves, stem removed and coarsely chopped (optional)

for the salad:

scant 2 cups shredded red cabbage
1 red bell pepper, seeded and sliced
2 cups bean sprouts
8 scallions, sliced diagonally
2 (7 oz.) cans sliced water chestnuts, drained
4 canned hearts of palm, drained and sliced diagonally
4 fresh mint sprigs, leaves stripped
oil, for deep-frying
10 pappadams
10 leaves from a round lettuce, washed and thoroughly dried
3 tablespoons sesame seeds, toasted
2 limes, cut into wedges
8–10 edible flowers, such as pansies or nasturtiums (optional)

method

To make the dressing, mix everything in the blender until smooth and set aside until required. Toss the first seven salad ingredients together lightly and keep cool.

Fill a deep skillet with 4 in. of oil and heat until it starts to smoke (375°F). Using tongs, carefully place a pappadam in the oil, then use a ladle to press down in the center—the pappadam will form a basket around the ladle. Drain upside down on paper towels. Repeat with the other pappadams and allow to cool.

Line each cooled pappadam with a lettuce leaf. Toss the dressing through the vegetables and spoon into each basket. Sprinkle with the toasted sesame seeds and finish with a lime wedge and an edible flower (if using).

think ahead

Pappadam shells can be fried four hours in advance and kept in a dry place.

ginger-spiked avocados **vegan**

If there is a way to improve the heavenly, buttery flavor of ripe avocados, then this is it. Ginger and avocado have a surprising affinity. Prepare these as close to serving time as you can.

ingredients

serves 6

3 perfectly ripe avocados
juice of 1–2 lemons
2 tablespoons dark soy sauce
1 tablespoon balsamic vinegar
2 teaspoons finely grated fresh root ginger
freshly ground black pepper
sprigs of dill, to garnish

method

Slice the avocados in half and remove the pits. To extract a complete half from the skin, soak a large spoon in a cup of boiling water for a few seconds, then use it to quickly slide between the skin and the flesh at the narrow end of the avocado. The warmth of the spoon should "melt" the flesh slightly, allowing you to scoop the avocado flesh out in one smooth move. Alternatively, cut the avocados into fourths and peel away the skin. Sprinkle lemon juice over the avocados and use your hands to gently coat them all over. Place on a platter or individual serving plates.

Mix together the soy sauce, vinegar, and ginger and drizzle over the avocados or pour into the pit cavity. Finish with a good grinding of black pepper and decorate with sprigs of dill.

roasted spiced squash soup with tamarind **vegan**

Imagine if velvet could bite, and you get some idea of what this soup tastes like. Buy a dense-fleshed squash weighing about 3 lb. for the recipe, to allow for peeling and seeding.

ingredients

serves 4–6

2 lb. squash flesh, peeled and cut into chunks
1 teaspoon coriander seeds
1 teaspoon cumin seeds
6 garlic cloves
2½ in. piece of fresh root ginger, peeled and chopped
salt and freshly ground black pepper
3–4 tablespoons extra-virgin olive oil
4 cups vegetable stock
2 tablespoons tamarind cream (page 17) or 1 tablespoon brown sauce or 2 teaspoons Worcestershire sauce

to garnish (optional):

heavy cream or plain yogurt
hulled squash seeds

method

Preheat the oven to 400°F. Place the squash in a roasting pan and sprinkle with the spices, whole garlic cloves, ginger, salt, and black pepper. Drizzle the olive oil on top and toss with your hands to coat evenly. Roast in the preheated oven for 30–40 minutes, stirring once or twice, until the squash is very soft.

Let cool slightly, then scrape into a pan and add the vegetable stock and tamarind cream. Bring to a boil and simmer very gently for 10 minutes. Process into a totally smooth purée, then serve in warm bowls with a drizzle of cream or yogurt and squash seeds sprinkled over the top.

beet & coconut soup vegan

This soup is an absolute stunner. Coconut and beets are often cooked together in southern India, which is the inspiration for this exciting soup. The shocking pink beets are made even brighter on a canvas of milky coconut—and the exotic flavors really do match up to the brilliant appearance. Any soup can be served as a canapé out of tiny espresso cups or shot glasses (allow the soup to cool slightly before pouring into delicate cups or glasses). This one is particularly impressive served in this way.

ingredients

serves 4–6

1 lb. 2 oz. fresh beets, leaves removed, scrubbed
7 oz. block of creamed coconut, chopped
4 cups vegetable stock
4 garlic cloves, peeled, coarsely chopped or halved
1 teaspoon ground cumin
grated zest of 1 lemon
juice of 1/2 lemon

to serve:

Cucumber Salsa (see below)
pita breads or chapatis, cut into strips and toasted

method

Bring a large pan of water to a boil and salt it well. Add the beets and boil for 30–40 minutes, until tender throughout (test with a skewer or sharp knife). Drain, then rinse under cold running water and rub off the skins, tops, and spindly roots. Chop coarsely.

Bring the vegetable stock to a boil in the rinsed-out pan, then stir in the coconut until dissolved.

Place the chopped beets, garlic, cumin, lemon zest and juice, and 3/4 cup water in a blender and process until smooth.

Add the beet purée to the boiling coconut stock. (You can swirl some coconut stock around the blender to get out every last bit of purée.) Bring to a boil and simmer for 10 minutes. Serve in warm bowls with a spoonful of Cucumber Salsa on top, with strips of toasted pita bread or chapati on the side.

cucumber salsa vegan—a clean-tasting salsa that lightens up the soup.

ingredients

2 in. piece of cucumber, peeled, seeded, and very finely chopped; 1 shallot, finely chopped; 10 fresh mint leaves, finely chopped; 1 fresh red chili, seeded and finely chopped; a squeeze of lemon juice; a pinch of salt

method

Simply mix all the ingredients together thoroughly. It benefits from standing for awhile, allowing the flavor to develop.

a small feast for friends—For a laid-back weekend afternoon with friends, escape from the routine appetizer-main-dessert format—try a casual six-course meal. If you think that sounds like a contradiction in terms, think again. It's an invitation to eat lavishly, but informally. I promise you won't be shopping, chopping, and washing up for days.

The idea is simple: Six consecutive small dishes, each to be considered and savored, one after the other. Choose six simple recipes, including something sweet. Some courses could be as simple as boiled artichokes with lemon and mayonnaise, a bowl of twinkling olives, or slices of sensuous, ripe mango. Don't reveal the menu. It's fun to maintain a sense of excitement and curiosity between courses.

shopping Seek out an unusual food store or deli in the morning or the day before. Don't be rigid about your menu. Go with an open mind—you might find a special cheese, some irresistible tomatoes as sweet as cherries, or a bizarre morsel you've never discovered before for everyone to sample.

presentation You won't need six sets of dishes for this six-course affair. One or two small plates and maybe one small bowl per person will suffice. Don't even think about washing dishes until after everyone leaves—or the next day.

drinks Beer seems to encourage laughter more than other drinks. Try buying a selection of different types of beer and ale and sampling a new one with each course. If it's a hot day, serve the beer in chilled glass mugs.

the menu

avocado soup with toasted cheese topping

The avocado is a sensuous and moody creature. When overripe, its incredible buttery texture can almost forgive a slightly off flavor. When underripe, it's totally inedible. Avocados are vulnerable—rough handling destroys them, as does fierce heat. However, as they have the highest fat content of all fruits, a careful warming brings out the best in them. This recipe, inspired by a soup I ate in Mexico, is essentially a guacamole diluted with hot stock. It's a breeze to make, but be careful not to cook it—merely warm it through.

ingredients

serves 4–6

for the soup:

4 medium ripe avocados
juice of 2 limes
generous 3/4 cup crème fraîche or sour cream
1 small onion, finely chopped
2 tomatoes, chopped
1 garlic clove, crushed
1 fresh red chili, seeded and finely chopped
salt and freshly ground black pepper
3 cups hot vegetable stock

for the topping:

3 1/2 oz. corn tortilla chips (unflavored)
1 cup grated cheddar or Monterey Jack cheese
4 scallions, chopped
1/2 cup crème fraîche or sour cream

method

Preheat the oven or broiler to its highest setting. Scoop out the avocado flesh and mash it with the lime juice. (A potato masher is the perfect tool for the job.) Stir in the crème fraîche or sour cream, onion, tomato, garlic, and chili and season to taste with salt and black pepper. Place the individual serving bowls on an oven tray and slide them into the oven to warm slightly.

The stock should be hot but not boiling. Stir the stock into the avocado mixture, then ladle into the warmed serving bowls. To make the topping, sprinkle a few tortilla chips on top of each bowl and sprinkle with the grated cheese. Put the bowls in the oven or under the broiler for just a few minutes, until the cheese melts. To serve, top with a few chopped scallions and a dollop of crème fraîche or sour cream and eat immediately.

think ahead

The avocado mixture can be made up to two hours in advance. Cover with plastic wrap and keep in the refrigerator, then bring up to room temperature before adding to the stock.

top tip

Presentation is most impressive out of individual bowls, but you can also pour the soup into one large ovenproof dish, allowing plenty of surface area for sprinkling the tortillas and cheese, then serve from the dish.

serve with

This is quite a filling soup and can be made into a complete meal with a salad on the side.

warm mushroom salad with creamy caper dressing

Use any mushroom you fancy for this simple yet sophisticated salad. It's easily converted to a main course by adding hard-boiled eggs or fried haloumi cheese.

ingredients

serves 4

2 tablespoons butter
1 tablespoon olive oil
2 garlic cloves, sliced
14 oz. exotic mushrooms or cremini or portobello mushrooms, stems removed, thinly sliced
salt and freshly ground black pepper
3 tablespoons finely chopped mixed herbs, such as rosemary, sage, thyme, marjoram, and parsley
grated zest and juice of 1 lemon
7 oz. mixed lettuce leaves
crusty bread, to serve

for the dressing:

1/2 cup crème fraîche or sour cream
2 tablespoons capers in vinegar, plus 1 teaspoon caper vinegar
1 tablespoon snipped fresh chives
1–2 tablespoons water, optional

method

Melt the butter in a large skillet or preheated wok over moderate heat and add the olive oil. Add the garlic and cook until fragrant. Add the mushrooms and season well with salt and black pepper. Stir-fry until the mushrooms are soft, then add the herbs and cook for about 5 minutes, until most of the pan juices have evaporated. Squeeze the juice of half a lemon over the mushroom mixture and remove from the heat.

To make the dressing, combine all the ingredients with the remaining lemon juice and zest. If desired, thin slightly with the water. Spoon the warm mushroom mixture over the mixed lettuce leaves and drizzle with the dressing. Serve with bread.

honey-roast parsnip & pear salad with blue cheese dressing

Parsnips, pears, and any blue cheese are a harmonious trio. This is an elegant winter salad that starts off a meal in style. It's well-balanced nutritionally, with the buttery macadamia nuts for extra protein, so it can also be served as a light main course.

ingredients

serves 4

4 small parsnips, peeled and cut into fourths lengthwise
2 tablespoons olive oil
1 tablespoon honey
salt and freshly ground black pepper
4 handfuls of arugula
2 dessert pears (such as Bartlett), sliced into wedges
3/4 cup macadamia nuts, toasted

for the dressing:

5 1/2 oz. Gorgonzola or other strong blue cheese
3 tablespoons white wine vinegar
1/2 cup olive oil

method

Preheat the oven to 400°F. Place the parsnips in a roasting pan and coat with the olive oil. Drizzle with the honey and season to taste with salt and black pepper. Roast in the preheated oven for about 20 minutes, until golden. Let cool.

To make the dressing, mash the Gorgonzola in a bowl. Stir in the vinegar and whisk in the olive oil with a little salt and black pepper until fairly smooth.

Arrange the arugula on individual plates and follow with the pears, toasted nuts, and roasted parsnips, then pour the dressing on top. Finish with more black pepper.

no-knead honey seed bread

If you love bread with a granular texture, you'll love it even more having made it yourself. To make this sturdy loaf, you will have to get your hands stuck in, but very little elbow grease is required. Seek out hemp seeds—available from health-food stores—they have a wonderful, nutty crunch, a bit like popcorn.

ingredients

serves 6–8

2 tablespoons honey
1 tablespoon active dry yeast
2 cups whole-wheat flour
1 1/2 cups all-purpose flour
2 teaspoons salt
2 tablespoons hulled pumpkin seeds
2 tablespoons hulled sunflower seeds
2 tablespoons hemp seeds
butter, for greasing
milk, for brushing (optional)
1 tablespoon poppy seeds, for sprinkling (optional)

method

Dissolve the honey in 1 1/4 cups hot (but not boiling) water in a small bowl or pitcher. Whisk in the yeast and let stand in a warm place for about 15 minutes, until frothy.

Combine the two flours in a mixing bowl. Using a wooden spoon, stir in the salt and the pumpkin, sunflower, and hemp seeds. Gradually add the yeasty water and mix to a dough. As the dough draws together, put the spoon aside and start using one hand to press the dough into a ball and the other hand to turn the bowl, incorporating everything into a soft, pliable mixture that leaves the sides of the bowl fairly clean. If the mixture is very sticky, sprinkle in a bit of flour to form a soft dough; if it is dry, sprinkle in a few drops of water and work it through until the flour disappears.

Grease a cookie sheet. Place the dough on it and form into a tapered "eye" shape—or whatever shape you fancy. Dust with flour and cover with a damp dish towel. Let rise in a warm place for about 1 hour, until doubled in size. Preheat the oven to 400°F. Use kitchen scissors to make decorative snips down the middle of the bread. Brush all over with milk and sprinkle with poppy seeds, if desired. Bake the loaf in the preheated oven for 30–40 minutes, until golden, firm, and hollow-sounding when tapped. Let cool on a wire rack.

hot brie fondue

—If you're fortunate enough to have access to a serious cheese shop, ask for the *Vacherin du Mont d'Or Sancey Richard*, which is perfect for this treatment. The same method will work with any soft, mature cheese with a washed rind, ideally in a box. If there's no box, you can still wrap the cheese itself in foil—the objective is a hot package of sinfully creamy goo to dip the bread in.

ingredients

serves 6–8; *mature soft cheese in a box; a little white wine*

method

Preheat the oven to 400°F. Take the lid off the cheese and drizzle a little white wine over the rind. Replace the lid and wrap the cheese in its box in foil. Place in the preheated oven on the middle rack for 15–20 minutes, after which time the cheese should be liquified right through. Unwrap and dunk slices of the Honey Seed Bread into the warm, runny cheese.

4

lunch & dinner meals

main dishes, some to serve with all the trimmings

The vegetarian main course seems to be the biggest stumbling block of all for the inexperienced. If you've planned a meal that revolves around a joint of meat, what do you do for the vegetarian? How do you create a meat substitute?

The answer is—don't. Soy-based "mock meat" products just don't fit the bill, and the days of the nut roast are now firmly behind us. Most vegetarians will be happy with all the trimmings of a roast, like potatoes and vegetables, supplemented with a dish that has lots of flavor and, ideally, a little protein. All of the dishes in this chapter can be slotted into that format. Don't forget, however, that many people will want to share the veggie dish! Make enough to go around the table—it's no fun to be alienated as the lone vegetarian.

A more interesting way of designing a menu is to give all the elements of the meal equal focus. If meat is being served, let it be one of the elements, but not the main event. Choose four or five dishes that balance each other perfectly. Provide a range of textures, for instance something crisp or crunchy, like lightly cooked green beans with toasted almonds, to contrast with a soft and creamy food like mashed potatoes. Avoid serving foods that are all the same color, especially brown. Consider the various tastes and aim to balance sweet and sour elements. Always serve one very clean-tasting dish, such as a simple salad or a steamed green vegetable, especially if the rest of the meal is very salty or spicy.

Avoid overcomplicating matters, however, especially if you're only cooking for a few. All the dishes in this chapter can, of course, be served as meals on their own.

ricotta & herb dumplings with vodka & cèpe butter sauce

The Italians would call these dumplings *malfatti*, meaning "badly made," because they are irregular in an endearing kind of way, meaning less fuss for the cook. The vodka fleshes out the sauce and turns this into a seriously good dish. It could easily be slotted into a roast meal—serve from a sizzling casserole on a wooden board, or transfer to a warm serving dish to be passed around with freshly grated Parmesan.

ingredients

serves 4

10½ oz. baby spinach, washed
2–6 tablespoons all-purpose flour
a large handful of fresh herbs, such as basil, parsley, or oregano, chopped
1 lb. 2 oz. ricotta cheese, drained
3 eggs
2 oz. fresh Parmesan cheese, grated
2 tablespoons semolina
salt and freshly ground black pepper

for the sauce:

1 tablespoon dried cèpes (approximately ¼ oz.)
¾ stick butter (3 oz.)
2 garlic cloves, chopped
⅓ cup vodka
freshly grated Parmesan cheese, to serve

method

First prepare the cèpes for the sauce. Place them in a bowl and pour in enough boiling water to cover. Let soak for 15 minutes, then drain, rinse again, and chop. For the dumplings, bring a large pan of salted water to a boil, then reduce to a simmer.

Meanwhile, place the spinach in a colander and pour boiling water directly over until it is wilted, then drain well, pressing out as much moisture as you can. Squeeze in a clean cloth to dry out further. Place the spinach in a food processor with the remaining ingredients—start with 2 tablespoons flour and pulse until well mixed. Alternatively, chop the spinach and herbs, then beat with the other ingredients in a bowl. The mixture should have the consistency of cottage cheese—it should just drop off the spoon.

The water in the pan should be simmering gently. Drop one test spoonful of the mixture into the water—don't panic if it falls apart, just add more flour to the mixture, then drop in spoonfuls and boil until they rise to the top, about 2–3 minutes. Drain thoroughly in a colander lined with paper towels. Cook in batches and keep warm in a dish in the oven.

To make the sauce, melt the butter in a skillet. Add the garlic and prepared cèpes and cook for 2 minutes. Add the vodka and season to taste with salt and pepper. Return to a boil, then simmer for 2 minutes, until the alcohol fumes are gone. Spoon over the dumplings and be generous with the Parmesan.

broiled tofu & mango skewers **vegan**

Anyone who doesn't like tofu should consider this: It just needs a little TLC to transform it from boring to irresistible. Cooking in hot oil gives it a crisp texture, and marinating kicks its spongy talents into action as it drinks up a pungent sauce.

ingredients

serves 4–5

for the sauce:

4 tablespoons dark soy sauce
2 tablespoons corn syrup or honey
1 tablespoon chili sauce or 5–6 dashes Tabasco sauce
2 tablespoons lime juice
1 tablespoon finely grated fresh root ginger

for the skewers:

4 tablespoons cornstarch
10½ oz. tofu, drained and patted dry
vegetable oil, for pan-frying
1 small, ripe but firm mango, cubed
10 kaffir lime leaves (optional)
10 lime wedges

method

Pour boiling water over ten long wooden skewers and let cool; this should prevent them from burning on the broiler. Mix together the sauce ingredients and set aside.

Sprinkle the cornstarch over a plate. Cut the tofu into twenty ½ in. chunks and roll in the cornstarch, shaking off any excess. Heat about a ½ in. depth of oil in a wide skillet until hot but not smoking. Cook the tofu, turning once with tongs, until crisp and golden all over. Keep the pieces from touching or they may stick together. Drain on paper towels briefly, then transfer to a plate. Spoon half the sauce over the hot tofu and let cool. If you have time, it will improve further if marinated for 1–2 hours in the refrigerator.

Thread a piece of mango, a piece of tofu, a lime leaf (if using), another piece of tofu, mango, and finishing with a lime wedge onto each skewer. Heat a ridged grill pan over high heat or heat the oven broiler to high. Broil the skewers, using tongs to turn them, until lightly charred all over. If the pan is hot, the cooking process should be quick, as the tofu is already fried. Use any remaining sauce to flavor accompanying noodles or rice.

smoked eggplant relish **vegan**—A sensational complement to the skewers.

ingredients

1 long, thin eggplant; ¼ cucumber, seeded and diced; a handful of fresh chives, snipped; 1 fresh green chili, seeded and chopped; 2 tablespoons chopped fresh mint; 1 tablespoon fresh lime juice; 1 tablespoon light soy sauce; 1 teaspoon superfine sugar

method

Push a fork into the stem of the eggplant and carefully place the body directly onto a high gas flame. Turn the eggplant occasionally until completely soft and collapsed; the skin should be blackened to the point of ash in places, and steam should be escaping through the fork holes. Alternatively, prick with a fork and broil until blistered all over.

Transfer to a plate and let cool, then peel off the charred skin and chop up the flesh. Don't worry if a few little charred bits remain, as they will add to the flavor. Combine the flesh with the remaining ingredients and serve.

sweet potato gnocchi with dolcelatte sauce

Gnocchi, the classic Italian potato dumplings, can be a little stodgy, so here's a new twist. Orange-fleshed sweet potato lightens them up beautifully. This minimalist cheese sauce is rather sinful, but goes outrageously well with sweet potato. When choosing sweet potato, rub a tiny speck of the skin off to be sure the flesh is orange. This is a rich dish and a little goes a long way—small portions are best; it's also very appetizing as a first course.

ingredients

serves 4–6

for the gnocchi:

1 lb. 2 oz. orange-fleshed sweet potato, scrubbed
salt and freshly ground black pepper
2 egg yolks
heaping 1/2 cup all-purpose flour
1/3 cup semolina, plus extra for dusting

for the sauce:

2/3 cup light cream
7 oz. dolcelatte or Gorgonzola cheese, cubed

method

Preheat the oven to 425°F. Prick the sweet potatoes and roast in the preheated oven for 45 minutes to 1 hour, until soft. Let stand until cool enough to handle, then peel.

Mash the flesh with a potato masher and fold in the remaining ingredients. Using wet hands, roll the dough into little dumplings and place on a large cookie sheet dusted with semolina. Bring a large pan of salted water to a boil, drop the dumplings into the boiling water, and boil until they rise to the surface, about 3–4 minutes, then drain.

To make the sauce, heat the cream gently to boiling and stir in the cheese until it melts. Grind in some black pepper and serve immediately, poured over the gnocchi.

roasted eggplants & haloumi with almond sauce

Based on a fifteenth-century Italian recipe, this exotic-tasting sauce uses pomegranate molasses, an amazing sweet-and-sour syrup made from pure concentrated juice. It is also delicious drizzled over soft white salty cheese.

ingredients

serves 4

2 medium eggplants
olive oil, for brushing
salt and freshly ground black pepper
9 oz. haloumi cheese, thinly sliced (vegans: use tempeh)
10½ oz. baby spinach, washed
a handful of fresh mint leaves, torn

for the sauce:

4 tablespoons ground almonds
1 tablespoon pomegranate molasses (or 1 tablespoon balsamic vinegar) blended with 4 tablespoons water
1 teaspoon superfine sugar
1 teaspoon cinnamon
1 teaspoon grated fresh root ginger
1 small garlic clove, crushed

method

Preheat the oven to 425°F. Cut the stem end off the eggplants and discard, then cut into four long wedges. Score the flesh in one diagonal direction, without piercing the skin. Brush thoroughly with olive oil and season to taste with salt and black pepper. Roast for 15–20 minutes, until soft and golden. Keep warm.

Now cook the cheese in a dry skillet until golden on both sides. To make the sauce, pound everything together in a mortar until smooth. If allowed to stand, the sauce will thicken; dilute with more water if necessary—it should have the consistency of creamy hummus. Arrange the spinach on a serving plate, then top with the cooked eggplant and cheese. Spoon the sauce on top or on the side. Sprinkle the torn mint on top and serve.

truffle-scented stuffed mushrooms

Wild about mushrooms? Well, here's a real fungi-fest. There's something so seductive about the deep, dark hue, rich flavor, and a texture that can only be described as, well, meaty.

ingredients

serves 6, or 3 generous servings of two mushrooms each

6 medium portobello, flat, or cremini mushrooms, similar in size, plus an extra 5 1/2 oz.
2 tablespoons olive oil, plus extra for brushing
2 tablespoons truffle oil, plus an extra 1 1/2 tablespoons
salt and freshly ground black pepper
9 oz. shiitake mushrooms, stems removed
5 garlic cloves, sliced
1/2 cup Madeira wine, sherry, or vermouth
2 teaspoons fresh thyme leaves
a good grinding of nutmeg
2 oz. fresh Parmesan cheese, grated
a generous handful of fresh Italian parsley leaves

method

Preheat the oven to 400°F. Cut the stems out of the six stuffing mushrooms, then brush the caps generously with olive oil and lay gill-side up on a cookie sheet. Drizzle a teaspoon truffle oil over the gills of each mushroom and season to taste with salt and black pepper. Coarsely chop the remaining mushrooms, including the shiitakes.

Heat the olive oil in a skillet. Add the garlic and cook for a couple of minutes until fragrant. Add the chopped portobello and shiitake mushrooms, salt, and a generous grinding of black pepper. Cook over medium-high heat until the mushrooms have collapsed. Pour in the Madeira wine, add the thyme and nutmeg, increase the heat, and cook until the juices have mostly evaporated. Let cool briefly, then place in a food processor with the grated Parmesan, parsley, and the remaining truffle oil. Process until a purée results, then spoon the mixture into the mushroom hollows and bake in the preheated oven for 20–30 minutes, until shrunken and lightly golden on top.

think ahead The filling can be made twenty-four hours in advance.

top tip If you are fortunate enough to have a fresh truffle, by all means use it—1 tablespoon of shavings in the filling mixture would be enough, plus a little more shaved over the finished article. In lieu of truffle oil you could also use 1–2 tablespoons of truffle paste, sold as "salsa truffina." I don't recommend truffles in brine.

serve with Delicious with cornbread, especially broiled, for added bite; or bruschetta, to accommodate the juices. These go beautifully with the trimmings for a roast meal.

a fancy Sunday roast—The Sunday roast is a bit of a dinosaur, but it's not yet extinct. It's a valuable ritual of family security, when loved ones gather to share gossip, relive old tales, and revel in unlimited comfort food. All too often these days, it's reserved for holidays like Thanksgiving and Christmas, but it could be welcomed any weekend. These occasions should be spoiling, but never strenuous; dinner's ready when it's ready. Relax and have fun introducing a little adventure into the traditional menu.

Roast potatoes are an absolute must-have for this menu, and here's the winning formula: Peel potatoes and boil for 5–10 minutes, until slightly floury on the outside but hard in the middle, then drain. Shake them around in a roasting pan to rough them up, coat with plenty of olive oil, season, and roast in a 425°F oven for 40–50 minutes until golden brown and crispy.

shopping This is an indisputably wintry menu, characterized by the seasonal, rib-clinging ingredients and substantial cooking time. Shopping might involve a trip to an outdoor market. If you've got several guests coming, make your life easier and delegate shopping or even whole cooked dishes.

presentation If you've got a fine set of china, now's the time to get it out. Polish the silver, shine the glasses, light the candles, and relish the ritual.

drinks A top-notch, full-bodied red wine is the ideal choice. A moderately priced Shiraz or Rioja seems to go miles further than inferior wine, as every sip is savored.

the menu

gratin of roasted garlic & squash *80*

ricotta & herb dumplings with vodka & cèpe butter sauce *67*

roast potatoes *74*

steamed tender-stem broccoli

radicchio & tomato salad drizzled with balsamic vinegar

cranberry torte with hot toffee-brandy sauce *90*

simple asparagus tarts

I affectionately call these "asparagus in a frame." I first devised this recipe for a large party on a minuscule budget, to be inexpensive (it was asparagus season) as well as easy to prepare. Afterward, I got calls from many of the guests, asking me to make them one or two, which I gladly agreed to because they only take ten minutes to make.

ingredients

serves 4–8

1 lb. 2 oz. medium-thickness asparagus spears, trimmed
2 teaspoons semolina or cornmeal
13 oz. ready-rolled puff pastry
2 egg yolks
scant 1/2 cup crème fraîche or sour cream
a pinch of salt
freshly ground black pepper
heaping 1/2 cup freshly grated Parmesan cheese

method

Preheat the oven to 425°F. Bring a pan of salted water to a boil. Add the asparagus, return to a boil, and cook for 3 minutes. Drain under cold running water until cool, then pat dry.

Sprinkle the semolina or cornmeal over a large cookie sheet, or over two small ones. Divide the puff pastry into two rectangles and place on the sheet. Using a sharp knife, score a 3/4 in. border around the edge of the pastry, not cutting through completely. Arrange the asparagus inside the pastry frames. To ensure that each slice has a fair share of the delicious tips, alternate the direction of the tips. Mix together the egg yolks, crème fraîche or sour cream, and seasoning in a measuring glass. Pour the mixture evenly into the middle of the two pastry frames, which should allow the borders to puff up in the oven before the custard runs off the edge. Quickly sprinkle the Parmesan over the two pastries and place in the preheated oven immediately.

Bake for 20–30 minutes, until the pastry is deep golden and the custard is patched with gold. Serve warm, each tart cut into four pieces. Cold tarts can be successfully reheated in an oven at 400°F for 5–7 minutes.

potato, garlic, & smoked mozzarella strudel

Strudel literally means "whirlwind," but this one is a breeze to make. Ready-made puff pastry is an honorable convenience, and when ready-rolled is easy to use. All-butter pastry has the best flavor and flakiest texture.

ingredients

serves 6–8

1 lb. 10 oz. mealy potatoes (such as Russet), peeled and cut into chunks

3 small garlic cloves

1 teaspoon coarse sea salt

9 oz. smoked mozzarella, or other smoked cheese, cut into 1/2 in. cubes

3–4 tablespoons finely chopped, fresh Italian parsley

freshly ground black pepper

13 oz. ready-rolled puff pastry

1 egg yolk mixed with 1 tablespoon milk, for glazing

method

Bring a pan of water to a boil and salt it well. Add the potatoes and simmer for about 15 minutes, until soft. Drain and mash, then let cool. Using a mortar and pestle, pound the garlic with the coarse salt until a smooth purée results. Add the purée to the cooled potatoes, along with the smoked mozzarella and parsley. Grind a good dose of black pepper into the mixture and stir until thoroughly combined.

Lay the puff pastry out on a cookie sheet. Spoon the potato mixture into a long, well-compacted sausage shape on one side of the pastry edge, leaving a border on that side and plenty of pastry to fold over the top of the mixture on the other side. Smooth the mixture and fold the pastry all the way around, forming a stuffed tube. Seal the ends by pressing them together. Press together the long seam, then roll the strudel over to rest with the seam underneath.

Cover and chill in the refrigerator for 30 minutes or up to 48 hours. When ready to bake, preheat the oven to 425°F. Using a sharp knife, make diagonal slashes on the top of the strudel about 3/4 in. apart and brush all over with the egg/milk glaze. Bake in the oven for 30–40 minutes, until deep golden and crispy all over. Let cool for at least 5 minutes, then slice into portions along the slashes.

sweet onion & ricotta cheesecake with cranberries & sage

This is my holiday version of Viana La Place's "Tortino di Cipolla" from *Verdura*, her brilliant book of Italian vegetable recipes. I have gussied it up with cranberries—a little vulgar maybe, but very seasonal, and a nice, tart contrast to the sweet onions. When cranberries are out of season, make it without.

ingredients

2 lb. 4 oz. fresh ricotta cheese
3 tablespoons olive oil, plus extra for greasing and drizzling
12 oz. onions (approximately 2 large), chopped
4 garlic cloves, chopped
10 fresh sage leaves, coarsely chopped
4 eggs, beaten
6 tablespoons freshly grated Parmesan cheese
salt and freshly ground black pepper
1 cup fresh or frozen cranberries
2 oz. cracker crumbs (cheese crackers or saltines), finely crushed
whole, fresh sage leaves, to garnish (optional)

method

Preheat the oven to 375°F. Place the ricotta in a strainer and place over a bowl or the sink. Let drain thoroughly while you cook the onions.

Heat the olive oil in a large skillet over low heat. Add the onions and cook gently, stirring frequently, until very soft but not colored. Add the garlic and sage and cook for 1–2 minutes, until fragrant.

Beat together the drained ricotta, eggs, Parmesan, salt, and pepper (ideally in a food processor) until totally smooth. Stir in the onion mixture and cranberries and mix thoroughly.

Brush an 8½ in. springform pan generously with olive oil. Sprinkle the cracker crumbs evenly over the bottom and sides, then pour in the ricotta mixture and smooth the surface with a spatula. Garnish the top with whole sage leaves and drizzle a little olive oil over the top, especially over the sage leaves. Place on a cookie sheet and bake in the preheated oven for 45 minutes to 1 hour, until firm and golden. Let cool for about 10 minutes, then transfer to a serving plate. Serve warm or cold.

think ahead

This recipe can be made up to twenty-four hours in advance. Let cool, then cover and keep in the refrigerator. If serving warm, return to room temperature before reheating.

top tip

Try to get ricotta from an Italian deli or high-quality cheese store, as it will probably be less watery and more suitable for cooking than the tubs sold in most supermarkets.

serve with

Trimmings for a roast meal

gratin of roasted garlic & squash

This is serious comfort food—a pretty outrageous dish that always pleases everyone. The squash family is huge and some members are more agreeable than others. Choose one with a dark orange, creamy, dense flesh. Butternut, kabocha, acorn, and onion squash are all good bets.

ingredients

serves 4–6

3 tablespoons extra-virgin olive oil
2 butternut squashes or other sweet-fleshed squashes (approximately 4 1/2 lb.)
8 garlic cloves
8 fresh sage leaves
9 oz. Swiss cheese, cut into 1/2 in. cubes
salt and freshly ground black pepper

method

Preheat the oven to 425°F. Chop the stem off the squash, then use a vegetable peeler or paring knife to peel off the skin. (This is much easier to do at this stage than after cooking.) Slice the squash in half lengthwise, then scoop the seeds out with a spoon and lay the squash on a cookie sheet, cavity-side up. Place two whole cloves of garlic in each cavity, along with two sage leaves. Pour about 2 teaspoons of olive oil over the garlic and sage and, using a dough brush, paint the oil all over the surface of the flesh. Bake in the preheated oven for 30–40 minutes, until tender and lightly browned around the edges. Let cool slightly.

Place the flesh in a bowl along with the roasted garlic and sage. Mash it all together with a potato masher until crushed but not entirely smooth. Stir in the Swiss cheese cubes. Spoon into a presentable, greased gratin dish and bake in the oven for 15–20 minutes, until golden and bubbly. Serve right away.

think ahead Roast the squash one day in advance.

top tip If you can't find a good squash, use red sweet potato. Roast whole in the skin at the same temperature, adding the garlic and sage for the last 20 minutes, lightly oiled alongside, then let cool and peel before mashing.

serve with Roast meal accompaniments; salad; steamed green vegetables

PAPAYAS

5

desserts

little candies and naughty bites

As if you haven't spoiled your guests enough already, you can really go to town with dessert. It's your gratifying grand finale, and no time to be judicious—everyone should feel they can dive into a dessert with reckless abandon, even if they thought they couldn't manage another bite. Dessert brings out the greedy child in all of us.

At canapé parties, some little sweet bites toward the end of the evening are a great way to inject some sugary stimulation, but can also be a signal that the party may be nearing an end. Make Baby Lemon Curd Meringues (page 96) or make the Pecan Chocolate Ripple Cheesecake (page 98) in a large, square baking dish and cut into bite-size portions.

If you're feeding a big crowd, choose Rhubarb Soup with Ginger-Studded Meringues (page 88) or one type of Eton Mess (page 87). If you're really pressed for time, they won't know what they're missing if you buy one, giant, delicious, ripe cheese—or two or three; any more and it's overkill—and some delectable savory crackers. Avoid buying lots of little pieces of different cheeses; the cheeseboard will quickly look unappetizing, and people will feel they can only take a small portion. Encourage your guests to surrender to temptation.

marrons caramelises au cognac

Chestnuts in a cognac sauce (sorry, but it just sounds so much better in French)—a quick and easy way to turn plain old ice cream into something unforgivably wicked. It's a great emergency dessert.

ingredients

serves 4–6

9 oz. whole, peeled, cooked chestnuts (sold in a vacuum pack, or in cans)
4 tablespoons salted butter
3 tablespoons sugar
1/3 cup cognac or brandy
chocolate ice cream, to serve

method

Carefully separate the chestnuts. Melt the butter in a skillet over moderate heat. Add the chestnuts and cook gently for 2 minutes. Sprinkle in the sugar, stir, and boil until it dissolves, about 1 minute. Pour in the cognac, stir, and turn off the heat. Let stand until just warm, then spoon over the ice cream.

think ahead

This is a last-minute recipe, but chestnuts and cognac are kitchen cupboard must-haves.

top tip

Make this as soon as the meal is finished. In the time it takes to cool off and thicken a little, your appetite should have had just enough time to come back for more. (If you have a very efficient freezer, you may want to get the ice cream out to soften as well).

serve with

Vanilla ice cream is also delicious with this treat.

tropical eton mess

Eton Mess is the absolute best dessert to feed a large, discerning crowd, as I'm sure the dinner ladies at the English boys' school know all too well—traditionally it's been served at Eton College's Founders' Day and Fourth of June celebrations. The classic version is a demure strawberry affair. Here are my two showstoppers.

ingredients

serves 8

8 individual hard-cooked meringue nests
2 1/2 cups heavy (whipping) cream
4 tablespoons white rum (optional)
1 papaya, peeled, seeded, and chopped
1 small mango, peeled and chopped
1 baby pineapple, peeled and chopped, or 1 lb. 2 oz. fresh, prepared pineapple
2 ripe passion fruit
cape gooseberries, to decorate

method

Break up the meringues into bite-size pieces in a large bowl. Whip the cream until it holds its shape—do not overbeat—then stir in the rum.

Just before serving, fold the crushed meringues and whipped cream together until evenly mixed. Spoon into a serving bowl and top with the prepared fruit. Slice open the passion fruits and drizzle the juice and seeds over the top. Decorate, if desired, with cape gooseberries.

strawberry rose eton mess

—Follow the recipe above, replacing the fruit with about 1 lb. 2 oz. fresh, hulled strawberries, halved if large. Instead of the rum, beat 4 tablespoons rose water through the cream. Provide extra strawberries in a bowl on the side.

rhubarb soup with ginger-studded meringues

This one is excellent for a crowd, as the portions are quite flexible and people can easily serve themselves. It looks beautiful served from a big, wide, shallow bowl, with the marshmallow-centered meringues floating on top.

ingredients

serves 10–12

4 1/2 lb. rhubarb, trimmed and sliced into 1/2 in. pieces
1 1/2 cups superfine sugar
crème fraîche or thick and creamy yogurt, to serve

for the meringues:

3 egg whites
generous 3/4 cup superfine sugar
1 teaspoon cornstarch
1/2 teaspoon vinegar
1/3 cup candied ginger, chopped

method

Place the rhubarb in a pan with the sugar and 1 3/4 cups water. Cover, bring to a boil, and simmer for 20–30 minutes, until a moderately thin compote results. Pour into a bowl, let cool, then chill thoroughly.

To make the meringues, preheat the oven to 250°F and line a large cookie sheet with parchment paper. Beat the egg whites until stiff, then beat in the sugar, a tablespoon at a time, until the mixture is very stiff and glossy. Whisk in the cornstarch, vinegar, and ginger pieces. Spoon egg-size mounds onto the cookie sheet, allowing a little space between them for expansion. Bake in the oven for 30 minutes, until crisp on the outside but still gooey in the middle. When cooled, dislodge the meringues from the paper by sliding a large knife under them.

To serve, pour the soup into a wide, shallow bowl and float the meringues on top. Serve with crème fraîche or yogurt.

kaffir lime ice cream

The splendid perfume of kaffir lime leaves gives this ice cream a subtle, fragrant undertone. I implore you, make the ice cream without kaffir lime leaves if you can't find them, as this is fantastically easy and delicious made just with lime juice or even lemon juice. You don't need an ice cream maker, just a freezer.

ingredients

serves 10–12

2 1/2 cups heavy (whipping) cream
2 1/2 cups whole milk
2 cups superfine sugar
6 kaffir lime leaves
2/3 cup fresh lime juice
zest of 2 limes

method

Mix together the cream, milk, and 1 cup sugar in a large plastic container and stir until the sugar dissolves. Cover tightly and place in the freezer.

Tear the lime leaves away from their tough stems, then pound them using a mortar and pestle to release the fragrant oils. Alternatively, whack them with a rolling pin or mallet. Mix together the lime juice, zest, kaffir lime leaves, and remaining sugar in a small plastic container and stir until the sugar dissolves. Cover and place in the freezer.

Freeze both containers for about 3 hours, until slushy—the creamy mixture should be the consistency of a milk shake. Scrape the lime mixture into the cream mixture, stirring well and scraping crystals away from the edge of the container. Freeze until solid. The ice cream freezes very hard, so it's a good idea to thaw it ever so slightly in the refrigerator for about 1 hour before serving.

cranberry torte with hot toffee-brandy sauce

This incredibly luscious cake is the perfect, lighter alternative to that heavy Christmas pudding or laborious pumpkin pie. It's a pan full of sharp fruit and nuts just fused together with a little cardamom-spiked cake batter, then drenched in hot, boozy toffee.

ingredients

serves 8–10

1 lb. 2 oz. fresh or frozen cranberries
3/4 stick butter (3 oz.), melted, plus extra for greasing
1 cup superfine sugar
1 cup chopped pecans
1 egg, beaten
1/2 cup sifted all-purpose flour
1 teaspoon cardamom seeds, crushed in a mortar
3 tablespoons light brown sugar

for the sauce:

scant 1 cup dark brown sugar
1 stick butter (4 oz.)
1/2 cup heavy (whipping) cream
3 tablespoons brandy

method

Preheat the oven to 350°F. Wash the cranberries and drain well. Grease and line the bottom of a 9½ in. springform cake pan with parchment paper. Place the cranberries in the pan, then sprinkle with half the superfine sugar and the pecans and mix well.

Next, make the batter. Beat the remaining superfine sugar with the egg in a bowl until well blended. Add the flour, melted butter, and cardamom, mix well, and pour evenly over the cranberries. Sprinkle the granulated sugar evenly over the top and bake in the preheated oven for 40–45 minutes. Let cool in the pan.

To make the sauce, place the sugar, butter, and cream in a pan. Stir together over a gentle heat until the sugar is dissolved and the sauce is bubbling. Remove from the heat and stir in the brandy.

Use a sharp knife or cake slicer to gently unmold the torte, letting it stand on the pan base. Slice into wedges and serve warm or cold, with warm toffee-brandy sauce.

think ahead

The torte can be made eight hours in advance. The sauce can be made up to two days in advance; cover, keep in the refrigerator, and reheat before serving.

top tip

Cranberries have a short season, but they freeze incredibly well—so stock up while they're available and use straight from the freezer in this recipe, any time of the year.

a garden party—A relaxing and indulgent English-style tea party is a comfort zone where kids, adults, and the elderly are most at ease together. It can also be a useful context for gathering people who don't know each other too well. It's a refreshing way to make the most of sunny days: nibbling, gossiping, and celebrating for the sake of it.

The menu here is for an all-out garden party, a truly lavish affair. For a simpler version, the Cucumber & Herbed Mascarpone Bites (page 15) are essential, then choose one of the three sweet recipes. Supplement with scones (easy to bake, easier to buy) and crumpets or madeleines from a reputable bakery. Don't forget the butter, cream, and jam!

shopping Decorate your table. Buy flowers, lots of fruit, and plenty of sugar cubes for tea.

presentation If you're short on tableware, ask a friend or two to bring what cups and saucers they have, then create a funky new set by mixing cups with nonmatching saucers. Extra teapots will be a godsend.

drinks Not everyone likes black tea (such as Earl Grey); provide some herbal alternatives. Green tea is delicious, but it's not caffeine-free. To make the perfect pot of tea: Warm the teapot with a little boiling water and swirl; discard the water; add teabags or loose tea; then add water that is on a rolling boil. Brew it fairly strong and provide a teapot of plain hot water for those who like it weak.

the menu

broiled stuffed peaches

Good peaches can be hard to come by. Sometimes they look perfect, but have been picked unripe and taste sour and woolly. If you can, buy one from the batch and take a bite—it should be bursting with sweet juice. White peaches are often the best choice.

ingredients

serves 6

3 ripe peaches, halved and pitted
1 tablespoon sugar
high-quality vanilla ice cream, to serve

for the stuffing:

2 tablespoons butter, softened
1/4 cup shelled pistachios, finely chopped
2 tablespoons sugar
3 tablespoons brandy
a pinch of ground cloves
1 tablespoon chopped candied ginger

method Preheat the broiler to its highest setting. Beat together the stuffing ingredients until smooth. Place the peach halves in an ovenproof dish. Divide the stuffing evenly between the peaches and sprinkle with the remaining sugar. Cook under the broiler for about 7–8 minutes, until the stuffing is golden and the sugar is melted. Serve with small scoops of vanilla ice cream.

think ahead This recipe can be made and assembled up to four hours in advance. Cover and chill in the refrigerator, then allow to return to room temperature before broiling.

top tip Vegans should use margarine instead of butter. Do not store peaches in the refrigerator, as their texture may deteriorate. Ready-shelled pistachios are not the easiest ingredient to find, but you don't need masses of them, so you could shell them yourself. Hulled pumpkin seeds can be substituted.

serve with Ice cream is ideal, though creamy yogurt or crème fraîche will do.

baby lemon curd meringues

Make these just bite-size for a sweet canapé or slightly larger for a light dessert. The meringues can be made up to two days in advance and kept in an airtight container in the refrigerator.

ingredients

serves 8

butter, for greasing
1–1 1/4 cups crème fraîche, sour cream, or softly whipped cream
2/3–3/4 cup top-quality lemon curd
pomegranate seeds, red currants, or blueberries, or a mixture
confectioners' sugar, for dusting

for the meringues:

6 egg whites, at room temperature
a pinch of salt
2 cups superfine sugar
2 teaspoons cornstarch
1 teaspoon vinegar

method

To make the meringue mixture, follow the recipe on page 88, adding the salt with the sugar and omitting the candied ginger. Place egg-size fluffy mounds on a lined cookie sheet, with a little room in between each. (You may wish to make them even smaller for bite-size canapés.) Flatten the tops very slightly and remember, irregularity is beautiful.

Bake the meringues in the preheated oven for 30–40 minutes, until crisp and light golden on the outside but still a little gooey in the middle. Let cool completely on the sheet. Loosen the cold meringues with a spatula and place on a tray. Top each with a spoonful of crème fraîche, sour cream, or whipped cream, and a small spoonful of lemon curd, and finish with pomegranate seeds, red currants, or blueberries. Dust with confectioners' sugar, if desired, and serve immediately.

chocolate strawberry truffle pots

These exquisite, rich little pots are ideal after a satisfying meal, when all you want is a few mouthfuls of naughty sweetness without the bulk. Make them up to eight hours in advance.

ingredients

serves 10

1 cabbage or large apple, for holding strawberries
7 oz. high-quality white chocolate
10 equal-size strawberries, hulled
10 silver dragées (candy decorations)
9 oz. high-quality semisweet chocolate
4 tablespoons butter, cubed
1 1/4 cups heavy (whipping) cream

method

Cut a slice off the bottom of the cabbage or apple to help it stand firmly, and place on a plate; this will act as a "pincushion" to hold the strawberries while the chocolate sets. Clear a space in the refrigerator that will accommodate the plate and some space above it. Melt the white chocolate in a bowl set over a pan of simmering water. Dip the pointed end of a strawberry into the melted chocolate to come halfway up the berry. Pierce a toothpick through the hulled end and then stick the other end of the cocktail stick into the "pincushion." Press a dragée into the chocolate at the very tip, if desired. Repeat with all the strawberries, then chill.

Arrange ten shot glasses or bowls on a tray, ready to be filled. Place the semisweet chocolate, butter, and cream in a pan and place over very gentle heat. Stir constantly until absolutely smooth, then remove from the heat. (If the mixture curdles from overheating, add more cream.) Divide the truffle mixture between the shot glasses or bowls, then place a chilled strawberry, with the white chocolate side pointing up, on top of the truffle mixture. Let chill for about 30 minutes, until set. Allow to return to room temperature before serving.

pecan chocolate ripple cheesecake

I created this for my mother's seventieth birthday, to be the very embodiment of delectable chocolate nuttiness, her favorite combination. She was not disappointed.

ingredients

for the shell:

7 oz. semisweet chocolate–covered graham crackers

4 tablespoons butter, melted

2 tablespoons unsweetened cocoa

for the filling:

9 oz. high-quality semisweet chocolate

2 cups cream cheese

1 1/4 cups mascarpone cheese

2 teaspoons pure vanilla extract

1 cup superfine sugar

2 organic eggs

for the candied pecan topping:

1 1/4 cups pecan halves

2 tablespoons sugar

2 oz. high-quality semisweet chocolate

method

Preheat the oven to 350°F. Crush the graham crackers in a food processor. Mix with the melted butter and cocoa, then press into the bottom of a 9 1/2 in. springform cake pan. Pack it down firmly with your fingertips or smooth down with the back of a spoon. Bake the cracker shell in the oven for 10 minutes, then remove and let cool. Reduce the oven temperature to 325°F.

To make the filling, melt the chocolate in a bowl set over a pan of simmering water. Alternatively, melt the chocolate in the microwave. Whip the two cheeses together until smooth. Add the vanilla extract and sugar, and finally the eggs, one at a time. Pour half the mixture into the cake pan. Add the melted chocolate to the remaining mixture and stir until smooth. The chocolate mixture will be considerably thicker than the vanilla one. Spoon into the cake pan in patches over the vanilla mixture, then, using a sharp knife, swirl the two mixtures together by drawing several zigzag patterns through the mixture. Bake in the oven for 30–40 minutes, until just set. If it wobbles slightly, remember that chilling will make it set firmer.

Let the cake cool in its pan on a wire rack, then chill for at least 3 hours or overnight. Meanwhile, make the candied pecans. Place the pecans in a dry skillet over moderate heat. Sprinkle the sugar on top and stir until the nuts are toasted and the sugar becomes sticky and caramelized. Let cool.

Run a knife around the edge of the cake, then unmold, leaving the bottom of the pan attached to it, otherwise you risk breaking up the crust. Place on a large serving plate. To finish, melt the chocolate, then sprinkle the candied pecans over the top of the cake. Drizzle melted chocolate over the top to fuse the pecans in place and chill in the refrigerator until ready to serve. Allow to return to room temperature. Soak a sharp knife in hot water, dry, and use immediately for cutting each slice. Indulge.

top tip

This cake can be made as a sweet canapé. Cook in a rectangular baking pan, then chill and cut into tiny squares and separate them. Top each square with a caramelized pecan, then drizzle with chocolate.

6

at the last minute

high-speed recipes, with minimal shopping

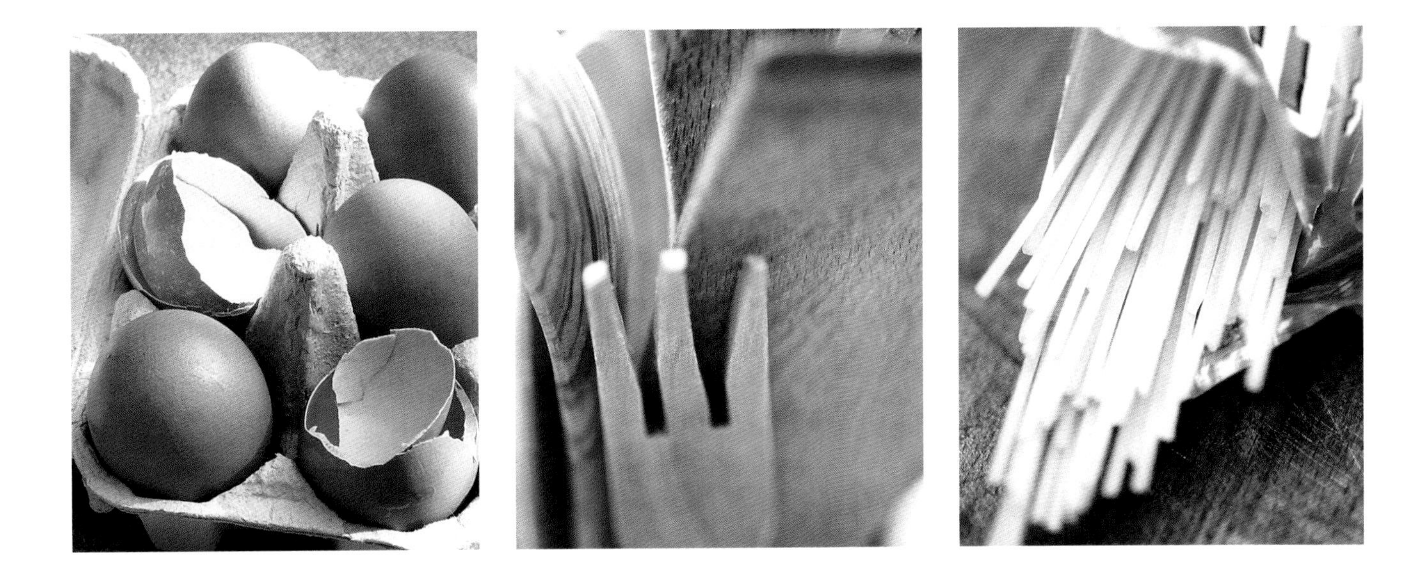

Spontaneity delivers some of the most memorable and relaxed occasions. This chapter is for those unexpected times in life—when old friends blaze into town without warning, when the weather is so beautiful you just have to invite some friends over after work to eat in the garden—when you can't be bothered to shop but have some hungry hangers-on to feed and you don't want them to know you can't be bothered!

Alas, a delicious last-minute meal can't be pulled out of thin air, but it can be rustled up from a well-stocked kitchen. See "The Entertainer's Bag of Tricks," page 11, and take the book with you when shopping and enjoy stocking up. If unexpected guests pop by, you can even just grab some of those tasty morsels from the cupboard and make a meal of it with some couscous and chickpeas dressed in lemon and olive oil.

Here are some superquick ideas:

Spicy soba salad Cook soba noodles, drain, and cool under cold running water. Make a dressing of sesame oil, soy sauce, chopped chilies, and scallions. Stir through the noodles and serve with lime wedges.

Cèpe cornmeal Make soft, instant cornmeal, according to the package instructions, using water in which you have first soaked a good clutch of dried cèpes for 10 minutes. (Add the cèpes too!) Stir in lots of butter and Parmesan at the end.

Fig & walnut pasta While the pasta cooks, heat some onions in olive oil until soft. Drain the pasta and stir in chopped dried figs, chopped walnuts, cubes of blue cheese, and the cooked onions.

Saffron aïoli platter Pound a garlic clove with coarse salt until smooth. Stir in 2 pinches of saffron threads soaked in 1 teaspoon of hot water, a squeeze of lemon, and 3 tablespoons of mayonnaise. Serve with potatoes and a selection of steamed vegetables.

hot & sour noodle bowl with chili oil **vegan**

Thick and toothsome udon noodles are available ready-cooked in vacuum packs for the quickest soups and stir-fries. They're satisfyingly slurpy in this zingy broth, but you could also use dried ramen or egg noodles, adding them to the broth early on, to cook with the vegetables.

ingredients

serves 4–6

1 lb. 2 oz. chopped, mixed vegetables from the refrigerator or freezer, such as broccoli, cabbage, cauliflower, peas, and zucchini

6 tablespoons dark soy sauce

6 tablespoons lime juice or rice vinegar, or a mixture

2 tablespoons sugar

1 1/4 in. piece of fresh root ginger, finely grated

14 oz. udon noodles or other cooked noodles

for the chili oil:

1 fresh red chili, coarsely chopped

1 garlic clove

1/2 teaspoon coarse sea salt

2 tablespoons sesame oil

method

Put 4 cups of water in a pan and bring to a boil while you make the chili oil. Pound or process the chili, garlic, and salt in a mortar or spice grinder. Whisk in the sesame oil, then set aside until required.

Add the vegetables to the pan of boiling water and return to a boil, adding the soy sauce, lime juice or vinegar, sugar, and ginger. Simmer until the vegetables are tender, then add the noodles. Cook for 1 minute or long enough to warm the noodles through.

Divide the soup between individual bowls. Drizzle the chili oil over each bowl and serve immediately.

artichoke soufflé omelette

This seriously sexy omelette will make a big impression—especially since it can be whipped up almost effortlessly. Serve with a salad or just basking in its own loveliness.

ingredients

serves 2–4

5 eggs, separated

2 whole eggs

4½ oz. artichoke hearts in oil, drained and sliced

½ cup freshly grated Parmesan cheese

10 fresh basil leaves, shredded

salt and freshly ground pepper to taste

1 tablespoon butter

2 tablespoons olive oil

method

Using a fork, lightly beat together the five egg yolks and the two whole eggs. Using a handheld electric mixer, beat the egg whites until stiff, then fold the whites carefully into the yolks, keeping it light and airy. Fold in the artichokes, Parmesan, basil, and seasoning, again being careful not to lose the fluffiness.

Heat the butter and olive oil in a wide, nonstick skillet over moderate heat. Pour in the omelette mixture and cook for about 5 minutes, until golden and crisp underneath. Depending on the size of your skillet, it may not be possible to flip the omelette with a spatula, so you can try this method: Slide the omelette onto a large plate, discard any excess oil so as not to risk getting burned, then invert the skillet over the top of the omelette and flip the plate and skillet over. Remove the plate and cook the omelette for an additional 1–2 minutes, until softly set. Slide onto a warm serving plate, cut into wedges, and eat immediately.

practically instantaneous pasta sauces

Prepared and cooked in less time than it takes to boil your pasta, these fresh sauces will knock the socks off any store-bought sauce. Don't forget that fresh pasta sauce freezes beautifully, so you can always have it on hand.

lemon spinach sauce

ingredients

serves 4

pasta of your choice
4 tablespoons olive oil
2 garlic cloves, crushed
1 small, fresh red chili, chopped, or 1/4 teaspoon dried chili flakes
10 1/2 oz. fresh or frozen leaf spinach
salt and freshly ground black pepper
6 tablespoons strained plain or thick and creamy yogurt
juice of 1/2 lemon

method

Bring a large pan of salted water to a boil. Cook pasta according to package directions or until al dente. Heat the olive oil in a wide skillet and cook the garlic and chili for 1 minute. Add the spinach leaves, season with a little salt and black pepper, and stir. Cover the skillet while the spinach wilts, about 2 minutes for fresh, 4 minutes for frozen. Take the pan off the heat and stir in the yogurt and lemon juice. Cover and let stand for 1 minute, then stir into the pasta.

fried tomatoes & hazelnut pesto

ingredients

serves 4

pasta of your choice

for the pesto:

1/2 garlic clove
1 teaspoon coarse sea salt
1 teaspoon pink peppercorns
scant 1/4 cup blanched hazelnuts
2 handfuls of fresh basil and parsley, coarsely chopped
3 tablespoons freshly grated Parmesan cheese
4 tablespoons olive oil

for the tomatoes:

2 tablespoons olive oil
2 medium tomatoes, thickly sliced
2 teaspoons balsamic vinegar
a pinch of sugar
salt and freshly ground black pepper

method

Bring a large pan of salted water to a boil. Cook pasta until al dente. Meanwhile, make the pesto. Place the garlic, coarse salt, and peppercorns in a mortar and pound to a paste. Add the nuts and pound a bit, then add the herbs and grated Parmesan. Pound and grind until a coarse paste results. Add the olive oil and stir until incorporated. While the pasta cooks, heat the oil for the tomatoes in a wide skillet over moderate heat. Add the sliced tomatoes, vinegar, and a little sugar and cook until slightly colored on both sides. Season with a little salt and pepper.

Drain your pasta, then return to the pan. Scrape all the pesto into the pasta and stir vigorously to incorporate evenly. Serve topped with fried tomatoes.

an impromptu dinner—Here's the strategy for the menu opposite: The Kerala-Style Egg Curry (page 113) takes no more than 30 minutes to make, including preparation. So, to keep your guests nibbling happily in the meantime, prepare some delicious toasted flatbread and luxury hummus.

Turn the oven on to 400°F. Cut the flatbread into triangles and place on an oven tray. Drizzle with olive oil and sprinkle with a few sesame seeds, if you like. Toast in the oven until crisp, approximately 7–10 minutes. Scoop the hummus onto a plate; taste and stir in a little lemon juice if you think it needs it. Sprinkle with some dried mint, a few drops of olive oil, and finish with a cluster of capers. Stand some of the flatbread crisps in the hummus. Place a few pickled beets in another bowl with a few cocktail sticks.

shopping If you do have time to shop, fresh hummus is always better than canned. Serve savory crackers in lieu of flatbread. Canned hummus is just one of the ingredients included in "The Entertainer's Bag of Tricks" (page 11), which lists useful staples to keep in the kitchen for impromptu entertaining.

presentation At the last minute, anything goes.

drinks If your impromptu guests come expecting to be fed, it's fair to remind them to bring a bottle of wine or a few cans of beer. Save washing up and serve beer from the can or bottle. Beer promotes good cheer, is a successful appetite curber, and tastes great with spicy food.

the menu

hummus topped with dried mint, olive oil, & capers *108*

pickled baby beets

turkish flatbread toasted with olive oil & sesame seeds *108*

kerala-style egg curry *113*

ice cream with hot toffee-brandy sauce *90*

wok-fried noodles singapore-style

It's the curry powder, pepper, and flat rice noodles that make this Singapore-style, but it's flexible, depending upon what you have in stock. Stir-fries are quick to cook, but what's the use if you're shredding, chopping, and mincing for half an hour? Preparation is kept to an absolute minimum here.

ingredients

serves 4 (more than this will be too slow and unwieldy in the wok)

5 1/2 oz. flat rice noodles
1 lb. 2 oz. mixed vegetables—whatever you have on hand from the refrigerator or freezer; no more than 4–5 types, such as broccoli, zucchini, bell peppers, mushrooms, peas, and cabbage
2 tablespoons mild curry powder
1/2 cup water
2 tablespoons soy sauce
1 teaspoon salt
2 teaspoons sugar
1/2 teaspoon ground black pepper
1/2 teaspoon dried chili flakes
2 handfuls of cashew nuts (approximately 1/2 cup)
8 garlic cloves, peeled and left whole
4–6 tablespoons sunflower or corn oil

method

Boil a generous amount of water. Place the noodles in a bowl and pour boiling water over them. Let stand for 2 minutes—no more—then drain. Rinse under cold running water. They should be just cooked.

Cut up the vegetables so that they are in similar-size chunks. Place in a bowl and sprinkle the curry powder over them. Stir and set aside.

Mix together the water, soy sauce, salt, sugar, black pepper, and chili flakes.

Heat the wok as hot as you can—do not add oil. Toss in the cashew nuts and stir until they take on a little color, then remove from the wok. Toss in the garlic cloves (still, no oil) and char them in the dry wok, shaking occasionally, until they are blackened. Now add the oil and, very quickly, the vegetables. Stir vigorously. (Add a little more oil if it seems dry.) Stir-fry for 1–2 minutes, then add the noodles, cashew nuts, and the sauce mixture. Stir-fry for 2–3 minutes, until the vegetables are crisp and tender, the liquid is reduced, and the noodles are cooked through. Serve immediately.

think ahead

Noodles are a great quick food, so keep a selection in stock.

top tip

A traditional steel wok with a round bottom is probably the most useful pan in the kitchen if you have a gas stove. On an electric stove, you'll need a wok with a flat bottom. Large ones are best so you can really move the food around without spilling it over the sides. Traditional steel woks are thin and get very hot, which is the secret of quick wok cooking. If the wok really is searing hot, you may need a little extra oil, which is why I've given two quantities in the recipe. Always heat the wok first without oil to prevent sticking.

bulgur wheat in a spiced tomato sauce

This one is easy, fast, filling, warming, and cheap—the ideal quick-fix dinner. Inspired by an Iranian dish called *haleem*, which is a sort of thick, savory porridge, it becomes even thicker as it stands.

ingredients

serves 4

14 oz. can chopped tomatoes
1 fresh chili, sliced and seeded if large, or 1/2 teaspoon chili powder
2 plump garlic cloves
2 teaspoons ground cumin
1 teaspoon brown sugar
1/2 teaspoon wine vinegar
salt and freshly ground black pepper
scant 1 cup bulgur wheat
1 tablespoon dried mint
2 pieces of cinnamon stick or cassia bark (optional)

to serve:

thick and creamy yogurt
extra-virgin olive oil
a little ground cumin or cinnamon, for sprinkling
fresh parsley leaves (optional)

method

Empty the can of tomatoes into a blender and save the can. Add the chili, garlic, cumin, sugar, vinegar, salt, and black pepper and process into a smooth purée. Pour into a pan.

Pour two cans full of water into the blender in order to rinse it out, and then empty out the water into the pan. This will ensure that every last drop of purée is used. Add the bulgur wheat, dried mint, and cinnamon or cassia bark. Bring to a boil and simmer for 10–15 minutes, stirring frequently, until the bulgur is cooked. Taste for seasoning. Ladle into bowls and serve with a dollop of yogurt, a drizzling of olive oil, and a pinch or two of cumin or cinnamon on top of each bowl. Garnish with parsley leaves, if desired.

kerala-style egg curry

"Curry" is a Westernized concept meaning "stewed in sauce," and some curries are cooked to develop flavor over many hours or even days. This dazzling dish from southern India takes no more than 30 minutes to prepare.

ingredients

serves 4

4 eggs
4 tablespoons sunflower oil
2 teaspoons black mustard seeds
2 large onions, finely sliced (approximately 14 oz.)
3–4 garlic cloves, sliced
1 1/2–2 in. piece of fresh root ginger, peeled and chopped
4 fresh chilies, halved lengthwise
2 teaspoons ground turmeric
2 teaspoons cumin seeds
3 tablespoons dry, unsweetened coconut
salt and freshly ground black pepper
4 plump vine tomatoes, chopped, or 14 oz. can chopped tomatoes
1 cup yogurt
fresh cilantro leaves, to garnish (optional)
freshly cooked basmati rice, to serve

method

Place the eggs in a small pan and cover with cold water. Bring to a boil and simmer for 5 minutes. Drain, rinse under cold running water until cooled, then peel and set aside.

Heat the oil in a wok or large skillet until quite hot. Add the mustard seeds, and when they start to pop, reduce the heat slightly, add the onion, and cook until soft and golden. Add the garlic, ginger, chilies, turmeric, cumin, coconut, salt, and black pepper. Cook for a couple of minutes until fragrant, then add the tomatoes and eggs. Stir gently until heated through, then remove from the heat. Stir the yogurt into the mixture, then cover and let stand for 2 minutes. Sprinkle with whole cilantro leaves if using, and serve with the freshly cooked basmati rice.

7

fire & ice

outdoor food—picnics, barbecues, and campfires

Where there's fire, there's often ice—if you're eating outdoors. You'll be some distance from the fridge and oven, and you'll be either warming yourself—or cooking—with fire, and icing down your drinks; or, in the case of a picnic, icing down your food. Whatever the case, food always tastes better in the fresh air.

Picnics Clever containers and cool storage are paramount. Seek out cans of all shapes and sizes to fit nonliquid foods snugly—metal stays cool longer than plastic as well as preventing squashing and leaking. Indian stainless steel "tiffin" cans and spice jars are ideal. Keep sandwich bags full of ice to wedge between your containers. A cooler with a refrigerating device, which plugs into your car's cigarette lighter, is the perfect modern picnic basket. Make a checklist—don't forget plates, napkins, cups, glasses, and a corkscrew.

Barbecues My guess is that nine out of ten vegetarians will prefer a separate barbecue grill. If you only have one, and you're cooking meat on it, borrow another or get a disposable grill. Once the coals are lit, it will take around thirty minutes before they're ready to be used for cooking. Wait until the flames have subsided; the coals should appear ashen. They should still be too hot to get close to; long-handled tongs and a long fork are essential for turning and rearranging the food.

Campfires Who said alfresco eating had to be a warm-weather affair? One of life's most exhilarating experiences is eating a hot meal by a toasty campfire in winter. Stick to one rich soup or stew, eaten out of a disposable cup with a disposable spoon, and sip mulled wine or hot cider. Discard leftovers into the fire and take your garbage home.

pressed tuscan sandwich vegan

This sandwich resembles its Tuscan sister, the famous "panzanella," a salad of bread marinated in garlic, tomato, and peppery olive oil. Here, the process of pressing squeezes these gorgeous Mediterranean flavors through the bread, which, as well as making it delicious, creates a nice, tidy package that is easy to eat on a picnic.

ingredients

serves 4

1 medium ciabatta loaf
1 garlic clove
1 medium vine tomato, chopped
10 fine black olives, stoned
2 teaspoons capers in vinegar, drained
5–6 sun-dried tomatoes in oil, drained and coarsely chopped
a small handful of fresh basil leaves, coarsely chopped
a small handful of Italian parsley leaves, coarsely chopped
3 tablespoons extra-virgin olive oil
1 teaspoon red wine vinegar
a pinch of salt
freshly ground black pepper

method

Slice the ciabatta in half lengthwise, then cut the garlic in half and rub all over the surface of the bread.

Place the remaining ingredients in a food processor or mortar and pulse or pound until blended to a coarse paste. Spread over one side of the bread and top with the other piece.

For the pressing, you can either tie the sandwich up with raffia or cotton string, which is very pretty, or slip it in a large plastic bag and roll up, which is easier and more practical.

Place a flat board or large book on top of the sandwich and weigh down with a heavy object—a bag of sugar, a heavy mortar, or a large container of water all work well.

Leave the sandwich to squash flat for about an hour before packing in your cooler.

think ahead This sandwich is best made not more than four hours before eating.

top tip Don't forget to bring a board and bread knife for slicing if taking this on a picnic. Alternatively, before departing, slice the sandwich into four pieces, then stack and tie with string or wrap in plastic wrap.

serve with Cheese, salad

lemony lentils with radishes vegan

The cooking time of all legumes is determined by how old they are, which is the one thing they never tell you on the package. Puy lentils usually take about half an hour, so taste after that long—they should melt in the mouth without being mushy. This nutritious but delicious salad tastes great on a picnic, either packed into a well-sealed container (such as the tiffin can shown), or stuffed into a pita. It also makes a tasty side dish at a barbecue.

ingredients

serves 6–8

2 1/4 cups green lentils, ideally Puy lentils
juice of 1 large lemon
2 tablespoons olive oil
salt and freshly ground black pepper
1 teaspoon fresh ground cumin
2 scallions, sliced
8 radishes, halved
a handful of fresh parsley, chopped

method

Rinse the lentils in a strainer, then place in a small pan. Cover generously with water, bring to a boil, and cook at a moderate boil, without salt, until tender. Meanwhile, mix together the lemon juice, olive oil, salt, black pepper, cumin, and scallions. When the lentils are tender, drain them and mix with the dressing while still hot. Let cool completely, stirring now and then. Mix in the radishes and parsley. Ideally, it should be served at room temperature.

think ahead

This can be made one day ahead, keeping radishes separate. Stir in radishes just before serving.

top tip

Any lentil can be used in this recipe except red ones—they are too soft and lose their shape. Lentils do not have to be soaked overnight before cooking, but larger legumes, including field peas and mung beans, are safer to eat after soaking and cooking.

picnic wraps

The globalization of the tortilla has made "wraps" a popular sandwich alternative. These fillings can also be enjoyed on their own as salads: Sprinkle the chickpeas with extra parsley and paprika; omit the cream cheese from the beet.

chickpea, zucchini, & paprika wraps

ingredients

2 tablespoons olive oil
2 small zucchini, thinly sliced (approximately 5 1/2 oz.)
2 garlic cloves, chopped
2 teaspoons smoked paprika or mild chili powder
14 oz. can chickpeas
a pinch of salt
a squeeze of lemon juice
a small handful of fresh parsley, coarsely chopped
4 tablespoons yogurt
4 medium flour tortillas

method

Heat the olive oil and cook the zucchini until soft and golden. Add the garlic and, when golden and fragrant, add the paprika. When it changes color, add the chickpeas with a pinch of salt. Cook for about 2 minutes, so the chickpeas heat through and become infused with flavor, then remove from the heat. Squeeze lemon juice over them and tip into a bowl. When cooled slightly, stir in the parsley and yogurt.

Take a tortilla and place a spoonful of the filling near the bottom. Fold over the sides, then fold over the bottom and roll up tightly. Place on a plate, cover, and chill until ready to eat. Slice in half diagonally before serving.

beet, blue cheese, & walnut wraps

ingredients

3 1/2 oz. baby beets in sweet vinegar, drained and coarsely chopped
1/2 cup walnuts, coarsely chopped
5 1/2 oz. blue cheese, such as Stilton or Roquefort, chopped or crumbled
2 heaping tablespoons cream cheese
freshly ground black pepper
1 1/2 oz. baby spinach leaves, washed and trimmed
4 medium flour tortillas

method

Combine the beets, walnuts, blue cheese, and cream cheese in a bowl. Grind in a little black pepper and mash together with the back of a spoon until evenly combined. Proceed as above for stuffing, adding a pile of spinach leaves to each wrap.

melting mushrooms

Soft, fleshy mushrooms oozing rich, dark juice and garlicky cheese—what more could you want? Serve them with bread so you can mop up every last drop that runs out of them.

ingredients

serves 4

8 large, open-cap or cremini mushrooms of roughly equal size
salt and freshly ground black pepper
4 tablespoons vermouth or white wine
2 garlic cloves, chopped
2 teaspoons fresh thyme leaves
4 oz. Swiss cheese or other melting cheese, grated
extra-virgin olive oil, for brushing
fresh crusty bread, to serve

method

Preheat the barbecue grill. Cut the stem out of the mushrooms, then score with a knife over the gills, not cutting through to the other side. Choose pairs of equal size. Lay one of each pair gill-side up on a clean counter, then season to taste with salt and black pepper. Add 1 tablespoon vermouth or white wine, followed by a little garlic and thyme, and finishing with grated cheese. Place another mushroom on top and drive a toothpick or skewer through from the top to secure together. Brush all over with olive oil.

Cook over hot coals, turning frequently and carefully, until very soft, juicy, and melting inside. Serve with crusty bread.

broiled miso-glazed eggplants vegan

If you're not familiar with miso, it's a fermented soybean paste with a strong, salty flavor. There are many types, each with different characteristics; I prefer the lighter colors to the darker ones. Miso gives a lovely depth to this glaze, which could be used for other vegetables—or anything you put on the grill.

ingredients

serves 4

large eggplant

wooden skewers, soaked for 30 minutes

for the glaze:

1 garlic clove, coarsely chopped

2 tablespoons miso

1 tablespoon tomato paste

1 tablespoon lemon or lime juice

2 teaspoons dark brown sugar

2 tablespoons sunflower or corn oil

method

Preheat the barbecue grill. Cut the eggplants into ½ in. thick circles and drive a presoaked wooden skewer through each piece.

To make the glaze, mix all the ingredients together in a small blender or spice grinder. Alternatively, pound the garlic with the miso paste until crushed, then whisk in the remaining ingredients until emulsified.

When the coals are hot, brush the eggplants on both sides with the glaze and cook, turning frequently with tongs and basting regularly, until very tender. Serve immediately.

broiled shiitake & tofu skewers vegan

Tofu has been around for two millennia, during which time the Japanese in particular have evolved some amazing and sophisticated recipes with the stuff. The simple teriyaki-style marinade—salty soy sauce, sweet mirin, and nutty shiitake liquor—is a long-standing winner. My "tofu mantra" is this: Keep it in its Asian home.

ingredients

serves 4

24 small, dried shiitake mushrooms
1 lb. 2 oz. fresh tofu
wooden skewers, soaked for 30 minutes
8 shallots, peeled
4 tablespoons dark soy sauce
4 tablespoons mirin (Japanese cooking wine) or sherry
sesame oil

method

Place the dried shiitake mushrooms in a bowl or large measuring pitcher and pour 2⁄3 cup boiling water over them. Let soften for 20 minutes, stirring now and then. Meanwhile, drain the tofu and pat dry with paper towels. Cut into sixteen chunks.

Pick out the softened mushrooms and set the liquor aside. Thread the mushrooms and tofu onto eight presoaked wooden skewers, with two pieces of tofu nestled between three mushrooms. Finish with a shallot on the end. Place the skewers in a container without stacking, so they can absorb the marinade.

Stir together the soy sauce and mirin, plus 4 tablespoons of the reserved mushroom liquor. Pour over the skewers and let marinate in the refrigerator for at least 1–2 hours. Turn the skewers over from time to time so they absorb the marinade evenly.

When ready to cook, brush the skewers with sesame oil. Cook over hot coals or on a ridged grill pan, turning over with tongs, until lightly charred on all sides.

think ahead Skewers can be prepared up to the cooking stage one day in advance.

top tip Don't use "silken" tofu—it won't hold together. Very fresh tofu can be bought at Asian markets and health-food stores. Try using tofu that has been frozen and thawed: It changes completely, taking on an amazing, fibrous texture.

serve with Broiled Miso-Glazed Eggplants (page 123).

a campfire party—An open fire brings out the pagan reveler in us. In the U.S., tailgate parties started as a gathering of football fans, beer, and fire, and have evolved into thoroughly gourmet affairs embracing the principle of enjoying the warm huddle while sharing food and drink, whatever the occasion and at any time of the year.

Before you consider hosting a party featuring an open fire, you should obtain permission and advice for building a fire; consult your local fire department. They can offer advice and guidance on where and how to construct a safe fire. Use your common sense and never abandon a lit fire.

shopping Army surplus stores often have a good selection of camping goods that might be useful (thermoses, outdoor candles, flares, etc.).

presentation This is one occasion for strictly disposable ware, ideally sturdy paper, which burns up in an eco-friendly fashion. Do not, however, burn polystyrene or plastic.

drinks To make mulled wine, buy plenty of inexpensive wine. Make an infusion of one bottle of wine with cinnamon sticks, cardamom pods, and an orange stuck with cloves in a large pot. Simmer for thirty minutes, then pour in more wine and heat until hot—not boiling, or the alcohol evaporates. Fortify with brandy if desired.

the menu

giant marshmallows on long sticks, for toasting on the fire

parsnip & coconut soup vegan

The clever thing about this soup is that it is thick. This means it won't slosh around easily, and it stays hot while you have steamy-breathed conversations outdoors by the fire. It's rich and warming too—a meal in itself.

ingredients

serves 8–10

4 tablespoons butter (vegans: use oil)
1 large onion, chopped
3 celery sticks with leaves, chopped
1 lb. 2 oz. parsnips, coarsely chopped
10½ oz. carrots, coarsely chopped
3 plump garlic cloves, chopped
1 tablespoon plus 1 teaspoon ground cumin
salt and freshly ground black pepper
5½ oz. block of creamed coconut, chopped
4 cups strong vegetable stock
a squeeze of lemon
Corn Salsa, to serve (see below)

method

Melt the butter in a large pan, add the onion, and cook until soft and translucent. Add the celery, parsnips, carrots, garlic, and cumin and season to taste with salt and black pepper. Stir, cover, and cook over low heat, giving it an occasional stir, for about 10 minutes.

Meanwhile, place the chopped creamed coconut in a large bowl and add 2 cups boiling water. Let stand for a few minutes, then stir until dissolved. Pour the coconut milk and vegetable stock into the pan and bring to a boil. Reduce the heat to a simmer and cook until the vegetables are very soft, about 15 minutes. Let cool briefly, then process into an absolutely smooth purée. Add a squeeze of lemon juice, process again, then taste for seasoning. Serve on its own or with Corn Salsa.

corn salsa vegan—Spicy, crisp, and juicy, this is the perfect garnish for the velvety soup.

ingredients

scant ¾ cup corn kernels, blanched if fresh, or from a can, drained; ¾ in. piece of fresh red chili, seeded and finely chopped; 1 scallion, finely chopped; a few cilantro leaves, chopped; a pinch of salt; 1 teaspoon lemon juice; 1 tablespoon olive oil

method

Combine all the ingredients in a bowl and serve a small amount on top of the Parsnip & Coconut Soup.

oven-roasted hotchpotch vegan

This richly warming dish requires minimal preparation. It's one of those genuine "throw it all in the oven" kind of recipes. The choice of vegetables is entirely flexible. Mushrooms and tomatoes are good because they're juicy; the rest can be any choice of seasonal veggies up to about 2 lb. in weight. A can of beans of some sort adds flavor and protein.

ingredients

3½ oz. shiitake mushrooms
7 oz. tomatoes
9 oz. celery root
9 oz. sweet potato
2 red onions
1 red bell pepper
3½ oz. string beans
14 oz. can chickpeas, drained and rinsed
4 garlic cloves, chopped
finely grated zest of 1 lemon
a handful of chopped fresh basil and parsley
1 teaspoon coriander seeds, crushed
a good grinding of nutmeg
salt and freshly ground black pepper
cayenne pepper to taste
4 cups carrot juice, fresh or canned
to serve (optional):
thick plain yogurt
chopped fresh herbs

method Preheat the oven to 350°F. Cut up all the vegetables into bite-size pieces and place in a deep roasting or casserole dish. Sprinkle in the rest of the ingredients and pour in the juice. Stir, then cover with foil and bake in the preheated oven for 45 minutes. Remove the foil and stir again. Reduce the oven temperature to 300°F and bake uncovered for an additional 30–40 minutes to let the juices thicken.

think ahead Serve from the dish into warmed bowls. Garnish with a dollop of yogurt and some more chopped herbs, if desired.

top tip Although this can be cooked in advance, there's something so appetizing about the cooking smells wafting out of the oven—it's part of the enjoyment of the dish. If guests are standing, serve the hotchpotch in mugs or cups.

serve with Couscous, bulgur wheat, rice, quinoa, or even baked potatoes. Delicious with Mustard Garlic Bread.

mustard garlic bread—This delicious diversion from the norm is always a hit. Cook it in the oven, on the barbecue, or in the embers of the campfire.

ingredients *1 stick butter (4 oz.), softened (vegans: use margarine); 1 large garlic clove, crushed; 1 tablespoon coarse-grain mustard; freshly ground black pepper; 1 long French baguette (approximately 30 in.)*

method Preheat the oven to 400°F. Beat together the butter, garlic, mustard, and black pepper. Cut the bread into ½ in. slices, but do not slice all the way through the bottom. If it is too long to fit in the oven, cut into two pieces. Spread the butter mixture generously between each slice. Wrap the bread up tightly in foil and bake in the preheated oven for about 15–20 minutes, until thoroughly heated through and slightly crispy. Serve immediately.

8

brunch

easy dishes that taste great early in the day

Brunch, a fusion of breakfast and lunch, is, not surprisingly, an American concept, occupying a traditional slot at Easter and on Mother's Day. Served anytime between 10:00 A.M. and noon, it can also be the party-a-day-after-the-party, usually Sunday. The hair of the dog might be required—Bloody Marys or mimosas are the order of the day.

When lots of people get together for a wedding or a big event, there is often a sequence of gatherings, culminating in a grand finale. Brunch bridges the gap between that finale and returning to normal life. It squeezes out that last bit of feasting and provides an opportunity for a relaxed winding-down from the previous night's event.

Brunch should be languorous and unfussy. No matter how few guests, brunch is a buffet—one course of many things, sweet and savory, available for refilling over and over if desired. Always provide fruit, especially melons and berries, pots of coffee, juice, and in the spirit of celebration, champagne.

turmeric potatoes with lemon & coconut

For me, crispy potatoes take the prize for the tastiest morning food. Turmeric essentially dyes these potatoes a blinding yellow while imparting a faintly earthy note in the flavor. The turmeric water turns an alarming blood red as it boils—this is OK! It's just doing its job.

ingredients

serves 6–8

2 lb. 4 oz. new potatoes, washed and halved
salt and freshly ground black pepper
2 teaspoons ground turmeric
3 tablespoons olive oil
6 garlic cloves
6 shallots, peeled
1 green bell pepper, chopped
1 lemon, thickly sliced
3 tablespoons dry, unsweetened coconut

method

Preheat the oven to 425°F. Place the potatoes in a pan, cover with plenty of water, and add a generous amount of salt and the turmeric. Bring to a boil and cook for 5 minutes. Drain thoroughly and let cool slightly. Transfer them to a roasting dish and add the olive oil. Add the remaining ingredients and toss gently with your hands, ensuring that everything is coated with a light slick of oil.

Roast in the preheated oven for about 30 minutes, stirring and dislodging sticky bits, until everything is thoroughly soft and crispy in places. Serve hot.

morning quesadillas with hot red sauce

"Quesadilla" is quite a loose term describing a Mexican-style fried tortilla encasing melted cheese, usually combined with beans, meat, or vegetables. It's usually served as a snack, but also loves the company of eggs—always yummy for breakfast. This simple, oven-baked version, though far from traditional, is handy to make in quantity.

ingredients

serves 2–4

for the hot red sauce:

14 oz. can chopped tomatoes
2 small garlic cloves, crushed
a few slices of pickled jalapeño chilies
1 tablespoon jalapeño chili juice from the jar
1–2 teaspoons mild chili powder
salt
a pinch of sugar

for each quesadilla, you will need:

about 1 tablespoon butter or olive oil, plus extra olive oil for brushing
1 flour tortilla
3 heaping tablespoons refried beans
2 tablespoons cream cheese
1 scallion, chopped
1 organic egg

method

Place the sauce ingredients in a small pan and bring to a boil. Simmer very gently while you cook the quesadillas.

Preheat the oven to 400°F. Spread the beans on one half of the tortilla and the cream cheese over the other half. Sprinkle with scallions and fold over. Brush generously all over with olive oil and place on a cookie sheet. Repeat with the remaining tortillas. Bake in the preheated oven for 10–15 minutes, flipping once, until golden brown and heated through.

Meanwhile, heat a little butter or olive oil in a skillet and cook the eggs to your liking. Serve the quesadillas with an egg and a little hot red sauce spooned over the top or in a dish on the side.

think ahead

The tortillas can be filled up to four hours in advance. Cover and keep in the refrigerator. The sauce can be made the day before and refrigerated.

top tip

If serving as part of a buffet, each quesadilla can be cut in half with a pizza cutter or knife to make smaller portions. Serve the hot red sauce in a separate bowl.

pine nut flatbread **vegan**

Flatbread makes a sassy alternative to toast. If you make the dough the night before, the pine nuts soften, forming little "stained glass" windows in the bread. Give it a whirl—it's dead simple, yet stunningly good.

ingredients

approximately 3 1/2 cups bread flour, plus extra for dusting
1/4 oz. package active dry yeast
2 teaspoons fennel seeds
2 teaspoons coriander seeds
3–4 tablespoons pine nuts
1 teaspoon salt
2 tablespoons honey (vegans: use brown sugar or malt extract)

method

Mix all the dry ingredients together in a large bowl. Dissolve the honey in 1 1/4 cups warm water, then add the water to the bowl gradually to form a soft dough. Add more flour if it's unmanageably sticky, but it should be just workable, not too stiff. Place the dough on a clean, flat counter (I use my kitchen table for breadmaking) and knead for about 5–6 minutes, until springy and elastic. Transfer to an oiled bowl and turn the dough in the oil. Cover the bowl and let stand in a warm place until doubled in size. Alternatively, place in the refrigerator and let rise slowly overnight.

Preheat the oven to 450°F. Sprinkle flour over a clean, dry counter. Gently punch the air out of the dough. Divide the dough into eight pieces and roll out with a rolling pin into flat, oval shapes. Irregular shapes are also beautiful. Place the flatbreads on a baking stone or oven tray and cook in the preheated oven for 6–8 minutes, until golden and slightly puffed. (If you have a large, flat griddle or hot plate, you can cook the bread directly on the griddle.)

whole-wheat cheese crêpes

These light and healthy crêpes require so little effort, I often make them for breakfast half-asleep, but they're good enough for entertaining, too. Tart fruit preserves are best with these, but they don't mind a little maple syrup, either.

ingredients

serves 2–4

scant 1/2 cup whole-wheat flour
1/2 teaspoon baking powder
2 teaspoons light brown sugar
1/2 teaspoon salt
2 eggs, beaten
heaping 1 cup cottage cheese
1/2–1 teaspoon butter

method

Combine all the dry ingredients in a bowl and stir in the eggs and cottage cheese. Heat a heavy skillet or grill pan until moderately hot and add the butter, swirling it around to coat the surface. Cook heaping tablespoons of batter until slightly dry and bubbly on top, then flip over and cook until golden. Serve hot with yogurt and fruit preserves.

think ahead

The batter can be made, omitting the baking powder, twelve hours in advance. Add the baking powder just before cooking. The crêpes can be cooked one hour in advance and kept warm, though they are best cooked fresh—leftover crêpes are, however, delicious reheated.

top tip

Cottage cheese usually has a plastic or foil covering under the lid—leave it in place after opening and it will keep longer.

a late morning buffet—The morning after a long night's sleep, particularly after a long night's partying, leaves most people with cravings, either for sweet things or for a complete refueling. Eggs, potatoes, fruit, and pastries are the cornerstones of brunch. Individual espressos and cooked-to-order food have no place in this laid-back, grazing affair.

A note about eggs: The most important food to buy organic, if there had to be only one, is eggs. Compared to regular eggs, organic eggs taste much better—they have a richer, buttery yolk and a soft, creamy white. The chickens have been reared to maximize their well-being, not to maximize egg production. They are able to roam free and are fed a natural, hormone- and additive-free vegetarian diet.

shopping Morning gatherings will be much easier if the shopping, and much of the food preparation, has been done the day before. However, a sudden surge in numbers might warrant a trip to a bakery for some croissants or pastries.

presentation Warm up large dinner plates in the oven for the main dishes, and offer smaller cold plates for fruit and sweets.

drinks On a hot day, make iced coffee. First, brew a triple-strength pot of coffee. For those who take sugar, pour out half and sweeten with sugar while hot. Fill two pitchers with ice and pour hot, sweet coffee into one, unsweetened into another. The ice will melt and dilute the strong coffee while chilling it. Top up with milk. Make more for those who like it black.

the menu

turmeric potatoes with lemon & coconut *135*

eggs baked in tomatoes *145*

whole-wheat cheese crêpes *139*

banana, coconut, & lime muffins *142*

melon and berries

strained plain yogurt and honey

banana, coconut, & lime muffins

Let's face it—muffins are just a crafty excuse for eating cake for breakfast. As with all good cakes, the secret is to avoid overmixing. Don't worry if there are patches of unmixed flour in the batter; they will sort themselves out.

ingredients

makes 6 large muffins or 12 small ones

1/2 stick butter (2 oz.), melted, plus extra for greasing, or 1/3 cup sunflower or corn oil
scant 2 cups all-purpose flour
1 teaspoon baking powder
1/4 teaspoon fine sea salt
1 cup superfine sugar
2 eggs
grated zest and juice of 2 limes
1 teaspoon pure vanilla extract or 1 tablespoon rum
1/2 cup yogurt
1 large, ripe banana, mashed
3 tablespoons dry, unsweetened coconut

method

Preheat the oven to 350°F and grease a muffin pan. Sift the flour, baking powder, and salt into a bowl. Beat together the remaining ingredients in a separate bowl, then fold in the flour mixture in a few swift strokes, until barely combined and still lumpy. Spoon into the greased muffin pan and bake in the preheated oven for 25–35 minutes, until golden, firm, and springy to the touch.

Let cool in the pan for 10 minutes, then turn out onto a wire rack. Eat hot with butter.

apple marzipan muffins—deliciously fruity with a knockout almond flavor.

ingredients

From the above recipe, omit the lime zest and juice, banana, and coconut and substitute: *zest and juice of 1 lemon; 1 cooking apple or large tart apple (such as Granny Smith), peeled, cored, and diced; 3 1/2 oz. marzipan, cut into 1/4 in. dice*

method

Proceed as for above recipe.

eggs baked in tomatoes

This idea first came to me in a dream. I made it for breakfast that morning, and it was gorgeous. A few days later, I was flicking through a newly acquired copy of Margaret Costa's *Four Seasons Cookbook*, a timeless book first published in 1970. In it, I found Margaret's Eggs Baked in Tomatoes. She recommends them as a summer appetizer, and adorns them with lashings of garlic, cream, and bread cooked in olive oil, which I'm sure could only make them even tastier if you're in that kind of mood. Still, the great collective cooking consciousness works in mysterious ways.

ingredients

serves 4, or 8 as part of a brunch buffet

8 plump vine tomatoes
4 tablespoons olive oil
salt and freshly ground black pepper
8 fresh basil leaves
8 small to medium organic eggs
4 tablespoons freshly grated Parmesan cheese

method

Preheat the oven to 400°F. Slice a tiny piece off the bottom of the tomatoes so they don't wobble, then slice off the tops of the tomatoes and scoop out the cores, being careful not to pierce the shells. Place the tomatoes on a lightly oiled cookie sheet and season the insides of the tomatoes with salt and black pepper. Lay a basil leaf inside and drizzle with olive oil. Break an egg into a cup or small glass, then carefully pour the yolk into a tomato, leaving much of the white behind (discard extra). Repeat with all the eggs. Sprinkle grated Parmesan on top and bake in the preheated oven for 15–20 minutes, until set to your liking. Serve immediately.

think ahead

The tomatoes can be hollowed out four hours in advance, wrapped in plastic wrap, and kept in the refrigerator.

top tip

If plump vine tomatoes aren't available, use beefsteak tomatoes. Cut in half equatorially, scoop out cores, and proceed with the recipe. If serving as part of a brunch buffet, place each tomato on a round of buttered baguette toast.

serve with

Buttered toast

9

when they eat fish

simple fish and seafood recipes for "pescetarians"

The concept of fish-eating vegetarians may seem contradictory, but the fact is, they are a growing population. While everyone has their personal reasons for restricting their diet, the morality issues are not always the strongest. Often it's just a matter of taste.

So, this chapter is for the fish lovers!

Freshness, of course, is absolutely paramount with fish, perhaps more than any other food. Here are some guidelines on how to choose the best:

Go to a seafood store, not a supermarket—it's likely to be fresher, cheaper, and cleaner.

Don't shop for fish on Monday—it may have been caught on Saturday, or even Friday.

Ask questions. What's good today? Where's it from? If the fish merchant knows his stuff, there's plenty of interesting information to glean. Don't hesitate to ask for your fish to be completely prepared for cooking (cleaned, filleted, etc.)—that's the fish merchant's job, not yours. Save yourself the hassle. Fresh fish should look as though it's still alive and about to swim away. The eyes of the fish give a good indication of freshness. They should be clear, bright, and bulging, not cloudy or withered. Look for sparkle!

Trust your nose. If the fish smells of anything other than the sea, reject it.

For this chapter, I have selected sustainable types of fish and seafood. However, this is unlikely to apply in every corner of the world, or forever. People who are concerned about these issues must make their own educated decisions. There are many helpful Internet sites that offer information on this subject; two of the more useful ones are: The Marine Conservation Society at www.mcsuk.org and the Monterey Bay Aquarium at www.montereybayaquarium.org.

chili crab cakes with fresh sweet chili dip

Fresh is always best, but frozen crab is perfectly acceptable for this recipe, and is likely to be cheaper than fresh. Get all white meat if possible, as brown meat can taste unappealingly gamey and has a rather mealy texture. I have never been able to find crab available in any weight less than a pound, so this recipe uses it all up and makes a lot of crab cakes. Many types of crab are overfished—choose snow crab, Dungeness, or king crab.

ingredients

makes about 24, serves 8 as an appetizer

2 oz. cheese crackers or saltines, finely crushed
1 lb. 2 oz. white crabmeat, thawed if frozen, squeezed dry and picked through
2–3 fresh red chilies, chopped
1 tablespoon Thai fish sauce or light soy sauce
a handful of fresh cilantro, chopped
juice of 1 lime
1 plump garlic clove, chopped
1 organic egg, beaten
sunflower or corn oil, for pan-frying
lime wedges, to serve

for the dip:

1⁄3 cup light corn syrup
1 tablespoon light soy sauce
1 tablespoon lime juice
2 tiny scallions, finely sliced
1 large, fresh red chili, chopped, or 2 small, fresh red chilies, finely sliced

method

To make the dip, stir all the dip ingredients together in a bowl until thoroughly combined, then set aside.

Crush the crackers in a food processor until they are a crumbly powder. Add the remaining ingredients and pulse until evenly and thoroughly combined, but not smooth. Form into 1 1⁄4–1 1⁄2 in. wide cakes, no more than 1⁄2 in. thick.

Heat a shallow pool of oil in a wide skillet over moderate heat until a tiny bit of the mixture sizzles immediately. Add the crab cakes and cook until golden and crispy on both sides, then drain. Serve with lime wedges and dip.

slow-cooked fennel & squid with pink peppercorns

The general rule when cooking squid is: Cook it for under two minutes or over twenty minutes. In between is the unappetizing rubbery zone. Always get your fish merchant to clean the squid for you—unless you fancy an icky lesson in cephalopod anatomy.

ingredients

serves 4

4 tablespoons butter
2 tablespoons olive oil
1 large fennel bulb (approximately 9 oz.), trimmed and cut from top to bottom into wedges
9 oz. squid, cleaned and cut into 1/2 in. rings
1 tablespoon pink peppercorns
salt
1/3 cup Madeira wine
2 heaping tablespoons bread crumbs
14 oz. bok choy or other leafy green vegetable, cleaned
1 tablespoon chopped fresh Italian parsley

method

Melt the butter with the oil, which should prevent it from burning, in a large, heavy-based skillet over moderate heat. Add the fennel and squid and cook, stirring frequently, for 15 minutes.

Add the pink peppercorns, a few pinches of salt, then pour in the Madeira wine. Cook until the wine reduces, then add the bread crumbs and cook for an additional 10 minutes, stirring frequently, so the fennel and squid turn a deep golden color and the bread crumbs are cooked to a crisp. Meanwhile, put the bok choy in a steamer and cook for about 5 minutes, until tender. Just before removing the squid from the heat, stir in the parsley. Serve on a bed of bok choy with any pan juices drizzled on top.

halibut with a warm tomato & basil vinaigrette

Flatfish like sole and halibut have a supremely delicate character. This warm, barely acidic vinaigrette lends itself well to feathery-textured fish. I cooked this for a wedding party of 130 people and it was devoured in no time.

ingredients

serves 4

4 tablespoons all-purpose flour
salt and freshly ground black pepper
1 lb. 2 oz. halibut fillets, washed, left whole, or cut into 4 portions
2–3 tablespoons olive oil

for the vinaigrette:

4 tablespoons olive oil
4 shallots, sliced
9 oz. tomatoes, chopped
10–12 fresh basil leaves, chopped, plus extra to garnish
2 tablespoons red wine vinegar
1/2 teaspoon dark brown sugar
salt and freshly ground black pepper

method

Preheat the oven to 400°F. To make the vinaigrette, heat the olive oil in a small pan and add the shallots. Cook until soft and translucent, then add the remaining ingredients. Cook until the tomato just starts to soften, about 2 minutes. Remove from the heat and set aside.

Sprinkle the flour on a plate and mix in a little salt and black pepper, then roll each fillet in the flour mixture. Heat the olive oil in a skillet over medium-high heat. Add the fish and cook on each side until lightly colored, about 2 minutes per side, then remove the fish to a roasting pan. (If your skillet is ovenproof, place it directly in the oven.) Roast in the preheated oven for 8–10 minutes, until slightly shrunken, sizzling, and cooked through. Serve immediately with the warm vinaigrette spooned over the top and a little extra chopped basil.

a thai-style feast

—Seafood is almost unavoidable in traditional Thai cooking—hardly surprising since Thailand is made up of thousands of islands. Like most Asian cuisines, it's built around creating a heightened sense of flavor through balancing the sweet, sour, hot, and salty aspects of taste. A few exotic ingredients like tamarind, lemongrass, and kaffir lime leaves give the cuisine its unique perfume. These ingredients may be difficult to acquire, but they freeze very well, so stock up if you can.

Ornamental carved vegetables are a traditional garnish for Thai dishes on an everyday basis. Use fresh, smooth red chilies or scallions. Hold the top firmly with your thumb and index finger and slice several thin strips lengthwise. Soak the scallions or chilies in a bowl of ice water for about thirty minutes to allow them to curl.

shopping If you can't locate a store specializing in Southeast Asian produce, investigate mail-order shops on the Internet. These recipes don't require anything too obscure—fresh chilies, limes, and mangoes should be easy to find. See notes on fish shopping at the beginning of this chapter. Note that the ice cream can be made without the kaffir lime leaves.

presentation Thai food is traditionally eaten with forks, spoons, and fingers, not chopsticks. If you can get fresh banana leaves, they make a gorgeous lining for plates and platters. Trim to size and sterilize by pressing into a very hot, dry skillet. The leaf will turn bright green and natural waxes in the leaf will come through to a brilliant shine.

drinks Jasmine tea is the traditional drink with food in Thailand. Fruity white wine with a bit of sweetness is a good choice.

the menu

pappardelle with scallops, saffron, & avocado

I will leave it up to you whether you want to leave the roe on the scallops—most pescetarians I've met prefer them without. This is a very subtly flavored summer dish. I first cooked it when staying in a friend's beach house; we got the scallops right off a boat from the diver himself. Strappy pappardelle carries the avocado-studded sauce nicely, but any long pasta will do. Make sure the water you cook the pasta in is as salty as the sea.

ingredients

serves 4 as a main course, 6 as an appetizer

12 scallops, cleaned and rinsed
sunflower or corn oil, for marinating
salt and freshly ground black pepper
2 tablespoons butter
4 shallots, finely chopped
1 red bell pepper, seeded and chopped into small dice
1 medium zucchini, chopped into small dice
1/4 teaspoon saffron strands, soaked in 2 teaspoons hot water
1 1/4 cups crème fraîche or sour cream
7 oz. pappardelle (long, flat pasta)
1 large, perfectly ripe avocado, chopped into chunks and dressed in the juice of 1 lime

method

Place the drained scallops in a bowl and add just enough oil to barely coat them. Season lightly with salt and black pepper and chill in the refrigerator.

Bring a large pan of well-salted water to a boil for the pasta.

Meanwhile, melt the butter in a large pan over gentle heat. Add the shallots, red bell pepper, and zucchini and cook, stirring frequently, until the shallots are soft and golden. Add the saffron water and stir in the crème fraîche or sour cream until heated through. Season with a little salt and black pepper, then remove from the heat, cover, and set aside.

Cook the pasta for about 6–8 minutes, until al dente. (Alternatively, follow the package instructions.) Heat a ridged grill pan until very hot, for cooking the scallops. When the pasta has 4 more minutes cooking time, place the scallops on the hot pan and cook for 90 seconds on each side, turning over with tongs, then remove from the heat. Drain the pasta and return to the pasta cooking pan. Stir the saffron sauce and the chopped avocado through the pasta until evenly coated. Divide the pasta between four warm plates and top with the cooked scallops. Serve immediately.

think ahead This dish is best prepared just before eating.

top tip Opt for diver-caught scallops, as dredging damages the seabed. Although I got my scallops from a diver, I still took them to a fish merchant to have them expertly removed from the shell.

thai tuna & mango salad

Fresh tuna is one of the meatiest fish around, and it's always a good idea to ask people how they like their tuna cooked, just like a steak. Most tuna lovers prefer it pink, as it does have a tendency to get leathery if overcooked. When selecting your fresh tuna, make sure it is labeled "dolphin friendly" and is not a bluefin tuna, which is an endangered species. Albacore tuna and yellowfin tuna are better choices, ideally if they are line-caught.

ingredients

serves 4

for the salad:

4 oz. egg noodles
1 tablespoon sunflower or corn oil
1 lb. 2 oz. fresh tuna steak, cut into cubes
1 medium mango, peeled and cut into strips
1 red bell pepper, cut into thin strips
1 small red onion, finely sliced
a large handful of fresh mint, leaves stripped
a large handful of fresh cilantro, leaves stripped

for the dressing:

1 garlic clove, finely chopped
1 fresh red chili, finely chopped
4 tablespoons light soy sauce
2 tablespoons Thai fish sauce or 2 extra tablespoons light soy sauce
4 tablespoons lime juice
2 tablespoons dark brown sugar

method

Boil the noodles for 5 minutes or cook according to package instructions. Drain, then rinse under cold water until cool. Place in a large bowl.

Whisk all the dressing ingredients together. Alternatively, mix in a blender.

Heat the oil in a nonstick skillet until very hot. Add the tuna and cook for a few seconds on each side until seared or cooked to your liking.

Pour half the dressing over the noodles and toss to coat evenly. Arrange the noodles on four plates. In the bowl that contained the noodles, combine the tuna with the rest of the salad ingredients and the remaining dressing and toss until well coated. Spoon on top of the noodles and serve.

index

NOTE: Green onions are referred to as "scallions" throughout this book.

for Dad

acknowledgments

My most heartfelt thanks to the dynamic team—Vanessa, Jan, and Nicky—sparks flew. Huge thanks to Stuart Cooper for keeping hold of the reins and for believing in me throughout, and to Lizzy Gray for her sharp focus and massive patience. Now for all the people who helped make this book the entity it is, with love:

Christiane Kubrick, Anya and Jonathan, Amy, Beth, and Mom, for your undying support

Suku, for auspicious friendship and the exquisite vegetable carvings, Emma, Andrew, Calum, Annette

Cathy Lowis

Tamsyn, Brent, and Shannon

Vanessa's Luke and Rosie and Mandy's Rebecca and Tilley the cat

Jennifer Joyce, Victoria Blashford-Snell

Lindsay Wilson

Recipe tasters Paula, Tracy, Ben, Kate, Paulie, Ying, Jill, Matt, Roland, Selene, James, Jessica, and little Sorrel (farther down the food chain), Rupert, Jeanne, and my lovely Dan

Rosie Kindersley and Eric Treuille and all the staff at Books for Cooks

Thanks also to: Lindy at Ceramica Blue—www.ceramicablue.co.uk; Camilla Schneideman at Divertimenti—www.divertimenti.co.uk; SCP—www.scp.co.uk; Little Book of Furniture—www.littlebookoffurniture.com; Aria—www.ariashop.co.uk; Patricia Michaelson at La Fromagerie—www.lafromagerie.co.uk; John Lewis Partnership; Renata at Giaccobazzi's; Steve Hatt fish merchants, Essex Road, London; James Elliot, Essex Road, London

Published in U.S. and Canada by Whitecap Books Ltd. For more information, contact Whitecap Books, 351 Lynn Avenue, North Vancouver, British Columbia, Canada, V7J 2C4

www.whitecap.ca

First Paperback Printing 2005

First published in Great Britain in 2003 by Pavilion Books, The Chrysalis Building, Bramley Road, London, W10 6SP

An imprint of Chrysalis Books Group plc

Senior Commissioning Editor: Stuart Cooper Editor: Lizzy Gray Art Director: Vanessa Courtier Styling: Celia Brooks Brown Styling Assistant: Nicki Hill

ISBN 1-55285-686-0

Printed and bound by Imago, Singapore.

1 2 3 4 5 07 06 05 04 03